Care and

Care
and
Commitment

Foster Parent Adoption Decisions

WILLIAM MEEZAN
AND
JOAN F. SHIREMAN

State University of New York Press

Published by
State University of New York Press, Albany

© 1985 State University of New York

For information, address State University of New York
Press, State University Plaza, Albany, N.Y., 12246

Library of Congress Cataloging in Publication Data

Meezan, William.
    Care and commitment.

    Includes index.
    1. Adoption—United States—Case studies. 2. Foster
home care—United States—Case studies. 3. Foster
parents—United States—Case studies. I. Shireman,
Joan F. II. Title.
HV875.55.M43   1985   362.7′34′0973   84-2730
ISBN 0-88706-103-6

ISBN 0-88706-104-4 (pbk.)

To those for whom we care
To those to whom we are committed
Michael
and
Charles,
Patricia, William and David

Contents

Preface

Projects such as the one reported here are not completed without the assistance of many persons. We are most grateful to all of those who have helped us complete this work. Unfortunately, only some can be named individually.

The very special contribution of our advisory committee is mentioned throughout the book and deserves primary recognition as we acknowledge the help of others. Its membership was drawn from the voluntary and public agencies who cooperated in our first sample selection, and included Kenneth Watson and Sylvia Raglan of the Chicago Child Care Society; Joan DiLeonardi and Dorothy Armstrong of the Children's Home and Aid Society of Illinois; Judith Schild and Charlotte Cohen of the Jewish Children's Bureau; and Gary Morgan and Carol Lemieux of the Illinois Department of Children and Family Services. These professionals worked with us throughout the project; they contributed ideas for us to explore, assisted us in multiple ways with the data collection, and helped us understand and interpret our data. In addition, we want to thank the staff of Lutheran Child and Family Services, and of Catholic Charities, who assisted us in collecting data on the sample of disrupted adoptions.

The project could not have been managed without the able assistance of our research associates, Gerri Outlaw and Theresa Kilbane. Their expertise consistently contributed to the smooth running of the project and its timely completion. Our interviewers, Dorothy E. Byrd, Margaret Gill, Patricia Haynes, Artemis Loberg, Lynn Merlone, Juan Y. Reed and Doris Tankersley had superb skills. They helped both the social workers and the foster parents to share complex material with us. The data reduction was dependent on the skills of our coders, Paula Bartlow, Barbara Berger, Linda Carnes, Judy Hirschman, Mary Ann Martello, and Yossef Meller. Their arduous labor allowed this phase of the research to be relatively problem free. Mary Hathcoat willingly typed our numerous drafts and revisions of the manuscript, always keeping her sense of humor about our compulsivity.

PREFACE

We are appreciative of the help of those experts in child welfare who read an early draft of our manuscript, and assisted us with questions, comments, and ideas for further elaboration. They were Dee Morgan Kilpatrick, Gary Morgan, Ann Shyne, Theodore Stein, and Kenneth Watson. John Schuerman provided us with critical comment on our statistical work, which was most helpful.

The project would not have been possible without funding from the Children's Bureau, United States Department of Health and Human Services, grant #90–CW–642. Additionally, we want to thank Charles Gershenson of that department for his sage advice, and his help throughout the project in mastering the intricacies of federal funding.

Nor would the project have been possible without the encouragement and support of Donald Brieland, the Dean of Jane Addams College of Social Work, University of Illinois at Chicago, who created a climate in which research was a pleasure, and helped us overcome more than one seemingly insurmountable obstacle.

As we acknowledge the help of others, we must express our appreciation for the most important help of all, that of the staffs of the cooperating agencies, and the foster families and adoptive families who worked with these agencies. These were the persons, too numerous to list, who shared with us their experiences, their feelings, and their ideas, in the hope that this information might be useful to others. Whatever of merit is in the data of this book is due to their sharing.

When two authors contribute equally to the development, implementation, and writing of a project such as this, there is no good way to decide the ordering of the names on the cover. The alphabet determined the order we have used. The work, however, reflects an equal input of ideas and effort, and many enjoyable and productive debates as we approached the issues raised from different perspectives. Our work together has been a rewarding venture.

William Meezan
Joan F. Shireman

CHAPTER 1

Introduction

When this research began, we believed that most foster parents who had cared for children for a long time would choose to adopt them when offered this opportunity. We questioned why some foster parents would not want to adopt. "What was different about these families?" And, when it was learned in the course of our work that some foster parent adoptions fail, we were even more intrigued. "Why wouldn't such an adoption work?" The need to understand the factors associated with these various outcomes directed the research.

Background

Adoptive homes have long been used to provide permanent families for infants whose biological parents cannot care for them. In recent years older children, children from minority group parentage, children with physical and emotional handicaps, and children who are part of sibling groups, have also been successfully placed in adoptive families. These homes, with their legal and community affirmation of the formation of a "family," have helped to meet the needs of children for continuity of care and for roots in a family of their "own." While the recent recognition of the need to know about one's biological heritage has added another dimension to the adoptive experience, it has not altered the promise that these homes hold for meeting the multiple needs of children who cannot be raised by their biological parents.

In contrast, foster homes have traditionally been considered transitional homes—homes in which children can receive good care, in a warm atmosphere, for a limited period of time, until they either return to their biological parents or move to an adoptive family. However, in recent years, child welfare workers have been dismayed by repetitive research findings showing that large numbers of children were "drifting" in foster care—simply

1

remaining in care for many years while those responsible for them made no plans for their future. As one expert commented in a 1978 publication:

> With disheartning repetitiveness the charge is made that . . . children get lost in the foster care system, temporary care becomes permanent care, systematic periodic review of case planning is often neglected, and there is a studied indifference to parental needs once the child has been removed; that the system operates against the achievement of permanence for many children. . . . The available evidence suggests that much of this is true.[1]

In order to remedy these and other identified problems within the service system, child welfare agencies have begun to evaluate their services using a new set of criteria. In the 1970s *permanency planning* became the watchword in child welfare, and the effort to preserve or find permanent homes for children was redoubled.

It is well to pause and examine the meaning of "permanence" as it is applied to children. What is meant, at the core, is that children should be provided with living situations which are expected to last indefinitely. This assures continuity of relationships for them. Thus, permanency planning dictates that children should remain with their biological parents whenever possible and that supports should be provided to maintain families at risk of separation. When this is not possible, and children must be removed from their biological homes, work to restore the family should be the primary objective of service. If intervention with the biological family demonstrates that the child is unlikely to return to their care, an alternative family situation, expected to last indefinitely, should be sought. Thus, because this study is concerned only with those children in foster care who cannot return to their biological homes, it examines only one aspect of permanency planning.

Permanence can be defined as "intent"[2]—the intent of parents to have a child grow up in their home. It is not a guarantee that this will occur. Most writers and practitioners add to this definition the concept of legal safeguards to permanency, and agency policies, court reviews, and research and demonstration projects have all emphasized the goal of legal permanence. Thus, permanence is often interpreted to mean adoption if children cannot return to their biological parents.

The attempt to find permanent homes for foster children unlikely to return to their biological families has pushed the field of child welfare toward a redefinition of foster care and the role of foster parents. Not only are foster families expected to fulfill their traditional functions of providing temporary care for children, but the question is now being asked: "If there are children who are unlikely to return to their biological homes from foster care, and they have successfully lived with the same foster family for a period of time, why shouldn't an adoption take place within that foster family?" Certainly this seems to be in everyone's best interest. For the child, the relationships formed within the foster family remain unbroken. For the foster parents, who were often the child's psychological parents, an adoption legally consumates their relationship with the child and eliminates any fear of the child's removal from their home. For the agency, the potential for foster care drift within their caseloads is diminished. Thus, the consideration of foster parents as adoptive parents has begun to take place, and the "right" of the foster family to adopt a child in their care has begun to emerge. Foster homes are no longer necessarily seen as temporary solutions for children needing care; they might well become adoptive homes.

Thus, the incorporation of permanency planning within child welfare practice has facilitated a recent acceptance of foster parent adoptions. Foster parents are now well received if they ask to adopt children in their care who cannot return to their biological home. They are often approached by the social worker if they do not mention this possibility, and are sometimes urged if they hesitate in this decision. If they finally decide not to adopt, their foster child might be moved to a potential adoptive home.

As agencies embrace the idea of foster parent adoptions, it is generally assumed that foster parents, when given the opportunity, will want to adopt a child who has been in their care, and that such adoptions will be successful. Workers know that bonds form between children and their foster parents. They have witnessed the difficulties of separation when a child is moved from a foster home in which such attachments have taken place. And, indeed, agencies have discovered that many foster parents want to adopt their foster children. Sam and his family are typical.

> Sam was three years old when his foster mother decided she was "too old" and asked to have him replaced. He came to his new home with reluctance, though for his new foster parents it was "love at first sight." Now he is six and these parents describe him as a "happy, spirited little boy, spoiled to death, who likes school, is observant, inquisitive, and very smart."

> Within a week after placement, cancer was discovered. There was surgery, and radiation therapy, and Sam was very ill for two years. During this time he and the foster mother grew very close. During this time, too, the family came to know Sam's social worker very well; they saw her daily at the hospital during Sam's crisis periods, and she helped them in their struggle to have Sam's feelings taken into account during his treatment.

As Sam grew stronger, the worker began to try to plan for his return to his biological parents, but as they repeatedly failed to keep appointments it gradually became apparent to the foster parents that there might be a chance of adopting Sam. They had always really wanted to adopt, and the worker encouraged them to hope. They met Sam's parents once, by accident, at the agency, but had little chance to talk. When the social worker finally raised the possibility of adoption with them they were overjoyed. They had no hesitation. After meeting the problems of his illness, they knew they "could care for him better than anyone else." Sam himself was excited by the idea of adoption. The family wanted to be sure Sam would remain with them, and Sam himself exclaimed "Now I'll never have to move again."

However, not all foster parents want to adopt, and little is known about the circumstances that lead this decision. Workers are often surprised and dismayed to find hesitation, reluctance and refusal when a foster family has been offered this opportunity. Often the child has been in the home for many years and attachments seem to have formed. It is often difficult for workers to understand this decision and to help the family feel comfortable with it. Such was the situation with Bruce and his family.

Bruce is a thirteen-year-old, apparently loved in his foster home and, according to the foster parents, "there to stay." The child of young, unmarried parents, Bruce was adopted as a toddler, and came to this foster home at the age of nine when the adoption broke down. The foster family was pleased; with grown daughters they had wanted a little boy, though they expected a younger child. Also, they were appalled at the rejecting behavior of the adopting parents, and their "hearts went out to him." They saw he "needed someone," knew he must not be rejected again, and stayed by him despite behavior problems which included fire-setting. Currently these extreme difficulties have ended, but Bruce can express neither joy nor hurt, nor can he allow much affectionate interchange with the family. He is working below grade level in school and does not have many friends. Yet he seems to feel this is his family, and asks to be adopted.

Bruce's caseworker has twice raised the possibility of adoption with this family, for she would like the child to have a permanent home. Each time the family has refused. They fear that Bruce will develop more severe problems as he goes through adolescence and they feel they cannot cope with them alone. The agency is a "back-up" they say. They also think he may need special schooling, and do not wish to take on this financial responsibility.

Subsidy has been discussed, but they are uncertain about whether it would really be approved, or whether it would really continue until he was adult. They do not seem to have had much contact with their social worker except around discussions of adoption. The family functions very independently; Bruce has a firm place in it. These foster parents do not see that adoption would make any real difference. They prefer not to take the risk. They will continue as foster parents to Bruce.

In recent years it has also become apparent that not all foster parent adoptions are successful. Some foster/adoptive parents return children to the agency and ask that another home be found for them. If workers do not understand why some foster parents choose not to adopt, they understand the reasons for foster parent adoption failure even less. After all, adoption has merely added a legal sanction to an existing, functioning family. The foster parents had known the children they were adopting and what it was like to live with them. Presumably the children had been integrated into the homes prior to the adoptions. Why, then, should the adoptions not succeed? Laura's situation is illustrative of the diverse families and children who seem to be involved in these devastating experiences.

Laura was seven when she and her younger brother came to the foster home. The foster parents, who liked children and had raised their own, were unprepared for the severe abuse to which the children had been subjected, and for the behavior problems they presented. They had been touched by Laura's frightened appearance, and by her protectiveness of her little brother, when they first met. Though from the start she stole "like a professional" and had behavior and learning problems in school, in many ways she was warm and sweet, and the foster parents thought that with love and understanding she would outgrow her problems. Her little brother adapted well to the family patterns. So when the caseworker told the family, about three years after the placement, that the children were now free for adoption, the family began to consider adoption. When the agency began actively looking for an adoptive home, the foster family decided that they would adopt in order to keep the children in their home. There was little discussion of the decision with the worker.

When Laura was tewlve she "became a different child." She stayed out late, became sexually active, truanted from school, and ignored family restrictions around dating. She was in constant conflict with the family. They felt helpless to control her behavior and began to fear that she would be a bad influence on the younger children. Finally they decided that they were no longer able to maintain a home for Laura, and called the agency which had placed her, asking that another plan be made. Laura was fourteen when she left the home.

"We tried everything we could," the foster mother said. "She had become a part of our lives, but we knew we couldn't do anything more."

Assumptions

This study is built on the assumption that one of the basic needs of children is the opportunity to form close affectional ties with their caretakers—ties which can be maintained through their growing-up years. The firmer the childrens' roots in the families in which they grow up, and the stronger their sense that they are family members, the better their situation. For most children these conditions are met in their biological homes. When it is not possible for children to remain with their biological parents, it becomes the responsibility of those who assume authority for planning their care to see that these conditions are approximated to the greatest degree possible.

In this report, attention is focused on children who have been removed from the biological home and strenuous attempts to reunite biological necessary that there be careful decision making at the point of initial removal from the biological home and strenuous attempts to reunite biological families. For the children who are the subjects of this study, the agency has decided that they cannot return to their biological parents and should be legally freed for adoption. It must be assumed that their work with the biological parents was appropriate and that their decisions were correct.

For the children in this study, the agency has also decided that the foster home in which they were placed would be an appropriate adoptive home. Again, it must be assumed that this judgment was correct. This research does not investigate those qualities which constitute a "good" adoptive or foster home. Rather, it is assumed that all of the foster families in this study are qualified to raise children successfully. The focus of the research is on the factors which differentiate the foster homes in which an adoption takes place from those in which either the opportunity to adopt is declined or where the adoption of a foster child has failed.

The Framework

In order to address these interests, the research focused on the characteristics and interactions of the major actors in the decision making process. Extensive inquiries and discussions with those most intimately involved with the decision—the foster parents themselves and the child welfare staff who worked with them—were conducted. A number of areas of inquiry were highlighted.

First, the investigation focused on *the family**** and its life. There was some retrospective inquiry about the family before the child arrived. The family's current life style—its flexibility, expectations, and desire for adoption—were explored. So, also, were the characteristics of the parents—their enjoyment of children and children's activities, their individualization of children and sensitivity to them, and their ability to nurture. Concrete factors such as age, health, stability of employment and income were also thought to be important.

The second focus of the study was on the characteristics of the *child*. Each child comes to a foster family with unique traits and behaviors. Even as a young infant, the personality, and perhaps handicaps or illness, present a unique configuration. The older child arrives with all the "baggage" of previous experiences. Often there have been multiple separations, and a primary question is always the extent to which these separations have damaged the child's ability to trust and to relate to new parents. The proclivity to disrupt a family, the display of unacceptable behavior, or even just the use of behaviors learned in another setting, can test a family's capacity to respond constructively.

Not only are the characteristics of the individuals important, but *their interactions and the "match" between child and family* may be important. To what extent do the children and families fit each other's expectation, and how flexible are those expectations? The process of attachment between parents and child is a phenomena about which relatively little is known. A sequence of behaviors and of feelings can be observed as the child and the family adapt to each other, but little is understood about how a bond that will hold the family together is formed. In his work, David Fanshel has used the term "embedment" to describe the child's final "fit" into the foster/adoptive home,[3] and it seems apt. The child's resolution of former ties and separations, the parents' acceptance of the child as he is, a positive working through of the attachment process, and just time in the home, might lead to deep embedment and help to turn a temporary foster placement into a permanent home.

The agency and the social worker who have contact with the child and the family might also influence the movement from foster care to adoption. The agency's policies and expectations can support workers in their roles, place

---

*The family on which this study focuses is the child's foster family. It will be identified throughout as "the family." If another family, such as the child's biological family, is meant, it will be so indicated.

constraints on them, and give their work direction. The agency's resources might impact the range of services which are available. Within this framework, workers' knowledge and attitudes about foster care and adoption are important in giving specific direction to their work. Their comfort with their agency, its policies, and its services, as well as the working climate in which duties are carried out, might also impact service.

While the above may structure their general position, social workers and families respond uniquely to each other. Social workers need to have detailed knowledge of the children they place and the parents they select for the child. Their skill in communicating with the family, their comfort and willingness to deal with disturbing material, and their perceptions of parents and child, might impact their relationship with the family. Their task is to prepare parents and children for each other, to effect a potentially good match, to provide support services to the family as the members adapt to each other, and to ensure that planning for the child's future is done in the best possible manner. The quality of service they receive and their relationship with the worker may be crucial in helping parents arrive at a sound decision and implement it.

The Inquiry

It is within this framework that the research was done. More specifically, the project was designed to answer the following questions about foster homes which the agency considered appropriate for adoption:

1. Are foster parents who choose to adopt their foster children different from those who choose not to adopt? Are foster parents who ask for the removal of an adopted foster child different from either, or both, of the above groups?

2. Do children who are adopted by their foster parents have different characteristics than children whose foster parents choose not to adopt, or for whom the adoption is not successful?

3. Do children who are adopted by their foster parents have different types of relationships with them than children who are not adopted by their foster parents? Are there similar patterns in relationships when adoptions fail?

4. Do foster families who choose to adopt have different perceptions of and experiences with the agency and its policies than those who decide not to adopt? Are these perceptions and experiences different from those who decide to adopt and then have the adoption fail?

5. Do workers' perceptions of critical factors in the fostering and adoption experience coincide with those of the foster parents?

These, then, are the questions which directed this investigation of foster parent adoption and which guided the selection of factors to investigate. The answers were sought in the most direct way; through asking the foster parents themselves, and the casewokers who worked with them. From the ranks of foster parents currently working with both public and voluntary agencies in metropolitan Chicago, a sample of foster parents who had cared for children for several years and had recently been offered the chance to adopt them was selected. Some foster parents had adopted, some had not. A small group of parents who had adopted foster children after caring for them for a long time, and had had so much difficulty that the children had been removed from the home and the adoptions set aside, was also identified.

The sample size in this study is relatively small and drawn entirely from an urban population. The sample of failed adoptions is very small and was not systematically selected. Though it is our impression that workers and families were open with us, the reliability of the information they shared cannot be assessed and distortions of memory are probably present. In any event, the research deals only with consciously available recollections in an area where the unconscious is believed by some to be important. These limitations do not detract from the value of the information that was obtained, but they do make clear that the study was a first look at this phenomena and that the results are subject to confirmation in further research, and in testing in practice.

The findings of the study were not always in line with the practice wisdom of the field. We were surprised at the large number of differences found between the adopting and non-adopting families. These differences were evident in all of the areas of inquiry. The exploration of factors associated with the failure of a small group of foster parent adoptions, though tentative in its conclusions, also revealed some interesting patterns and results.

It is evident that we are dealing with a complex matrix of interacting factors. Particularly because the analysis of the services provided by the agency to these groups of foster parents revealed a large number of differences and emerged as an important differentiating factor, the findings have many implications for service delivery. Our hope is that some of the findings may increase the understanding of family and child development, some provide practice guidelines for implementing current policy, and some suggest the development of new policy within the field.

CHAPTER 2
Background of the Study

Amy was three when she was placed with two younger sisters. Her grandmother had been unable to care for the girls after their mother's death. For the grandmother and the girls, the family seemed ideal. The grandmother, at first, visited monthly, and was welcomed by the foster family and the children. Over the years the visits grew less frequent.

When Eric was five months old, he was admitted to the hospital with bruises and human bite marks. It was his third admission, and this time he was discharged to a foster home. The foster parents felt he was not ready to leave the hospital, for he was not eating or taking a bottle. He was difficult to care for, cried constantly, was not responsive. The foster parents expected this would be a short term placement. During the first two years, Eric's mother's sporadic visits were upsetting; she frequently wouldn't show, and when she did he seemed frightened. He would scream and cry for hours afterward. The visits stopped aburptly, and there has been no contact for three years.

Throughout the country, children who have been in foster care for long periods of time are being freed for adoption. This trend is likely to continue as child welfare agencies embrace the philosophy of permanency planning, and as resources become available to implement planning.

Many of the children in need of permanent homes are older than those traditionally placed for adoption by child welfare agencies. Some have physical, emotional or developmental handicaps. Many are from minority parentage and some are part of a sibling group that should be placed as a unit. Many have spent long periods of time in foster care, and many are embedded in their current foster homes. The initial situations, detailed above, are typical.

Recent reports indicate that for many of these "special needs" children foster parents are an important adoptive resource.[1] In fact, demonstration projects concerned with permanency planning have found that foster homes are a *primary* adoptive resource, and often constitute the majority of adoptive homes found for such children.[2] Research has also found that many foster parents react positively to the idea of adoption; one study reported that over 70 percent of the foster parents approached reacted in this fashion.[3]

Recent federal legislation encourages adoptive planning for these children. Federal funds have become available for adoption planning and for subsidy. Both the Adoption Assistance and Child Welfare Act of 1980 (P.L. 96–272) and the Model State Adoption Act developed by the Department of Health and Human Services and published in 1981 seek to insure permanence for children who have spent time in foster care. Each of these initiatives encourages the adoption of children by their foster parents.

The Model State Adoption Act states:

> Good practice dictates that adoption first be explored with foster parents who have provided a stable, nurturing home for the child and who have a psychological commitment to the child; the Act requires that foster parents not be excluded from consideration as adoptive parents.

> Since the goal is to provide the child with a stable, nurturing home and since the field of social work acknowledges the validity of a variety of parenting styles, agencies cannot restrict the eligibility of applicants solely on the basis of such factors as age, race, marital status, income, religion, employment, physical condition or disabilities or the number of children already in the family.[4]

It goes on to state:

> The assessment of a foster family home for adoption varies from a regular family assessment. In a foster parent adoption, the agency must fully explore the situation of a child already living in the foster home. The discussion must focus on the meaning of permanency to a child, the agency's responsibility for subsidy, and postadoption services.

> If the foster parents want to pursue adoption of the child the original foster family assessment should suffice as the basis for the adoptive assessment, but should be supplemented with a current description of the child's adjustment and needs, the foster parents' commitment to the child, and any significant family changes. There should also be exploration with the foster family of significant differences between foster family care and adoption.[5]

P.L. 96–272, which establishes federal payments for adoption subsidy for the first time, specifically recognizes the special attachments which might occur between children and their foster parents. By exempting foster parent adoptions from the requirement that a placement in an unsubsidized home be sought before a subsidy is approved, this law grants special preference to these adoptions.[6]

Foster Parents as Adoptive Parents—A Shift in Philosophy

Until recently, agencies did not consider foster parents as possible adoptive resources for children in care. Foster care was believed to be a temporary arrangement for children who would eventually return to their biological homes or be adopted by other families, and foster parents were encouraged to keep emotional distance between themselves and their foster children. Foster parents were viewed as "clients" of the agency or as paraprofessionals, and were expected to accept the removal of a child from their home on very little notice. As late as 1974 almost two-thirds of the states had a cautionary note or a prohibition of adoption in their placement agreements with foster parents.[7]

Along with these formal barriers to foster parent adoptions, child welfare personnel have, in the past, raised a number of objections to this practice. These included: 1) foster parents were not as carefully selected or screened as adoptive parents and did not meet the same agency criteria as other adoptive applicants;[8] 2) such adoptions "drain off" valuable agency resources—the agencies' best foster homes may be lost to them;[9] 3) adoption of only one child in a home may create an emotional upheaval for other foster children in the home and may lead to their replacement;[10] 4) foster parent adoptions may not afford the traditional protections of adoption; biological and foster parents may be involved with each other and parents, siblings and other relatives may continue to have contact with the adopted child;[11] 5) matching of children with parents, long a tenet of adoption practice, may not take place because many foster children are placed under crisis conditions;[12] and finally, 6) the anticipation of a foster parent adoption might lead to diminished effort to restore the child to the biological family.[13]

In addition, these adoptions may have been resisted because many foster parents are not "typical" adoptive parents. Some are older; others have low incomes or limited education. Many were not initially motivated to adopt when they applied to the agency. Most will need an adoption subsidy, although money is not their primary motivation for the adoption.[14]

Even with repeated evidence that many children never return to their biological homes from foster care, many did not see adoption by foster parents as a viable alternative to foster care "drift." A 1971 experience survey of workers in the field revealed that while many of the respondents saw the need for expanding the pool of adoptive parents, only one-third recognized that foster parents might provide the needed resources.[15]

It was not until the mid-1970s, when agencies became increasingly concerned with formalizing permanent plans for children, that foster homes began to be considered for adoption. Caseload studies conducted at this time revealed that there were large numbers of older children, some with handicapping conditions, often of minority races, usually having no contacts with their biological families, continuing to live in foster homes. What could be more natural than to suggest that their foster parents adopt them? The concept of the foster parent/adoptive parent continuum emerged.[16] For the first time in many years, caseworkers approached foster parents about adopting their foster children.

Some agencies found the benefits of foster parent adoption so attractive that they created the "three option" or "legal risk" foster home[17] to maximize this possibility. Such homes serve as the child's initial foster placement. However, if it appears that the child cannot be returned to the biological home within a reasonable length of time, these families are willing to become their legal guardians (if the child cannot be legally freed for adoption) or their adoptive parents.

There seem to be a number of advantages when foster parents adopt. First, the child and the family are known to each other. Thus, they are aware of what they are "getting themselves into." Initial placement adjustments have been made and each has "settled in" with the other. The child does not experience an additional separation and remains within a familiar family and a familiar community. In addition, the children (depending on age) can be more fully involved in the adoption decision, since they know and have lived with the foster parents.

In recent years many of the legal barriers to foster parent adoptions in the United States have been removed by legislation or agency policy. Most states now grant foster parents preference in the adoption of children who have been in their homes either in law, policy or practice.[18] In fact, subsidy legislation in some states was initially designed solely to promote foster parent adoptions.[19]

The Adoption Decision

With the growing acceptability of foster parent adoptions the question has been asked: why are some foster parents approached and others not?; and when approached, why do some foster parents adopt and others decline? The existing literature on this topic is extremely limited.

Regarding why some foster parents are approached, the available evidence seems to indicate that foster parents are not given this option when they have been with the agency for short periods of time; when their child has experienced multiple placements; when their child has not been in the home for a long period of time; or when the child is placed with siblings or is still being visited by biological parents.[20] Surely there is also a clinical judgment involved in making this decision, although there appears to be no literature on this topic. It thus appears that agencies continue to remain cautious and approach foster parents who are well known to them and who are caring for children who are already embedded in their homes.

The literature provides some clues as to why some foster parents adopt when given the opportunity. In a large study in England, in which 105 foster parents who had adopted their foster children were compared with 145 non-adopting long-term foster parents, fear of losing the child was associated with adoption. A high proportion of the adopting parents feared removal of the child by either the agency or the biological parents. In addition, the foster parents who adopted were younger and better off financially. And, their children were more likely to have been placed in their homes as infants and to be better adjusted.[21] However, the authors of this study emphasized that these factors did not really explain why only some of the long term foster parents had wanted to adopt.[22]

Personality characteristics of adopting foster parents have also been associated with the decision to adopt. In the study just cited, an active and continuing desire to adopt was noted among those who eventually adopted, as was a configuration of motivations for caring for children which was slightly less altruistic than among those who did not adopt.[23] In another study of sixty-nine foster families, about half of whom adopted children in their care, caseworkers identified enjoyment of children (particularly on the part of the mother) and sensitivity to their needs as attributes of foster parents who adopted. They also identified "a combination of child-centered motives and narcissistic investment in raising children" as reasons for taking children into the home on a permanent basis. Attitude scale responses of those foster parents who had adopted showed a strong interest in children and an ability to respond to their differing characteristics.[24] However, these terms all lacked specificity.

The available literature also indicates that foster parents are reluctant to adopt for a number of reasons. Their age or health may deter them; so may the degree of the child's handicaps. Their fears regarding their ability to cope with the child's behavior upon entering adolescence, the possibility that agency support might be withdrawn if an adoption was completed, and a lack of attachment to the child have also been identified as deterrents to foster parent adoptions.[25]

Conditions for Foster Parent Adoption

In order for an adoption to take place: (1) children's ties to their biological family must be legally severed; (2) a bond must have formed between the foster family and the child so that a "psychological parent-child relationship" exists—the child must be free of impeding emotional ties and able to identify with the foster/adoptive family, and the family must make a commitment to the child; and (3) arrangements must be made so that adoption does not impose financial hardship on the foster family, either because they are relying on foster care board payments or because the child's condition will necessitate extraordinary expenditures in the future. Each of these conditions pose insurmountable blocks for some families. For others, each condition can be met and a legal adoption can be completed.

Whether they are adopted by their foster family or by a different family, children's ties to their biological family must be legally terminated—they must be "freed" for adoption. In foster parent adoptions this process may be simplified by the fact that an adoptive home, the foster home, has already been "found" and is "waiting" for the child. It has been observed that termination of parental rights is quicker and apparently more comfortable for the courts, and that parents find it easier to complete voluntary surrenders, if the children are already in homes in which they will remain.[26]

Ties to a biological family are not only legal, they are also emotional. Studies have repeatedly shown that parental visiting of children in foster care diminishes with time, but even children who have not seen their biological family for a long time may retain emotional ties to them. These ties may be those of unresolved anger, hurt or guilt; or they may be more positive affectional ties. Many children are conflicted in their feelings. If these feelings about separation and "own" parents remain, the child's new relationships in an adoptive or a foster home may be distorted.[27] In order to "free" themselves to become permanent members of a foster family, children often need help to resolve these feelings.

The complexities of the tug-of-war between loyalties to a biological family and loyalties to a foster family were apparent in three studies which examined the issue of conflicting attachments among foster children. Fanshel questioned children in long term foster care in New York City;[28] Weinstein worked with children in care in Chicago;[29] and Triseliotes interviewed forty young adults who grew up in foster care in Great Britain.[30] Other studies provide some supplementary information.

All three studies reported that most of the children had formed strong and positive relationships with their foster parents. The major dimensions associated with the child's being able to form an identification as a member of the foster family seemed to be (1) resolution of ties to the biological family; (2) placement at a young age; (3) length of time in the foster/adoptive home; and (4) the structure and expectations of the family.

Parental visits, as long as they were regular, appeared to hinder the resolution of ties to biological families and tended to delay the child's identification with the foster family. As visits diminished, as they often did over time, attachments to the foster family began to develop.[31] However, knowledge about the family of origin and an understanding of the circumstances which led to the need for foster care seem to "contribute to feelings of well-being and to better adjustment" in young adults[32] and in children.[33]

Interestingly, the presence of other relatives in the children's lives does not seem to complicate their adjustment; indeed, it may facilitate it. Brothers and sisters, particularly if they are in the same foster home, can be a source of support and mutual assistance. One study showed an appreciably smaller percentage of children displaying problems when siblings were in the same foster home.[34] Concerned grandparents, who cannot care for the child, are often accepted by the foster family. They apparently have little impact on the developing foster parent-child relationship.

Age at entry into foster care has been found to be associated with the attachment of foster parents and foster children. Children who enter foster care young and have little memory of any other home may quickly become a member of what seems to be their "own" home. Fanshel and Shinn's measures of embedment in foster care showed this clearly; children under two years of age when they entered foster care appeared more deeply embedded in their foster homes than other children.[35]

Many writers have noted, and common sense agrees, that the length of time in the foster home is associated with the foster parent becoming the "psychological" parent to the child; the data of the New York longitudinal study showed increasing embedment in the foster family as time progressed.[36] Weinstein also identified length of time in the foster home as important to the child's identification with the foster family.[37] Triseliotes did not find age at placement to be important, but all children in his study had been in foster care for many years.[38]

These findings are corroborated in another study by Fanshel in which caseworker reports of the relationship of 352 foster children, for the most part in long-term foster care, to their own and to their foster families were examined. The caseworkers reported that half of the children had no attachment or minimal attachment to their own families. Over three-fourths of the children were thought to be strongly identified with the foster family, and almost half were considered to be "at peace" with their living arrangements. However, age was related to each of these variables. As expected, younger children tended to have less attachment to their biological families, to be more deeply integrated into foster homes, and to more often be "at peace." Older children, despite their increased years in the foster home, demonstrated more conflict.[39] This last finding seems, at first, to be at odds with the previously cited studies. However, this was the only sample that had a high proportion of adolescents, and adolescence is the age of the search for self-identity.

Finally, family structure seems to be an important factor in the children's ability to form attachments to their foster parents. Triseliotis differentiated four types of foster families and found strong attachment less frequently in families that had cared for many children and that had a "professional" attitude toward fostering. Families under stress or with tension were also less likely to form attachments.[40] Weinstein found that homes "structured in a quasi-adoptive manner" by the foster mother were more conducive to the formation of a family identity by the child.[41] And, Rowe and her colleagues found that the foster parents' expectations of the length of stay were associated with the children's adjustment.[42]

From the perspective of the parents, the attachment to a foster child is also complex. That it is formed through the day-to-day interactions of the child and the caretaker is unquestionable, but isolating the elements of this attachment is difficult. Goldstein, Freud and Solnit write of a relationship in which the child is "truly wanted" and "feelings are totally involved" so that there is, in effect, a "common law adoption."[43] This is akin to the sense of "total commitment" of which Pike writes.[44] Ward isolates factors of "entitlement" to the child and "validation" of parenting—the sense that "parenthood is ratified or confirmed both by societal attitudes and experiences with the child."[45] These abstract concepts need to be studied in more specific terms.

In several studies foster parents have been queried, and there has been some attempt to differentiate homes in which a close attachment has formed from other homes. Some of the factors important to children also seem important to foster parents, as would be expected in an interactive process, but other factors also seem important.

The structure of the foster home seems as crucial from the parents' perspective as from the children's. Foster parents with close attachments speak of a very early absorption of the child into the family and about their intent (or hope) to adopt from the start of placement.[46] This seems related to receiving a child, often a young child, similar to one that they had pictured in their family. A sense of "likeness" between child and family, as perceived by the foster parents, emerges as important.[47]

Enjoyment of children and active involvement in their lives seems crucial in those families where strong attachments form.[48] Additionally, there must be enough time and energy for this involvement and enjoyment to be expressed.[49]

While the evidence is ambiguous, writers seem to indicate that there is some relationship between a family's ability to resolve their feelings about the child's biological parents and their ability to form close affectional ties with the child. On the basis of research data, Holman has developed the concept of "inclusive" and "exclusive" fostering; "inclusive" parents include the biological family in their thinking about and interaction with the child, and are generally more successful than foster parents who try to deny the child's biological heritage.[50] Triseliotis found the parents who formed the closest attachment to their children had "predominantly positive feelings about the family or origin" and were quite open in sharing what they knew.[51] However, in another report, Triseliotis reports that about three quarters of forty-four adopted young adults, and half of forty young adult foster children, said they had been told very little about their heritages and that this information was shared with them very late in their lives.[52] Surely this is a reflection of parental discomfort with this information, even in families with "inclusive" attitudes.

Thus, in the crucial process of family formation, the factors which emerge from the literature as important are (1) the child's resolution of ties to the biological home; (2) at least some acceptance by foster parents of the positive elements of the child's background and some ability to be open about it in discussion with the child; (3) a family structure in which the child is received as a family member and long term care (or adoption) is expected; (4) the placement of a young child; (5) the placement of a child who is perceived as similar to the family in some way; (6) enjoyment of children and energy to express it; and (7) length of time in the foster/adoptive home. Given the limited empirical data available on this topic, there are probably many other factors which could be added to this list.

As agencies began to embrace foster parent adoptions as a way of achiev-

ing permanency, it quickly became apparent that one impediment to this plan
was that foster parents often could not afford to adopt. For some families,
foster care board payments had become a part of their economy. For others,
heavy expenses would be incurred in meeting the child's physical, emotional
or developmental needs. If foster parent adoptions were to be encouraged,
these economic barriers had to be removed.

In order to address this issue, most states created adoption subsidy programs with state funds. However, even with these programs, some problems
remained. Particularly in states where an annual review was required, some
foster parents feared that subsidy payments would be discontinued before
their child reached majority. Others were disturbed by the administrative
procedures for establishing subsidy payments and felt that receiving a subsidy
had "welfare" connotations.[53]

Recent federal legislation attempts to remedy these problems. P.L.
96–272 provides federal funds for adoption subsidy and mandates that states
have adoption assistance programs. This has, already, increased both the
amount of money being used for adoption subsidies and the number of subsidized adoptions being completed.[54] Further, provisions within this law
which guarantee that assistance will continue until the children reach matur-
ity, unless they are no longer being supported by the family, may increase
foster parents' trust and acceptance of subsidies.

Failure of Foster Parent Adoptions

It is clear that as the field moves toward placing greater numbers of
"special needs" children in adoptive homes the possibility that adoptive
placements will not work increases. Research has shown that the rate of
adoption failure increases with the age of the child, the number of moves the
child has experienced while in foster care, and the presence of other children
in the home.[55] While disruption rates for infant adoption are usually under 3
percent, those for special needs children are reported to be between 11 percent and 14 percent.[56]

There has been some speculation as to why placements disrupt when
special needs children are placed in new adoptive homes. In some cases, it is
due to unforeseen or situational circumstances such as financial stress, a
death, etc. However, in the majority of cases the disruption seems to be
caused by a problem in the parent-child interaction. The family may be
unable to cope with the child's behaviors or its effect on the family. They may
have trouble accepting a child's atypical appearance. Their expectations of the

child may be too high. The child may not be able to respond to them quickly or change in the ways that they expect.[57] Whatever the reasons, the match between parent and child was not right.

These are unlikely to be the reasons for failure in foster parent adoptions. The child has been in the home, the parents have coped with the child's behavior and appearance for a long period of time, and family equilibrium has usually been achieved. Foster families are usually not approached about adoption until the placement appears to be working out and both the family's and child's initial adjustments have been made. Often, the child has agreed to the adoption.

In all special needs adoption, whether in a new home or in a foster home, it has been posited that disruption can retrospectively be traced to problems in the worker's assessment of the family and the child. Pre-existing problems in the family, the child, or the family-child interaction may not have been recognized. These problems may have been unknown, or may have been known but not explored by the worker. Or, there may have been a misjudgment in the capacity or readiness of either the family or the child to form a permanent attachment.[58] Further, the child's entering a new developmental phase, such as adolescence, may cause stress. Finally, the family's "need" for the agency, either in coping with the child's behavior or for personal support, may not have been addressed.

There is also some indication in the literature that practices thought to be important to help assure that the adoptions will "work" are not being followed with some foster parents. Two studies have reported that some foster parents have felt pressured or blackmailed to adopt their foster children. Some families were threatened with the child's removal if the adoption was not completed.[59] Further, it has been reported that social workers have, at times, done little to prepare foster parents or their children for the adoption. The results of these practices have included cases where the foster parents were not planning to discuss the adoption with a child who has been in their home since infancy.[60]

While many would agree that a full home study is not necessary when the family has been known to the agency, there are issues in adoption which are different from those in foster care. These need to be fully identified and understood, and their relative importance assessed. Only then will practitioners be able to adequately prepare foster families for adoption.

It has been recognized that supportive services provided during the transition from foster care to adoption can help to diminish emerging problems and decrease the possibility that they will escalate.[61] It is apparently important to let all parties know that disruption is a possibility. This gives them "permission" to ask for help before their feelings intensify to the point that nothing can be done to avoid the child's replacement. Workers should also watch for signs during placement which may signal a possible disruption; an intensification of discomfort within the home and the personalizing of unpleasant events have been identified as indicative.[62] Beyond this, however, very little is known about the reasons foster parent adoptions fail or the process involved in their failure.

Outcome of Long-term Foster Care

Some foster parents decide not to adopt the children in their care, and the dilemma then posed to the worker is whether to move them to another home, which may provide legal permanency, or to avoid another separation and let them remain in foster care. The place of long-term foster care as an agency service needs thought.

The assumption that adoption is preferable to long-term foster care has been examined only in research completed in Great Britain, where adoption and foster care have long been a single continuum of care. Triseliotis has directly investigated the issue, comparing forty-four young adult adoptees and forty young adults who had grown up in long-term foster care. His findings are ambiguous, for he finds more than half of each group to be both well pleased with their experiences and well adjusted as young adults. However, of the remaining subjects, he finds only a few adoptees, but about a third of those fostered, to be dissatisfied.[63] In another paper, drawn from the same data, various types of foster families were identified, distinguishing those who may do better in providing long term care.[64] He concludes that for some children, in some circumstances, in some foster homes, long term foster care may be a suitable plan, though when adoption is possible it is preferable.[65]

One cannot draw clear cut conclusions on this issue based on studies of children who have spent time in foster care. On the one hand, clinical experience and some research reports document the damage done to children by separations, and probably about one quarter of the children who enter foster care experience an unreasonably high number of placements.[66] On the other hand, most studies seem to show that a high proportion of children who remain in foster care for extended periods of time develop reasonably well.[67] The exception is the study done by Rowe and her colleagues, in which careful comparisons of maladjustment rates among populations indicated that foster care did not provide a secure enough base for children to recover from earlier traumas.[68]

There is ample reason for concern about those foster children who move from one home to another. The extreme difficulty which young children have in coping with separation from accustomed caretakers has been well documented in the child development literature. Even separation entailing movement into a benign environment has been demonstrated to produce considerable upset in young children.[69] Knowledge of the impact of separation on the children who move from their biological home to a foster home comes chiefly from the practice literature of child welfare, which abounds with descriptions of the negative reactions of young children to such moves.

As most of the empirical work on separation has been concerned with its effects on young children, it is difficult to know how to generalize these findings to older children. At least one study has found age at placement and age at the time of study to be associated with the child's realism in explaining the reasons for placement.[70] And, possession of a good understanding of the reasons and the need for foster care has been associated with a good adjustment[71] and a secure sense of self.[72] Lack of information about the reasons for foster placement is mentioned by adults as a source of resentment,[73] and Fanshel has detailed the misery of the children who did not understand what had happened to their biological home.[74] One follow-up study of foster children as adults notes the continuing effort of these individuals to find some circumstantial explanation for their parents' failure to care for them.[75]

There is considerable reporting of the damage done to children by extensive replacements within the child welfare system. It appears that children gradually lose their ability to trust and to form new relationships.[76] A recent follow-up study reported that children who experienced multiple placements in foster care fared less well as adults than those who did not.[77]

There are a few studies of children who have been in foster care for an extended period of time and a few follow-up studies of young adults. Both types of studies indicate the importance of the interpersonal qualities of the home to the child's future adjustment. There is also some indication that feelings of permanence and belonging can develop under some circumstances in foster care.

In the most detailed and sophisticated study of foster care to date, Fanshel and Shinn followed a cohort of 227 children remaining in foster care over five years. Their study provides a wealth of data about various facets of adjustment. Overall, neither improvement nor deterioration in the children's functioning was found. Social workers identified the provision of an environment in which growth and development could take place as beneficial for most children in this cohort. Detrimental effects of the environment were identified in 43 percent of the cases; the child's sense of "insecurity" was prominent in the examples cited.[78]

After review of eight major outcome studies, Kadushin concludes:

Children who were in foster care for long periods have in 70–80 percent of the cases grown up satisfactorily. Some of the associations usually thought to be related to outcome, such as age at placement and number of replacements, are not unequivocally supported in the studies. Outcome seems to be differentially related to the sex of the child and *directly related to the interpersonal quality of the foster home*.[79] (emphasis added)

A recent British study classifies long-term foster homes on the basis of the quality of relationships within them, and has found outcome differentially related to these classifications. In particular, a feeling of "well being" and a "capacity to cope with current life" were strongest among young adults who had grown up in foster homes in which relationships had been satisfying.[80] This differential assessment of foster homes may be an important first step in understanding the various outcomes of foster care.

How does one connect the troubled memories of foster care reported by adult foster children with the successful lives they seem to lead? One explanation may be that former foster children do not feel as secure about themselves as their outward lives would warrant, though there is little basis on which to compare these feelings with those of children who have grown up in more permanent homes. It is perhaps best summed up in the concluding paragraph of one of Meier's reports:

The vast majority of subjects have found places for themselves in their communities. They are indistinguishable from their neighbors as self-supporting individuals; living in attractive homes; taking care of their children adequately, worrying about them, and making some mistakes in parenting; sharing the activities of the neighborhood; and finding pleasure in their association with others. They do not always regard themselves as being indistinguishable, however, because they remember that, as foster children, they were different from their peers.[81]

There is some evidence that long term foster care may "feel" permanent to some foster families and children. Weinstein found that over two-thirds of the children he interviewed expected to remain permanently in the foster home (even if biological parents were visiting).[82] However, children for whom a move was imminent were excluded from this sample.

The potential permanence of foster homes for children is also emphasized in a study in which caseworkers judged over three-fourths of 386 foster children to be deeply embedded in their foster homes; 52 percent of these children were reported to consider the foster parents as their "own" parents. The youngest children were most deeply rooted in their foster homes.[83]

Foster parents may also see themselves in a role similar to biological parents, and be so defined by others in the community.[84]

Outcome of Adoptions by Foster Parents

Is adoption by foster parents a good plan for children? Logically it makes a great deal of sense, for the child achieves permanency without the disruption of an existing set of relationships. Many foster parents who adopt may have expected the placement to be permanent from the start.[85] Most follow-up studies of adoption show about 70 to 75 percent of the children do well,[86] and, in general, research has shown that foster parent adoptions seem as successful as other adoptions.

In England, the recollections and assessments of 160 adoptive families and 105 young adult adoptees, who had been in these adoptive homes since early childhood, were gathered by interviews. About half of these families had fostered before adopting, although all but fourteen had expected or at least hoped to adopt from the beginning of their fostering experience. In general, the adoptions had been satisfactory for both parents and children. The adult adjustment of 68 percent of the adoptees who were first fostered was good, a percentage just slightly below that found in most adoption follow-up studies.[87] However, the adjustment of children whose families had not initially expected to adopt was not wholly satisfactory. The number was small, but these fourteen foster parents found the adoption experience less satisfactory than other adoptive parents in the study, and their children did less well as adults. Many reported that a distance between the child and the family was always maintained.[88] A thread of "not belonging" ran through the interview material in these cases.

In Illinois, the experiences of fifty-six foster/adoptive parents and twenty four of their children were explored in some depth about two years after the adoption. This is the only study in which an attempt was made to assess, through interviews with the children, the impact of adoption on foster children. Seemingly, adoption was important only if the child had a history of placement in other foster homes. Few parents attributed behavior change in the child to the adoption, though all change reported was positive. No formal assessment of the children's adjustment was made, but the experiences of the families appeared, in general, to be positive. However, it is disturbing that almost a third of these families had not wanted to adopt, and almost a third indicated difficulty in discussing adoption with the child.[89]

In Oregon, as part of a follow-up study of children for whom various permanent homes had been found, fifty-two families were interviewed nine months to two years after they adopted their foster child. On all measures, the results indicated that foster parent adoptions were as good as other permanent plans implemented in the project, including return to the biological home and adoption in a new family. Eighty-eight percent of the foster/adoptive families were reported to be doing well.[90]

Some Conclusions

The literature suggests that for the foster parents and children involved, foster care and adoption may not be as distinct as they have been to social workers. Rather, there may be a continuum of foster care experiences. In some foster homes there is the intent and feel of permanence to as great a degree as in adoption. In others, for a variety of reasons, such attachments do not form.

Even adoption does not ensure permanence. About a quarter of the foster parents who adopt experience difficulties, and some of these adoptions end with the child's replacement. The policy changes of recent years, which have blurred the distinction between foster care and adoption, while on the whole useful, may have encouraged the expectation that any foster family that cares for a child for an extended period of time will want to, and be able to, adopt. This is not so. One can speculate that the foster families that will adopt have distinct characteristics and will not be unlike those foster families in which permanence is the intent.

In the experiences of children, one sees the continuity between foster care and adoption. In foster care continuity with the biological past is associated with "well being"; adult adoptees are teaching us that this is important in adoption as well. The need to understand the reason for coming into care, and to find a circumstantial reason which does not imply parental rejection, runs through the practice literature of both foster care and adoption.

There are, of course, also major differences between foster care and adoption. The main difference is the extra support that adoption gives to permanence. About a quarter of the children in long-term foster care experience a disturbingly high number of placements, and there is no question that continuity of parenting is one of the chief developmental needs of children. Older children may deal with separations better; they are also the children least embedded in their foster homes and most susceptible to replacement. Some older children in foster care experience severe behavioral problems, increasing the risk that a foster home will disrupt. Thus adoption, which adds legal sanctions to permanence, may be crucial for some children.

Some adoptions by foster parents do, however, fail. The literature concerned with the adoption of older children informs us that placements break down because parents and children do not "bond" into a family, because parents do not expect the extent of disturbance they find in a child, or because the child cannot meet their expectations. None of these reasons should apply when foster parents adopt children who have been in their homes and who are a part of their families. The reasons for the failure of these adoptions are intriguing. Perhaps these children were not really embedded in their foster homes or their parents were not really ready to adopt. Perhaps the child's behavior, thought to be manageable at one time, escalates to the point that it becomes intolerable to the parents. Perhaps there are other reasons.

It appears, from what has been studied and written, that adoption by foster parents can be a satisfactory permanent plan for both parents and children. This also appears to be true for long-term foster care under certain conditions. The progression from foster home to adoptive home is not, however, a "natural" transition. Extensive and sensitive service seems to be needed to help children resolve their ties to their former homes so that they can fully accept their current status. Similar services seem to be needed to help foster parents weigh and accept the particular responsibilities of adoption. Without this help, there is danger of unhappiness and feelings of "not belonging" or of disruption of the adoption. Such work is probably also needed to establish a foster home for long term care.

Foster homes are a valuable resource for children—all the more valuable with the discovery that some can become permanent adoptive homes. The field must be knowledgeable as it works with these transitions, so that the potential of the home is enhanced and permanence insured.

CHAPTER 3

The Design of the Research

We lack understanding of the meaning of adoption and how it would affect a child.

Matching of parents and child is chancy at best—a gut feeling, not what anyone tells you.

We don't really understand why foster parents become attached to foster children. The relationship has to grow or the placement will not work.

Preparation for adoption and support to the family afterwards are often lacking. We don't really know what elements are needed.

Placements don't work when families have fantasies about care of the foster child that are inaccessible to the worker. Fantasy and reality must match.

Some children cannot tolerate close family ties—we don't know how to identify those children.

Why do some foster-parent adoptions fail? That's a good question.

The workers quoted above were working with foster parents, and adoptive planning, when they shared these ideas with the interviewers. Their comments illuminate some of the gaps in knowledge—some of the information social workers need if the transition from foster home to adoptive home is to be made successfully. It is evident that there is much that the field needs to know. The practice wisdom developed during the years in which social workers provided foster care and adoption as separate services provides some guidelines, but the merging of these two fields is new. There is research in some crucial areas of child development, family formation, and the outcomes of various plans of alternate care, but only fragments of the research questions posed by this study have been investigated. As yet, there is no synthesis of theory from which hypotheses can be drawn for testing. Thus, the current study is, by design, descriptive and associational.

Initially, the investigation was to be limited only to those factors associated with the decision of foster parents to adopt or not adopt a child who had been in their care. However, during the first year of the research, 1981, it was learned that some foster parent adoptions failed and that these failures were a growing concern of agencies. Therefore, additional funding was obtained to study a small group of foster parent adoptions which failed. This additional inquiry took place during 1982.

The Setting

Though based in a university, this study was possible only because of the enthusiastic cooperation of the six child welfare agencies involved. The input of an active advisory board, composed of people from four of these agencies, kept the research in touch with the practice concerns of the field. Their mediation also ensured the availability of workers in their respective agencies, whose own interest and thoughtfulness contributed to the richness of the data.

The Illinois Department of Children and Family Service is a large, multi-service, public child welfare agency. The children in Cook County, Illinois (the Chicago metropolitan area) are served by four area offices, large semi-autonomous units where varying practices can develop. Two area offices which served large numbers of foster children of various ethnic and racial backgrounds were used in sample selection for the study of adoption decisions; the sample of failed foster parent adoptions was drawn from all four area offices.

Three voluntary child welfare agencies also cooperated in the development of the study and the drawing of the sample: the Children's Home and Aid Society of Illinois; the Chicago Child Care Society; and the Jewish Children's Bureau. Of varying size, they share the common framework of providing professional services by highly trained workers. All have been active in the development of innovative service patterns in various aspects of child welfare. These agencies provided the members of our advisory board from the voluntary sector. In the study of failed adoptions, cooperation was also received from Lutheran Children and Family Services and Catholic Charities of Chicago.

Data Collection Pattern

Though there were some modifications due to reality constraints,[1] the research followed the same basic pattern during all periods of data collection. First, the members of the advisory board were queried about their general ideas regarding foster parent adoptions or adoptions that failed. Next, a sample of children who were either adopted or not adopted, or whose adoption had failed, were identified. The children's workers were then interviewed about their general ideas concerning the genesis, implementation and assessment of foster parent adoptions; their attitudes about such adoptions and other related matters; and information about the specific families and children identified for the study and with whom they had worked. Available case material about the families and children of concern was also read at this time. Finally, interviews covering a wide range of topics thought to be related to the various decisions were conducted with the families themselves. Whenever possible, ideas generated by the advisory board were included in the interview schedules, and insights generated during the worker interviews were pursued in the discussions with the families.

Thus, the initial work of the study was an extensive exploration with the advisory board, as a group, about their ideas concerning the reasons foster parents adopted or did not adopt, and later concerning the reasons for the failure of such adoptions. Each advisory board member was also individually interviewed for two to three hours, principally by the project directors, about their knowledge and speculations on these issues. These discussions are not reported here, but formed the framework for the instruments used in the research.

Following these discussions, an appropriate sample of families and children were identified and their workers were interviewed. These interviews had a number of purposes. First, they were used to gather the general ideas of the workers in order to gain insight into the phenomena under study and determine the critical areas which should be explored with the foster parents. Second, these interviews were used to gather information about the specific families identified for the sample and with whom the worker had had contact. Finally, this contact with the worker was used to gather information about their perceptions of agency policy regarding foster parent adoption and to tap their attitudes in a number of areas thought to influence this phenomena.

Thus, after being interviewed about their general ideas, workers were asked about specific families in their caseload including their characteristics, the characteristics of the child in their care, the relationship between the family and the child, and the services provided to them. This information augmented case record material which was also collected about the specific child and family. This was not only important independent data, but its collection allowed comparisons to be made between the worker's perception and the family's perception (gathered later in the project) of the critical factors involved in the decision under study.

Following the data collection with the workers, interviews with the foster/adoptive families were conducted. As often as possible, both parents were interviewed. These interviews were designed to elicit the parents' perceptions about their decision and information about variables which might have been associated with it. Thus, they were broad-ranging. While focused on the parents' experience with the child and the parent-child relationship, the interviews also elicited the family's composition, the history of fostering, the affectional response of the child, the supports available to the family, the perceptions of the characteristics of the child, and the perceptions of the worker and agency service.

With those families whose adoptions had failed, the interview focused on the family expectations, hopes and experiences in fostering; the important elements in the decision to adopt; a description of the circumstances which led to the failure; and the impact of this experience. With data comparable in many ways to that collected from the other families, it was anticipated that interesting comparisons could be made.

In all instances the interviewer who spoke with the parents was not aware of the data generated about the family through discussion with their worker. Thus, neither the interviewer nor the data provided by the family was biased or influenced by the perceptions of the agency worker.

The Sample

Sample selection for this study was a complex undertaking. It involved: (1) deciding on criteria for inclusion in the sample; (2) selecting children meeting these criteria, the needs of the project, and the reality constraints imposed by the research environment; (3) locating and interviewing the workers of the children chosen for the study; and (4) locating and interviewing the families who made the decision to adopt, not adopt, or terminate their adoptions. Each of these will be discussed in turn.

The Sampling Framework

In order to insure that the children had had time to become well established in their foster homes, and that the foster parents had had time to consider the issues of adoption, the sample was limited to children:

1. who had been under the care of a cooperating agency for a continuous period of at least two years prior to the study;

2. who had spent at least eighteen continuous months in the home in which their adoption was being considered; and

3. who, if their adoption had failed, had been in the home at least twelve months as foster children, and at least six additional months after the decision to adopt was made.

In order to insure that concrete factors did not emerge overwhelmingly as impediments to adoption, the sample was limited to children in homes in which at least one parent was under sixty years of age. Attempts were made to include only children legally freed for adoption, but records were not always complete, and in the end it was found that there were children in the sample for whom the process had not been completed, though no difficulties were anticipated.

Additionally, the sample was limited to children for whom the decision under investigation had occurred recently; either the decision to adopt, not to adopt, or to request the termination of the adoption. Efforts were made to study only decisions arrived at within the last two years, but in some instances it was necessary to use a three year time span in order to obtain a sample of adequate size. It was hoped that by working within a relatively recent time frame retrospective distortion would be minimal, for the events under discussion, the circumstances that led to them, and their impact would still be fresh in the respondents' memory.

Because of record keeping systems and desired sample size, the process of selection used to study the decision to adopt or not differed from that used to study adoption failure. Though both samples were drawn within the framework outlined above, it is easiest to describe their selection separately.

Sample Selection: The Children Adopted or Not Adopted

Within the voluntary agencies, workers completed forms identifying any children on their caseloads who met the stated criteria. Within the public agency, records were used to identify appropriate cases.

At the beginning of the process, the proportion of children needed in each of the various sub-samples was decided upon. In order to ensure that an extensive analysis of the factors associated with adoption could be made, a higher proportion of adopted children was decided upon. Because of possible differing service patterns, it was also decided that an equal distribution of adoptions and non-adoptions between the public and voluntary sectors would be included. It was hoped that a stratified probability sample could then be chosen.

However, the realities of actual sample selection further modified the design. First, it was discovered that there were not enough cases to meet the desired sample size in the sub-sample of children served through the voluntary sector whose foster parents had chosen not to adopt. Rather than unbalance the public/voluntary ratio desired or decrease the number of non-adopted children in the sample, a decision was made to go back a third year and identify and study cases in this group which met the other sampling criteria.

Second, it was discovered that in a number of cases two (and in some cases more) children, eligible for the sample, had either been adopted or not adopted by the *same* family and that these decisions had been made at the same time. Rather than burden either the worker or the family with repetitive questions, one child was selected to be the focus of the interview. If the worker thought that the family's decision was, in actuality, based on their feelings about one child, that child was designated as the sample child; otherwise the sample child was randomly selected. However, in one instance, a family decided to adopt one child in their care and not another. Both of these children were included in the study and the family and worker were interviewed about both children. It was believed that this would add richness to the data and help to highlight differences in the decision.

Finally, in matching the selected cases with their workers, it was discovered that many of the children had had the same social worker. This was particularly true in the public sector. In an attempt not to overburden any single worker, the inquiry was limited to the worker's experience with a maximum of five families. In those cases where the worker had more than five families chosen for the sample, a choice was made as to which families to eliminate based on the sampling needs of the study. These cases were then randomly replaced from the pool of families remaining in the appropriate sub-sample whose workers did not already have five families included in the study.

This, then, was the basic framework of the sample through which the decision to adopt or not adopt was studied: children in their foster homes for a considerable period of time, for whom the decision was made recently, about half served by public and half by voluntary agencies, about two-thirds adopted and one-third not. There were thus four groups of children: (1) adopted through the public agency; (2) not adopted through the public agency; (3)

adopted through a voluntary agency; and (4) not adopted through a voluntary agency.

Sample Selection: The Children Whose Adoptions Failed

In order to obtain a sample of children who had been adopted by foster parents only to have the adoption fail, administrators, supervisors and workers in the large public agency were asked to recall cases which met the criteria outlined above, and in which work with the family was completed. Initially it seemed possible to draw a large sample from this agency, but of the thirty-eight cases "nominated," only twelve met the sampling criteria (see Chapter 8). Such is the impact of relatively few of these distressing cases! Only the public agency was used in selecting this sample because all cases of adoption failure are re-opened in the public agency where responsibility for future planning is lodged. However, in three cases, the worker who best knew the family and/or child at the time the adoption was disrupting was employed by a voluntary agency, and these workers were interviewed.

The Final Sample

The final sample of children chosen for study numbered ninety-five. Fifty had been adopted by their foster parents; half from the public and half from the voluntary sector. Thirty-three children had not been adopted by their foster parents; eighteen from the public and fifteen from the voluntary sector. Twelve failed foster parent adoptions, all identified through the public sector, completed the sample.

With the exception of the sample of cases in the voluntary sector for whom the decision not to adopt was made, the sample represented roughly equivalent proportions of the total number of eligible cases within the agencies. The sample of adopted children included about 45 percent of the population of adopting foster families in both the public and voluntary sector whose adoptions had occurred within the two years prior to the study. The final sample of children who were not adopted included all children in the care of the cooperating voluntary agencies whose foster parents had decided not to adopt within the three years prior to the study, and 54 percent of the children in the care of the public agency whose foster parents made this decision within the two years prior to the study. All identified cases of foster parent adoptions which failed were studied.

The Workers Interviewed

The workers interviewed were those who had worked with the children and families selected for the sample. The process of drawing the sample of workers was thus dictated by the process of selecting the children to be included in the study.

In all, forty-three workers were interviewed about ninety-two children living in ninety-one families chosen for the study. Fifty of these children had been adopted by their foster parents, thirty-three had not been adopted, and nine had been adopted only to have the adoption fail. Thus, all but three children's workers (all in the disruption sample) were able to participate in the research. The number of children about whom each worker was interviewed and the worker's affiliation are displayed in Table 3.1.

Table 3.1
Workers Affiliation and Number of
Specific Families Discussed with Worker

Number of Children	Affiliations				Total		Total	
Discussed	Public		Voluntary		Workers		Children	
	n	%	n	%	n	%	n	%
1	5	28	14	56	19	44	19	21
2	4	22	7	28	11	26	22	24
3	4	22	2	8	6	14	18	19
4	2	11	2	8	4	9	16	17
5	2	11	–	–	2	5	10	11
7*	1	6	–	–	1	2	7	8
Total	18	100	25	100	43	100	92	100

*This worker had five cases initially included in the study. However, she was also the worker for two failed adoptions included during the second year of the project.

As can be seen from the above table, fewer than half of the workers were interviewed about only one family. These tended to be workers in the voluntary sector, where cases were distributed among six agencies. Thus, while 58 percent of the workers interviewed were from the voluntary sector, they reported on only 46 percent of the specific cases in the sample. Half of the workers in the public sector were interviewed about three or more children compared to only sixteen percent of the workers in the voluntary sector.

The Families Interviewed

The ninety-five children who were identified for discussion with their workers formed the basic sample for this phase of the study. As is true with all studies requesting voluntary cooperation from families who have worked with social agencies, some sample loss was anticipated. This was the case in this study. Table 3.2 displays this sample loss.

Table 3.2
Children in Sample by Agency Affiliation
and Adoptive Status

Sample Status	Adopted				Non-Adopted				Adoption Disruption			
	Public		Voluntary		Public		Voluntary		Public		Voluntary	
	n	%	n	%	n	%	n	%	n	%	n	%
Included in Sample	25	100	25	100	18	100	15	100	12	100	–	–
Moved/not located	3	12	3	12	–	–	–	–	–	–	–	–
Refused	6	24	4	16	3	17	2	13	2	17	–	–
Interviewed	*16*	*64*	*18*	*72*	*15*	*83*	*13*	*87*	*10*	*83*	*–*	*–*

A total of seventy-one families were interviewed about seventy-two children in this phase of the study; thirty-two adopted children, twenty-eight children who had not been adopted, and ten children who had been adopted and had their adoptions fail. This represents about three quarters of the children and families eligible for inclusion.

With the exception of the failed adoptions, about half of the families were served through the public sector, half through the voluntary. Sample loss, however, was not equally distributed among the adopted, non-adopted and failed groups. Loss was greatest among families who had adopted children, and most profound among those who adopted through the public sector. Just over two-thirds of the adopting group were interviewed compared to 85 percent of the non-adopting group and 83 percent of the group that had adoptions fail. While only a few more of the adopting group who were located refused to be interviewed, six adopting families had either moved to places too distant to allow an interview or could not be located. It was this inability to locate adopting families that accounted for the differences in sample loss between the three groups. This pattern of sample loss was anticipated and accounted, in part, for the decision to interview workers about more adopting families than non-adopting families.

Based on consultation with the advisory board it was anticipated that many of the families whose adoptions had failed would find their experiences too difficult and painful to recount, and that others would be angry with the agency and therefore unwilling to cooperate with the research. This anticipated high refusal rate did not materialize; only two of these families contacted refused to be interviewed.

The Instruments for Data Collection

The instruments used in data collection were developed from the ideas of the advisory board, from ideas generated by the literature review and, in later data collection periods, from information gathered from the workers. They were designed to meet the data gathering needs of all phases of the research and included instruments for: sample selection and clarification; gathering the workers' general ideas about and attitudes toward foster parent adoptions; collecting information about the families from the workers; and obtaining information from the families themselves. For the most part, the instruments used to gather data from or about the adopting and non-adopting families had parallel items, so that comparable information could be collected and compared.*

Instruments for Sample Selection and Clarification

Four forms were used for the purposes of sample selection and clarification. Three were used as assignment sheets for the interviewers: one for the workers of the adopting or non-adopting families; one for the adopting or non-adopting families; and one for the workers and families whose adoption had failed. An additional form was used when the interviewer telephoned the worker in order to clarify information and to establish, when necessary, which child should be the focus of the interview. All of these forms allowed the interviewer to document efforts to locate the appropriate subject and arrange appointments, and all were destroyed after data collection so that anonymity of responses could be guaranteed.

---

*Copies of all data collection instruments are available from the authors.

Instruments to Gather the General Ideas of the Worker

These instruments were intended to gather the knowledge and speculations of workers about foster parent adoptions in general. A number of attitudes thought to be related to the adoption of "special needs" children were also tapped, as was demographic and professional data about the worker.

The major interview schedule gathered the workers' knowledge, ideas, and feelings about foster parent adoption. The first question asked their opinion about why some foster parents adopted and others did not. This question was not always answered fully at this point, but it was thought important to have these initial responses before the worker's ideas could be structured and, perhaps, modified by other questions. Content areas, such as their perceptions of the importance of adoption for children; the elements of bonding; agency supports for foster parent adoptions; and ideas about why these adoptions fail, were also covered.[2] Some questions, such as those concerned with parent-child attachment, were drawn from theoretical material found in the literature. Other questions were drawn from the practice wisdom of the advisory board. Questions in this schedule were very open in nature and were designed to elicit opinions, ideas and speculations. Workers had varying degrees of comfort in responding to it and generally took between thirty minutes and an hour to complete this portion of the interview.

Typical of the questions in this part of the interview were:

We know that some foster parents, when offered the opportunity, choose to adopt a child in their care and others choose not to when given the same opportunity. Why do you think this is so?

In your opinion, does adoption really make a difference for these children, or would long term foster care be just as good?

Writers tell us of the "magic" of the bond that sometimes forms between foster parents and children, and leads toward adoption. What are some of the elements of this bonding that you have seen in your work with foster families?

When it becomes evident that a child needs a home and is not going to be able to return to his own home, in your opinion:

a.   Should the foster home generally be given the first opportunity to adopt the child?   Y   N

b.   Under what conditions should the foster parent generally not be considered as an adoptive parent for the child in his care?

What kinds of services do you think foster parents who choose to adopt their foster children need after the adoption?

About 15 percent of adoptions by foster parents of children who have been in their care are said to fail. Why do you think this happens? Could you speculate about specific reasons?

An additional schedule was designed to identify personal characteristics of the workers and information about their background, including their experience with foster parent adoptions. No specific hypotheses guided the construction of these questions, though it seemed important to be able to pay particular attention to the ideas of experienced workers. Areas covered in this schedule included the workers position, age, race, marital status, education, experience in social work and child welfare, specific job functions, working conditions and work pressures, future plans, and involvement in other, non-work related social welfare activities.

Finally, the workers were given a self-administered schedule, containing items designed to elicit their attitudes about areas thought to be relevant to foster parent adoptions. It attempted to gather their perception of adoptable children; their attitude toward permanency; their commitment to child welfare; their attitude toward subsidy; and their attitude toward termination of parental rights. Some indices had been used in prior research,[3] some were developed for this study.

Other than collecting personal information, these schedules were not administered to the sample of workers who were included only in the small study of adoption failure, as their focus was on the decision to adopt. However, a few key items regarding the worker's knowledge, ideas, and feelings were incorporated in the schedule used to interview these workers.

Instruments to Gather the Workers' Knowledge of the Families

Questions concerning the workers' perceptions of specific families in the sample had to be asked for each sample family with whom the worker had contact; between one and five families. Thus, these schedules were repeated when necessary. This discussion of specific families took between two and eight hours to complete, depending on the number of cases involved.

These instruments were designed to record the workers' perceptions of the families and children in the sample, and to record the interviewer's impressions of the interaction between the worker and the family. Through their use the "professional" perspective on the families and children was gained. Also gained was an understanding of the interaction between the family and the agency in the process of decision making.

Two schedules gathered the workers' perceptions of the specific families in the sample and the children they had adopted and/or not adopted. They also gathered factual and historical information drawn from the case record. One pertained to adopted children; the other, identical in many respects, to children whose adoption was refused. To the extent possible, an attempt was made to obtain a picture of the family and the child prior to placement and of the placement process. The case record was helpful in this attempt, for workers had often changed in intervening years. When the record was relatively barren and the worker gone, a supervisor was occasionally able to supply supplementary information. The current functioning of the child and family, and the factors which were germain to the adoption decision, were known to the worker interviewed and were collected. Demographic information about the family was also collected. Again, questions were drawn from relevant theory, literature, and our advisors' ideas and observations of practice. For children in long term care, the worker's statements about long term plans and the reasoning behind them provided our only data in this area.

Typical of the questions in these schedules were:

Prior to the placement of the child, did this family express any preferences for a certain type of child (e.g., age, race, sex, etc.)?   Y   N
If yes, specify:

What preferences were met?

When the child was initially placed in this home, did the family expect that this might be a long term placement?

What circumstances led to this child's placement in *this* home?

Describe the mother's initial reaction to this child (for example, sorrow, concern, determination to modify behavior, etc.).

Did the parents think this child had special needs either at the time of placement or at the time adoption was discussed?

Do you think this family wanted to adopt a child when they applied to be foster parents?

Tell us about the effects the child's placement had on the family, parents, own children, other foster children in the home, initially and at the time adoption was discussed?

When adoption was first considered for the child, did the agency approach the foster parents, or did the foster parents approach the agency?

When adoption was first discussed, what was the family's initial reaction?

In the course of the discussions about adoption, how long did it take the family to make a final decision?

At the end of the interview, the workers were given a self-administered schedule which summarized their impressions of the family in a series of ratings. Some items were developed for this project; some were drawn from the work of David Fanshel.[4] Also, on a separate form, the interviewers evaluated the information given by the worker regarding the specific families in the study. This form also allowed for any additional comments or notes that the interviewer wished to record.

Instruments used to gather data from the worker on the adoptions which had failed paralleled these schedules. Sources of ideas were the available literature, content analyses of the relevant items in the worker and family interviews conducted in the first year of the project, and the continuing ideas of our advisory board.

One form was used in reading all records that could be located—usually the summary record of the adoption subsidy unit and the child's record. Factual information about the family and the child was recorded. Information about the structure of the family, their fostering experiences, and the characteristics and needs of the child were gathered. Data on the placement process and early adjustment of the child in the home were also taken from the record and later supplemented by the workers if they had known the family at this point in time. A chronological outline of the adoption and its disruption was also recorded.

The major form used in interviewing the workers of the families whose adoptions had failed asked a few general questions about foster parents, adoption, and the reasons adoptions fail. For the most part, however, it was concerned with the worker's perception of the experiences of this specific family, and was similar to the major interviewing schedule described above. Focus was on the family's expectations in fostering, the matching of child and family, and the preparation for adoption. In addition, it asked questions regarding the services used to support the adoption, the interaction of worker and family during the period the adoption was disrupting, the factors which led to the failure, and the effects of the failed adoption on the family. Subsequent planning for the child was also elicited. Typical of these additional questions were:

How committed did this family appear, at the time of adoption, to be to this child?

How did the agency first learn of the problems that eventuated in the disruption?

What were the specific circumstances of the disruption?

What services were recommended?

What services were used? (List, noting family members using service)

If services were recommended but not used, why?

At any time, did the foster/adoptive parents change their minds about requesting replacement?

Can you describe the impact of this adoption and disruption on the development of the child?

Instruments to Interview the Family

The instruments for collecting data from the foster/adoptive families were developed only after the data from the agency workers was gathered and content analyzed. This was done so that the insights garnered from the worker data could be utilized in their construction. In addition, information from the literature and ideas generated from the periodic meetings of our advisory board were again utilized.

The schedules designed for this phase of the study were intended to (1) record accurate demographic information about the family and child; (2) parallel items used in the worker interview, so that differences in worker and parent perceptions could be explicated; and (3) explore areas about which only the foster family had knowledge including the impact of fostering (and adoption) on the family, the role perceptions of the parents, the "feel" of accepting the child into the family and the process of bonding, the impact of the agency and worker on the decision-making process, the continuing needs of the family, and the nature and quality of the services provided by the agency. Four instruments were used in this phase of the project.

One schedule concentrated on the families themselves and their experiences in fostering. It included the amount of time and the number of children they had fostered; demographic and family composition information; their motivation for fostering; their experiences with the agency and with the biological parents of the study children; their perception of their role as foster parents; the "family style," demographic and developmental information about the child of concern; their initial experiences with, expectations of, and reactions to the child; their perceptions of this child; and the child's effects on the family homeostasis. Some of the questions used included:

What were the most important reasons you decided to become foster parents?

When you first applied to be a foster parent, did you think you might want to adopt a child?

Do you feel you knew what you were getting into at the time you became foster parents?

Before *any* foster children were placed with you, did you have any specific ideas about the type of child you hoped to have?

How many agency workers have you had?

How many workers have you felt really know you and your family well?

Was one of these workers the one who discussed adoption with you? Y N

Describe what _____ is like now? (health, physical handicaps, behavior, intelligence, school performance).

Describe your first meeting with _____.

Have you ever met the child's biological parents?

Tell us about the effects the child's placement had on the family, on you yourselves, on your own children, on other foster children in the home.

Can you describe how _____ has changed during the time in your home?

Can you describe how your feelings toward _____ have changed since he first came into your home?

Does _____ seem to be similar to (like) any members of your family?

A second schedule was asked only of foster parents who had adopted study children, and directs itself primarily to the adoption decision. This schedule included inquiries about the families' perceptions of the events which led to thinking about adoption; the process of making the adoption decision; the reasons for this decision; their feelings and agency experiences during this period of time; the reality factors which influenced this decision; the child's involvement in the process; the changes which had occurred as the result of the adoption; and their expectations for the future.

A third schedule paralleled the one just described but was asked of foster parents who did not adopt the study child and directs itself toward this decision. Areas covered in this schedule were similar, but some questions were reworded to collect data on the decision not to adopt and the reasons for this. Typical of the questions used in these two schedules are the following (questions for the adopting parents are reported):

How long had _____ been with you when adoption was first raised?

What was your initial reaction to this discussion?

When adoption was first considered, did the agency approach you, or did you approach the agency?

What were the main reasons you had for wanting to adopt _____ rather than remaining his/her foster parent?

How well did you know the caseworker who discussed adoption with you?

In the course of the discussions about adoption,
a. How long did it take you to make a final decision?
b. What hesitations or fears did you have? How strong were they?

What were the most important factors which led to the final decision to adopt this child?

Has there been a change in _____ since the decision to adopt was made?

Is an adoptive home the same as a foster home?

The final schedule used in this phase of data collection sought the interviewer's assessment of the family. It asked the interviewer to judge the family on a number of dimensions including integration of the child in the home; affection of parents toward the child and vice versa; the parent's understanding of the child's needs; the child's adjustment; the conditions in the home and of the family; and the outlook for the future. These rating scales had also originally been developed for use in another research project.[5]

The instruments used to gather information from those parents whose adoptions had failed were developed in the second year of the study. The major interview schedule focused on the family's expectations in fostering; their perceptions of the children they had adopted; the experience of adopting; and the circumstances which led to the disruption and failure of the adoption. Initial experiences with the child, the process of parent-child attachment, preparation for adoption, and support received during the adoption, were of particular interest. So, also, were the experiences of the family which led to the request for the child's removal and their feelings about this. It also attempted to gather information about how the family "put itself back together" after the experience. Thus, the initial portion of this interview was similar to that used with the parents in the other samples. Typical of the additional questions asked were:

Describe what _____ was like in his last year in your home.

Did things "feel" any different to you after the decision to adopt? Was adoption different from foster care?

Can you describe to me what happened that made you think your decision to adopt _____ was a wrong decision?

What happened when you contacted the agency?

What could have happened to make this placement work?

These events are very difficult to go through. Can you describe at all how it felt to you?

How do you feel now about your decision?

Is there anything the agency could have done to be more helpful?

As you look back over your experience in fostering and adopting are there things you wish had been different?

Through the final schedule in this phase, the interviewer evaluated these families and the services they received. It included all items from the rating schedule previously described, but went beyond this material to include judgments about the failure and the supports that these families received at that time.

Hiring and Training of Interviewers

Seven interviewers with strong qualifications (extensive experience in foster care, adoption or both; clinical interviewing experience; and a masters degree) were hired. This was believed to be desirable given the sensitive nature of the questions which were to be asked, the fact that the interviewers would be questioning agency personnel who were often highly trained, and the nature of the judgments which the interviewers were asked to make after each interview.

At the beginning of each round of interviewing the full project staff engaged in an extensive training session. This training included an explanation of the particular phase of the study and an exploration of the theoretical underpinnings of the data to be collected. The concepts underlying each instrument were explored and reviewed, as was the content of each question. The mechanics of administering the instruments were explained. Finally, each interviewer was given the opportunity to "role play" the interview, both as subject and as interviewer. In this way the actual interviewing experience for each party was simulated.

Training was continued through periodic group meetings between interviewers and project staff after the data collection was begun. During these sessions experiences were shared, problematic aspects of the instruments were reviewed, and modifications were made in the schedules when necessary. Difficult aspects of the interview situation were discussed and, when possible, resolved. Techniques for dealing with sensitive questions or situations were suggested by the project staff.

The final aspect of training was accomplished through individual meetings with the interviewers. After the interview schedules were completed they were edited. Problems in the interview were identified and discussed with the interviewer. Through this process, familiarity with the concepts underlying the interview and interviewing techniques were strengthened.

Data Collection

The staff began interviewing agency workers in mid-May, 1981. All interviews, including those concerned with adoption failure, were completed by the end of June, 1982.

The study was explained to agency workers through our agency-based advisory committee and, when necessary, interviewers provided further information about the study. Workers signed a consent to be interviewed and to have the interview taped. Three workers requested that they not be taped, and this was honored. Schedules were number coded to assure confidentiality. Workers considered the questions thought-provoking and interesting, and their cooperation was excellent.

This phase of data collection was free of major problems. There were instances of difficulties in scheduling, interrupted interviews due, in part, to the length of some of the interviews, etc., but no more than one would expect when agency workers are asked to set aside large portions of their work time.

Because most ot the interviews were taped, the interviewers could maintain a certain quality control by playing back portions of the tape after the interview was completed. This insured that their recording during the session was accurate and that missed information was included in the final schedule. Each completed schedule was then edited. In this process, tapes were again used for clarification when necessary. With this double schedule editing, frequent discussions between interviewer and research associate, and the periodic staff meetings which included the interviewing staff, it is believed that an acceptable level of reliability was maintained.

Beginning in late August, 1981, letters on stationery provided by the cooperating agencies, explaining the study and requesting participation, were sent to parents sequentially. Each letter contained a card which the foster family was asked to return to the project if they did not want to be contacted. Only eight families returned these cards; nine additional families refused to be interviewed after telephone discussion with project staff (sometimes an appointment had been set only to be broken or cancelled).

In order to extend funds to as many interviews as possible, assignments to interviewers were made solely on the basis of geography. However, none of the interviewers who had participated in the data collection with the workers interviewed families about whom they had knowledge. Thus, no interviewer was aware of information about a specific family that had previously been collected.

After signing consent forms, most foster/adoptive parents were interviewed in their own homes. Whenever possible, arrangements were made so that both parents could be present for the interview.

Reliability of recording was maintained in the same way for the parent interviews as it was for the worker interviews. Playbacks of tapes, editing of interviews, and staff meetings to resolve any problems, were continued during this phase of the project.

The interviewers' experiences with the families were generally positive and they reported that their contacts went well. Many interviews lasted more than two hours, as many families wished to show pictures of their children, reminisce, etc. It appeared that the families were interested in this project and saw their participation as an opportunity to make a contribution to knowledge, as well as to talk about their experiences. For the most part, the interviewers believed that they talked very freely and honestly with them. After each interview the family was sent a "thank you" letter and a check for $25.00 in appreciation of their time.

Data Reduction

Because of the nature of this study many of the questions within the interview schedules had to be open ended; many were far reaching. This necessitated spending a significant amount of time in the development of codebooks which accurately captured the essence of the respondents' replys. Codes were therefore developed from the actual responses of the workers and parents.

In many cases the responses of the workers and/or families to a given open-ended question contained a number of pieces of information, all of which might be important in distinguishing adopting, non-adopting and disrupted families from each other. Take, for example, the question we asked of parents: "Before any foster children were placed with you, did you have any specific ideas about the type of child you hoped to have? (If yes) Describe." Parents might have talked about their preference with regard to the child's age, sex, race, degree of physical, emotional, or the developmental handicaps of the child, the presence of siblings, etc. The number of combinations and permutations of these elements is enormous. Rather than attempt to capture the respondents complex response in a single code, each possible element present in the response was formed into an individual variable—a "dummy variable"—and the family's response was coded for each of these elements as "mentioned" or "not mentioned." Thus, the codebooks for the interviews were quite long, very detailed, and required that the coders fully read a response, digest it and understand it, before they began to code the answer.

Six staff members of high calibre were hired to do this task. All of the coders involved with the project were either masters or doctoral students in social work and had either previous coding experience, experience in child welfare agencies, or both. Again, such qualifications were necessary given the complexity of the material to be coded and the necessity for the coders to make judgments in a number of areas including change in the child, the family, etc. Most of the coders remained with the project throughout the coding of all the data and were therefore able to become quite proficient.

The coders were trained at the beginning of each phase of coding. An explanation of the particular phase of the study and the actual data to be coded were provided. The mechanics of coding open-ended items in the manner just described was thoroughly reviewed, and each coder had an opportunity to do a "dry run" on actual schedules.

Training was continued throughout the coding process through bi-weekly meetings. In these sessions problems in the codebooks, the mechanics of the coding operation, and problems in specific schedules were discussed. Codebooks were refined as problems were uncovered, and periodic memos went to all staff informing them of modifications in the codebooks and procedural considerations in dealing with specific items.

Coding Reliability

In order to insure that the coding of this material was reliable, two separate procedures were used. First, after all coding of a particular schedule was completed, twenty percent of the cases were randomly selected. These randomly selected schedules were then coded for a second time by another staff member. Procedures were developed to insure that this reliability coding was rotated among the coders, thus insuring that the same two coders were not consistently checking each other's work.

Results of the twenty percent reliability check showed that on all but one schedule the two coders were in agreement on at least ninety percent of the coding decisions made. This was considered sufficiently high, given the open-ended nature of the responses, to warrant no further checking at this stage and these data were entered into the computer. In the case of the interview schedule concerning the general ideas of the workers, reliability was less than ninety percent. In this instance, all schedules were independently coded by two staff members. Discrepancies between the two coders were identified and resolved by senior project staff who made an independent judgment. These data were then entered into the computer.

In retrospect, it is not surprising that the coding reliability was low on this particular schedule. It was the first schedule assigned and the staff's inexperience in coding this type of complex material was evident. It was also the first codebook developed by the project staff and the "bugs" in the coding procedures had not yet been worked out. Finally, this schedule contained the most difficult material to code, for it dealt with the workers general ideas and opinions. The responses were far-reaching and often discrepant among workers.

Once entered onto the computer the second reliability check of the data could be started. Using the initial frequency distribution on each schedule, the data was checked for internal consistency. All discrepancies discovered at this point were corrected by returning to the original schedule and making the needed corrections in the data. It is assumed that the initial estimate of ninety percent reliability was substantially increased through this operation. Final frequencies were then run to assure that the data were clean of detectable errors.

Data Analysis

Analysis of the data in this study was concerned primarily with uncovering differences between the adopted and non-adopted groups. Thus, for the most part, statistics for differences between groups were used. When more elaborate analyses had to be performed, either in the construction of indices or in the use of multivariate statistics to explain outcome, it is noted in the text. All statistical procedures were performed through the use of either the SAS[6] or SPSS[7] statistical packages.

Summary

The study deals with five groups of children and the workers who knew them best. They include:

1. children adopted by their foster parents, with the families later interviewed (n = 34)

2. children whose foster parents decided not to adopt them, with the family interviewed (n = 28)

3. children adopted by foster parents, whose adoptions later failed, with the family interviewed (n = 10)

4. children whose parents refused to be interviewed:
    a. children adopted (n = 10)
    b. children not adopted (n = 5)
    c. children whose adoptions failed (n = 2)

5. children whose families had moved or were not located (n = 6)

The primary analysis of factors associated with the decision to adopt or not includes the first two groups. The description of the third group should enrich understanding of this decision and its consequences. From record material and interviews with workers, it is also possible to search for any common characteristics of those who refused or could not be reached for an interview.

CHAPTER 4

Parents and Children

"Foster homes are really only good for smaller kids who don't really understand. Adoption is more like a home. The name business means a lot to them. The day they really realize the name is different, they start asking questions and having certain feelings."

——A foster mother

"In adopting you think of a life-time."

——Another foster mother

"Adoption is only a word. It doesn't express the feelings you have."

——An adoptive father

"We treat all the kids as our own. I'm all for adoption . . . but not wanting to adopt doesn't mean you're not a good parent."

——An adoptive mother

There were, in the sample, fifty children who were fostered for at least two years and then adopted, and thirty-three who were similarly fostered, but whose foster parents decided not to adopt. Of these, the families of thirty-four adopted children and twenty-eight children who continued to be fostered were interviewed. In this chapter the characteristics of these parents will be explored. However, one cannot simply describe the sample without quickly moving into the findings of the study, for the parents who adopted differed markedly from those who did not; so, also, did the children about whom they made their decisions.

In examining the factors that differentiated those who adopted from those who did not, it should be noted that the difference between these families was in their willingness to take on a legal commitment and responsibility. Many of those who decided not to adopt had every expectation and hope that the child would remain in their homes and grow up as their foster child. In fact, at the time of our data collection, twenty-one children remained as foster children in their foster homes and were expected to continue there.

The chapter begins with a description of the families—their compositions, demographic characteristics, socio-economic status, motivations to foster, and community involvements. It then moves on to describe the children, including their demographic characteristics; their histories within the foster care system and within these homes; their development within foster care; and their physical, emotional, intellectual and behavioral status at the time adoption was discussed.

Whenever possible, information about the full sample of families and children, collected either from the case records or the workers, will be presented first. These data will be followed by information on the same variable gathered during the interviews with the families. In this way, the reliability of the information between these two data sources can be judged by the reader.

In reading this chapter it should be noted that the worker interview preceded the family interview by as much as a year in some instances. Thus, differences in the two sources of data may be a reflection of changes which occurred in the families over the course of the year. However, differences between the data sources may also be due to the effects of sample loss (twenty-one families were not interviewed directly); missing information due to an interviewer error, an uncodable response, the informant not having the requested information or incomplete case records; or inaccurate reporting on the part of one of the interviewees. When such differences between data sources occur, an attempt will be made, whenever possible, to clarify for the reader the reason for the discrepancy.

One troublesome note pervades this description. The reader will remember that one family adopted one child in their care and did not adopt another. There are thus only 82 families for the 83 children. With the focus on comparison of those who adopted and those who did not, this family cannot be assigned to one group or the other. It thus appears twice. Because it is an interesting family, and in order that the reader can evaluate its impact on the comparison, it is briefly described at the end of the chapter.

The Families

Mr. A, a printer, is forty-one. His wife, a nurse, is thirty-six. They have a comfortable income. They had two daughters. When their six-year-old died after a long illness, they decided they would like to be foster parents. They describe themselves as idealistic, and saw themselves as helping needy children. They adopted a two-year-old boy. Then, soon after a four-year-old little girl was placed with them, they began to think about adopting her, and soon were urging the agency to consider it.

—— An adopting family

Mr. F has only a grammar school education, but supports his wife and three children quite adequately as a welder. He is fifty-seven, she is sixty-one. They had no children of their own, and over the years have cared for six foster children on a long-term basis. Three are now in their home, all teen-agers. They like children, like having them around, like to think of themselves as helping. They have considered adopting some of the children, but do not see that it makes much difference.

—— A foster family

The extent to which families who later adopted differed from those who did not was surprising. Some of the differences are illustrated in the examples above. Because of these differences, demographic and descriptive characteristics of both groups of families are explored in considerable detail, as are more subtle variables such as motivation to foster children, and the parents' expectations as they began to foster.

Family Composition

There was wide variability in the composition of the families in both the total and interviewed samples. While the "typical" family in both the adopting and non-adopting groups consisted of a husband, wife, and three children (including the sample child), only one quarter of the families fit this modal picture.

In the total sample, nine women were without husbands. Three of these single women adopted (6 percent of the adopting group) and six did not (18 percent of the fostering group). Only one single parent could not be interviewed. Within the smaller sample, there were also nine single parents; two who had adopted and seven who had not (the six reported in the full sample plus one foster mother who had recently been widowed).

The workers reported that only five families had extended family members living in the household. In three families there was a grandparent present; in two an aunt or uncle. The parents reported more people outside the immediate family living in the home than the workers. Eight of the interviewed families reported other relatives or friends present—three had grand-parents, three had in-laws (one mother, one brother, and one son), one had a great-grandparent and one had a friend. Six of these homes adopted; two did not.

As shown in Table 4.1, in the total sample there were six very small families in which the child in the sample was the only child. Two of these families adopted and four did not. Eleven families contained more than six children; seven of these adopted and four did not.

The overall picture of the families in the interviewed sample was very much like that of the total sample. There were five families in which the sample child was the only child. In ten families, seven adopting and three non-adopting, there were six or more children. Apparently, having either many or few children is not, by itself, related to the decision to adopt.

In both the total and interviewed sample, about half of the families who adopted and about sixty percent of those who did not had biological children living at home. This is rather surprising, for practitioners continue to find childlessness one of the major motivations for adopting. In both samples, slightly less than half the adopting parents and half of the fostering parents had adult biological children.

Table 4.1 also shows that the presence of other adopted or foster children in the home may be an indicator of the family's intent with the study child. In the total sample, only six of the families who decided not to adopt had other adopted children; one of these is, of course, the family who adopted one child in the sample and did not adopt another. Sixty percent of the adopting families had previously adopted another child, compared to less than twenty percent of the families who continued to foster. This difference is statistically significant (p < .001).* On the other hand, more than half of the non-adopting families had other foster children, as did only about one-third of the families who adopted.

This same pattern was reported by the families in the interviewed sample. As in the larger sample, the presence of other adopted children was associated with the adoption of this child. Just more than half of the adoptive families had adopted a child before this one, as had only six families who did not adopt (p < .01).

Parents were asked if they had any unusual responsibilities or concerns about family members living outside the home. Two-thirds of both the adopters and the non-adopters stated that they did not. Among the others, responsibilities included care and financial support for ill parents; extensive

---

*Unless otherwise specified, probabilities presented throughout the text are based on Chi-square calculations with one degree of freedom.

help to grown children; care of children in the extended family when parents were under stress; and nursing care through some serious illnesses.

Table 4.1
Children in Home by Adoption Decision of Family

Children	Total Sample Adoption Decision				Interviewed Sample Adoption Decision			
	Adopt		Not Adopt		Adopt		Not Adopt	
Biological								
	n	%	n	%	n	%	n	%
none	28	56	11	33	17	50	11	39
one	7	14	10	30	7	21	8	29
two or more	15	30	12	36	10	29	9	32
Total	50	100	33	100*	34	100	28	100
Adopted (Excluding Sample Child)	n	%	n	%	n	%	n	%
none	20	40	27	82	16	47	22	79
one	17	34	3	9	10	29	3	11
two or more	13	26	3	9	8	24	3	11
Total	50	100	33	100	34	100	28	100
Foster (Excluding Sample Child)	n	%	n	%	n	%	n	%
none	32	64	16	48	22	65	15	54
one	9	18	10	30	4	12	7	25
two or more	9	18	7	21	8	24	6	21
Total	50	100	33	100	34	100	28	100
Total (Excluding Sample Child)	n	%	n	%	n	%	n	%
none	2	4	4	12	2	6	3	11
one	10	20	9	27	6	18	9	32
two	16	32	7	21	11	32	5	18
three or four	15	30	9	27	8	24	8	26
five or more	7	14	4	12	7	21	3	11
Total	50	100	33	100	34	100	28	100

*Throughout the text, total column percentages are presented as 100%. Where the actual total does not add to this figure it is due to rounding error.

Age

Within the total sample, those foster parents who adopted children were younger, and the children in their homes were younger. On average, the parents who adopted were about seven years younger than the parents who chose not to adopt. The average age of adopting mothers was about forty-two years; for adopting fathers it was forty-four years. On the other hand, the average age of mothers who did not adopt was about forty-nine years and the fathers in this group averaged fifty-one years. This difference in age for both mothers and fathers was statistically significant ($t = 3.32$, df $= 81$, p $< .002$ for mothers; $t = 3.23$, df $= 72$, p $< .002$ for fathers).

There was, as would be expected, a large range in each group. The youngest mother in the total sample was twenty-three and the oldest sixty-eight. Both adopted. The two youngest fathers in this sample were thirty years old; one adopted and one did not. The oldest father was sixty-eight and adopted the sample child.

The children in these homes also differed in age. Twenty-one (42%) of the adopting homes contained at least one child under six, as did only seven (21%) of the non-adopting homes. Fourteen of the non-adopting homes (42%) had only children over the age of twelve, as did only five (10%) of the adopting families. Thus, the families who did not adopt were older in all aspects.

Ages of children and parents in the interviewed sample were in the same patterns as in the larger sample. The range of ages among the adopting and non-adopting parents were almost identical to those reported above, and the difference in the mean ages between the two groups remained statistically significant. Eighteen of the interviewed adoptive families (53%) had children under the age of six, compared to only eight (29%) of the non-adopting parents. Nine (32%) of the interviewed non-adopting homes had only children over twelve, compared to six (18%) of the adopting parents in this sample.

Race

Within the total sample, white families predominated among those who adopted. Seventy percent of all of the mothers who adopted were white, compared to only 33 percent of the mothers who did not adopt. Of the forty-six white foster mothers in the total sample, three-quarters adopted the children in their care, while of the thirty-three black foster mothers, only about 40 percent adopted (p < .001). There were four Hispanic foster mothers in the sample, two of whom adopted and two of whom did not.

Almost all of the marriages were to men of the same race. As can be seen in Table 4.2, patterns of adoption were the same for fathers, and the difference in adopting between black and white fathers was also statistically significant (p < .001). Patterns among the smaller group of interviewed families were very similar; whites were clearly more likely to adopt than blacks.

Table 4.2
Race of Foster Parents by Adoption Decision

Adoption Decision

| Race | Adopt | | | | Not Adopt | | | |
| | Mothers | | Fathers | | Mothers | | Fathers | |
	n	%	n	%	n	%	n	%
White	35	70	34	72	11	33	10	37
Black	13	26	10	21	20	61	14	52
Hispanic	2	4	3	6	2	6	3	11
Total	50	100	47	100	33	100	27	100

The white parents in both the total and interviewed sample were younger than the black parents. Seventy percent of the white foster mothers in the total sample were under age forty-five, as were only eighteen percent of the black foster mothers. It seems that it is the white foster mothers under age forty-five who tend to adopt; 88 percent of these thirty-two foster mothers in the total sample adopted. Black foster mothers over age forty-five tended to continue to foster; 63 percent of these twenty-seven mothers decided not to adopt. The pattern was similar for foster fathers and for the smaller sample of interviewed families.

Family structure of white and black families differed only slightly. White families were somewhat larger, and had more biological children still living at home. Half of the white families had adopted a child prior to deciding about this adoption, as had only a third of the black families. And, of the nine single women in the sample, eight were black. Only three of these eight adopted.

Socio-Economic Status

Workers were unsure about much of the information they reported concerning the socio-economic status of the families. They were unable to report on the educational attainment of fifteen of the mothers (18%) and thirteen of the fathers (18%), and on the incomes of twenty families (24%) within the total sample. Because of this missing information, and the possible unreliability of the information obtained, the data presented in this section are taken from the interviews with the families themselves.

There are trends within the data which suggest that there is an association between socio-economic status and the adoption decision. These relationships are displayed in Table 4.3. Almost half of the adopting fathers were employed in professional, technical or business capacities compared to about one quarter of the non-adopting fathers. Adopting fathers were also better educated—more than half had gone beyond high school (16% held graduate degrees) compared to only one third of the non-adopting fathers (none of whom held graduate degrees).

Disparities among the mothers were less evident. Only about 40 percent of both groups of mothers were employed outside of the home. Two-fifths of the non-adopting mothers did not complete high school compared to only one-quarter of the adopting mothers.

At the extremes, income also appears to be related to the adoption decision. Of the eight families that reported monthly incomes of under $500, six chose not to adopt. More than half of the families that adopted had monthly incomes above $1,500; only one-third of the non-adopting group had incomes this high. It should be noted that seven of the eight lowest income families were headed by single women, including five of the six non-adopting mothers.

Further analysis of these data demonstrated that measures of socio-economic status were related to the race of the parents. Black mothers and fathers were much less likely to have completed high school than their white counterparts. Of the ten men in the sample who were either unskilled or retired, all were black. And, of the eighteen families with incomes under $1,000 per month, about three-quarters were black.

From this analysis, it appears that measures of socio-economic status,

Table 4.3
Socio-Economic Indicators of Interviewed
Families by Adoptive Status

Socio-Economic Indicators	Adoptive Status			
	Adopted		Not Adopted	
Foster Father Occupation	n	%	n	%
Professional/Technical/Business	14	44	5	24
Clerical/Craftsman/Operator	14	44	10	48
Unskilled	2	6	3	14
Retired	2	6	3	14
Total	32	100	21	100
Foster Father Education	n	%	n	%
Less than High School	7	22	6	30
High School Graduate	8	25	7	35
Post High School	17	53	7	35
Total*	32	100	20	100
Foster Mother Education	n	%	n	%
Less than High School	9	26	11	41
High School Graduate	11	32	7	26
Post High School	14	41	9	33
Total	34	100	27	100
Foster Mother Occupation	n	%	n	%
Professional/Technical Business	5	16	6	22
Clerical/Craftsman/Operator	6	19	4	15
Unskilled	2	6	1	4
Homemaker	18	58	16	59
Total	31	100	27	100
Monthly Income	n	%	n	%
Less than $500	2	6	6	21
$500–$999	6	19	4	14
1,000–$1,499	7	22	8	29
$1,500 or more	17	53	10	36
Total	32	100	28	100

*In this and all other tables based on the interviewed sample of families, totals of less than thirty-four adopting mothers and twenty-eight non-adopting mothers and thirty-two adopting fathers and twenty-one non-adopting fathers are due to missing information. There are a number of reasons for this including obtaining vague answers which could not be classified, a lack of information on the part of the family, a failure on the part of the interviewer to ask the question, etc.

which were related to race, impact the decision to adopt. Previous analysis showed that the age of the foster parents, which was also related to race, was also associated with the adoption decision.

One must therefore wonder about the impact of age, income, and education on the apparent hesitancy of black foster parents to adopt their foster children. This question is explored in the multivariate analysis presented in Chapter 7.

Motivations to Foster

Both the families and the workers were asked to speculate about the families' reasons for becoming foster parents and their expectations as they did so. The whole concept of motivation is fuzzy, and as the parents' data is the most direct, it will be used to describe the families.

Foster parents gave a mix of answers to the question: "Was there anything in your growing up that led you to become foster parents?" Most common was enjoyment of children, mentioned by twenty-seven mothers. Positive family experiences with children were mentioned by eleven mothers. The most common experience given by fathers was coming from a large family (n = 14), which was also mentioned by seventeen mothers. Other experiences such as aloneness, loss, or distorted growing-up experiences, were mentioned by only a scattering of parents. There was no association between these experiences and the adoption decision.

Asked their motivation for fostering, again a mix of reasons was given. Twenty-five mothers and twelve fathers mentioned wanting more children. Six mothers mentioned wanting young children now that their own children were grown, though fathers did not mention this. Altruistic motivations were prominent, given by thirty-two mothers and seven fathers. Sixteen mothers noted that learning about the need for foster parents had been important. Enjoying children, so prominent in discussions of growing up, was not often mentioned as a motivation; perhaps it had just been discussed and was taken for granted. Finally, it should be noted that ten fathers, only 16 percent of the sample, stated that they "went along" with their wife's desire to have more children. These motivations were very similar for families who adopted and those who did not.

Expectations

The interviewers explored with the families their ideas about what kinds of children they thought they would like to care for as foster parents. Though subject to considerable retrospective distortion, particularly among those who had been foster parents for a long time, the data are nonetheless suggestive. Only about 20 percent of the parents had no specific ideas about the child they would like to foster. Infants were mentioned by ten of the parents who later adopted and by only three of those who continued to foster. Four foster parents and no adoptive parents specified that they did not want an infant. Nine parents who continued to foster and only five who later adopted wanted a child of a specific sex. Only five adopting parents and three parents who continued to foster wanted a child without physical handicaps. Thus, the only discernable difference between the groups in this area was that the adopting parents tended to have a stronger preference for fostering very young children.

The parents were asked if there were children they felt they could not care for, and forty families, twenty-three who later adopted and seventeen who did not, agreed that there were. Most commonly mentioned were physically handicapped childern (n = 16), teenagers (n = 12), developmentally slow children (n = 10), and children with behavioral problems (n = 7). Twenty-seven families had, at some point, refused a foster child, mainly because the child had behavior problems or was the wrong age. In this thinking about their limits as foster parents, there was no difference between those who later adopted and those who did not, with only one exception. Four families, three of whom later adopted, had refused to care for a child because there was no possibility of adoption.

At the time they were thinking about the placement of this child, the similarity in preferences between the two groups remained. Fifteen families who adopted and sixteen who did not had specific preferences at that time. Fourteen wanted a child of a specific sex. Eighteen, ten of whom later adopted, wanted an infant or pre-school age child.

It is interesting, however, that the workers perceived preferences somewhat differently. Workers reported that twenty-six of the families who were interviewed and who later adopted (76%) had specific preferences while they knew of preferences for only sixteen (57%) of the interviewed families who did not adopt. Most notably, they thought that twelve families who later adopted, and only four who did not, had a specific preference for an infant or pre-school aged child.

Parents were also asked if they had wanted to adopt when they first applied to be foster parents. Twenty-eight, fourteen of whom later adopted, said they did not. Twenty who adopted and twelve who did not said they had wanted to adopt when they became foster parents but had, for a variety of

reasons, applied as foster parents. The difference between the original intentions of the two groups was not statistically significant.

Families apparently communicated this intention accurately to workers,
for there was very little difference in the reports of families and workers on
this variable. However, in the full sample of eighty-three families, the difference in original intentions between the two groups, as reported by the
workers, was somewhat sharper and, as displayed in Table 4.4, reached
statistical significance (p < .05).

Table 4.4
Original Intention by Adoption Decision

Original Intent	Adoption Decision			
	Adopt		Not Adopt	
Full Sample	n	%	n	%
Foster	15	33	17	57
Adopt	31	67	13	43
Total*	46	100	30	100
Interviewed Sample	n	%	n	%
Foster	14	41	14	54
Adopt	20	59	12	46
Total	34	100	26	100

*In this and all other tables based on the entire sample of families, totals of less than fifty adopting
families and thirty three non-adopting families are due to missing information.

Thus the original expectations of the two groups seemed fairly similar.
There was some greater preference for infants or young children expressed by
those who later adopted, and this group communicated specific preferences
more clearly to workers. A larger proportion of the total group who later
adopted also admitted to an original hope that this would be the outcome of
fostering.

Living Patterns

A series of questions were asked of these parents about their patterns of
family living. Within the families, a pattern of shared decision-making regarding budget, purchases, family plans, etc. was found. The mothers tended to

be primarily responsible for household tasks and child care, while the fathers were more involved in discipline. Aside from the fact that seven of the foster homes were headed by a single woman, there were few differences between those who adopted and those who did not.

In patterns of belonging to organizations, those who adopted differed from those who did not. These relationships are displayed in Table 4.5.

Table 4.5
Organizational Participation by Adoption Decision

Participation	Adoption Decision			
	Adopt		Not Adopt	
Outside Organizations	*n*	*%*	*n*	*%*
Active in Fair Number	12	36	1	5
Active in Child-Centered Organization	15	45	11	50
Not Involved	6	18	10	45
Total	33	100	22	100
Foster Parent/Adoptive Groups	*n*	*%*	*n*	*%*
Active Currently	10	29	2	7
Active in Past	4	12	1	4
Plan to Join	1	3	1	4
No Interest	19	56	22	85
Total	34	100	26	100
Church Participation	*n*	*%*	*n*	*%*
Regular or Active	25	74	20	80
Occasional or None	9	26	5	20
Total	34	100	25	100

Those who adopted were significantly more likely to be involved and active in community organizations. More than one-third of the adopters were involved with organizations which were unrelated to their child, as compared to only one non-adopting family. About half of both groups were involved with child centered organizations, mainly the school. Almost half of the non-adopters reported no ties to outside organizations. This difference is statistically significant when lack of involvement is compared to involvement ($p < .01$).

Further, fifteen of the adopting parents had in the past, were now, or planned in the future, to be active in foster parent or adoptive parent organizations, as did only four foster parents. This difference was also statistically significant (p < .02).

Only in church participation did the two groups look similar. Most of the sample were Protestant (47%) or Catholic (36%) and 76 percent were regular participants in the work of their churches.

Most families seemed to be in fairly close contact with neighbors, relatives, and friends. Only eight were distant from relatives. Coders judged only five families to be isolated, with parts of the typical social network not present. Four of these were foster families, but numbers seem too small to attach much weight to this variable.

The Children

The children who were adopted also evidenced many differences from those who were not, in their ages, in the experiences they had had, and in the extent of their difficulties.

> By the time Adam was eight years old, he had survived extreme neglect and final abandonment by his mother, an abusive foster home placement, a second foster home placement, and a group home placement. At the time he came to the home in the sample, he was almost nine, an attractive, appealing child who seemed much younger than his years. By age twelve he was destructive and over-active at home, but was also responsive to his new parents, and attempted to be helpful. He was three years behind in school and found learning difficult. He fought constantly with other children and found conformity to school rules impossible. He was suspended numerous times during one school year. He continues as a foster child.

> Robert was fifteen weeks old when he was placed with his foster family. He was very tiny, having been seriously neglected, and had a healing broken leg. But soon he was described as "nice and frisky." At age twelve, he is a bright child who is described as not working up to capacity in school. He is mechanical and interested in building and repairing things. He is curious, very sensitive to others' feelings, well liked by children and adults. He is adopted.

Gender

Of the eighty-three children in the total sample, thirty (36%) were girls and fifty-three (64%) were boys. Twenty of the girls (67%) and thirty of the boys (57%) were adopted. Thus, sex of the child was not a discriminating factor between the groups within this sample. For some reason, almost all of the black children in the total sample were boys. Of the seven black girls in the sample, three were adopted and four were not.

Among the children in the interviewed sample the distribution of the children by sex was somewhat more even; the sample loss was skewed toward boys who had been adopted. There were thirty-six boys and twenty-six girls. Within this sample, boys were somewhat less likely to be adopted than girls. Forty-four percent of the boys were adopted compared to 69 percent of the girls. Thus, in the interviewed sample there were twenty boys and only eight girls who were not adopted.

In both the total and interviewed samples, children were adopted or not adopted irrespective of the sex of other children in the home. Thus, the balancing of the sexes of children within a home does not seem to be a motivation for adoption.

Race

Parents tended to both adopt and foster children of the same race as themselves. Thus, as can be seen in Table 4.6, black children were disadvantaged in terms of adoption in both the total and interviewed sample. There were, in the total sample, thirty-eight white children, twenty-nine black children, seven Hispanic children, and nine children of mixed race (combinations of black, white, Hispanic and American Indian, with no combination prevalent). Seventy-four percent of the white children were adopted, compared to only 38 percent of the black children, a statistically significant difference (p < .001). Hispanic children were also likely to be adopted.

The racial composition of the homes in the interviewed sample was very similar to the larger sample. In the sample of families interviewed, there were twenty-six white children, twenty-four black children, two Hispanic children, and nine children of mixed racial background. Nineteen of the twenty-six white children (73%) were adopted, while fifteen of the twenty-four black children (63%) were not adopted. This difference was statistically significant (p < .001) and identical to the one reflected in the entire sample.

Table 4.6
Race of Child by Adoption Decision of Family

Child's Race	Total Sample Adoption Decision				Interviewed Sample Adoption Decision			
	Adopt		Not Adopt		Adopt		Not Adopt	
	n	%	*n*	%	*n*	%	*n*	%
White	28	56	10	30	19	56	7	26
Black	11	22	18	55	9	26	15	56
Hispanic	6	12	1	3	1	3	1	4
Mixed	5	10	4	12	5	15	4	15
Total	50	100	33	100	34	100	27	100

Age at Interview

In the total sample, the children who were adopted were younger than those who were not adopted. The average age of adopted children was about nine years; of fostered children about twelve and one-half years. As is evident in Table 4.7, within the total sample 22 percent of the adopted children were pre-school children and an additional 44 percent were ten or under. In contrast, only about one-quarter of those children in this sample who were not adopted were under ten ($t = 3.58$, $df = 81$, $p < .001$). Thus, it appears that adoption was more problematic for children over the age of ten.

The difference in age between the adopted and non-adopted children was even more pronounced within the interviewed sample. Due both to sample loss (many of the adopted children whose families were not interviewed were older) and inaccurate reporting (probably from the worker), the mean age of the adopted children fell from nine to eight years in the interviewed group. The mean age of the children who were not adopted remained almost the same, somewhat more than twelve years.

As might be expected, there was some congruence between the children's age and their parent's age; and children in white homes were younger. Within the total sample, slightly less than half the children in white homes were ten years old or older, while two-thirds of the children in black homes were in this age group. However, as is shown in Table 4.8, more black families showed hesitance in adopting these older children; 68 percent of the white children age ten and over were adopted while this was true for only 23 percent of the older black children. This may well be due to the lower socio-economic status of the black families within the sample.

Table 4.7
Age of Sample Child by Adoption Decision

	Total Sample Adoption Decision				Interviewed Sample Adoption Decision			
	Adopt		Not Adopt		Adopt		Not Adopt	
Age	*n*	*%*	*n*	*%*	*n*	*%*	*n*	*%*
2–5 years	11	22	5	15	11	32	4	14
6–10 years	22	44	3	9	12	35	5	18
11–12 years	8	16	6	18	5	15	4	14
13 years or more	9	18	19	58	6	17	15	54
Total	50	100	33	100	34	100	28	100

Table 4.8
Adoption Decision by Race of Foster Mother and Age of Child

	Mother's Race								
	White			Black			Hispanic		
Adoption Decision	Under 6	6-10	10+	Under 6	6-10	10+	Under 6	6-10	10+
	n *%*	*n* *%*	*n* *%*	*n* *%*	*n* *%*	*n* *%*	*n* *%*	*n* *%*	*n* *%*
Adopt	9 75	11 92	15 68	2 50	6 86	5 23	– –	– –	2 50
Not Adopt	3 25	1 8	7 32	2 50	1 14	17 77	– –	– –	2 50
Total	12 100	12 100	22 100	4 100	7 100	22 100	– –	– –	4 100

Coming Into Care

Children came into care due to a variety of circumstances. According to the caseworkers, thirty-eight (46%) were either abused or neglected, and sixteen of these were abandoned. Parental problems accounted for the placement of thirty children; fourteen of these parents were unable to care for children due to death, physical illness, and/or simply being overwhelmed, while the remaining sixteen parents were absorbed by the problems of alcohol, drug abuse, mental illness, etc.

Asked what they knew of the circumstances of the child coming into care, parents painted a similar picture. The reason mentioned most often (n = 19) was parental inability to care for the child. Abandonment was noted in fifteen cases, abuse in twelve cases and neglect in twenty cases.

For the most part, the reasons given by adopters were the same as those given by parents who continued to foster. However, neglect was noted by fourteen of the parents who adopted and only six who did not; and abuse or abandonment was mentioned by ten of the parents who adopted and seventeen who did not.

Children's reactions to separation from their biological parents were described by the foster/adoptive parents as overt wishes to be reunited with the family (n = 7), fearfulness (n = 6), anger (n = 5), and denial (n = 5). Children displayed symptoms such as crying, bedwetting and sleep disturbances (n = 8), acting out behavior (n = 2), withdrawn behavior (n = 2), and other negative responses (n = 5). They also expressed relief at being away from a difficult situation (n = 5) and other positive responses (n = 6). Twenty-three were considered too young to react.

Placements

Placement histories are often difficult to trace. Foster parents usually do not have full information regarding their children prior to their entry into the home. Workers have often changed. Case records, although often sparse, are probably the most reliable available source. Thus, in discussing these data, only information for the full sample, based on case record material, is reported.

The histories of the children before they came into foster care were often vague, and there was probably more disruption in their lives than was reflected in the records. Eight children went "from family to family" (often various relatives) before entering care. Three other children entered care around the age of five and there is almost nothing known of their first years. Of these eleven children, who almost certainly had multiple separations before entering the child welfare system, nine were later adopted. Six of these were lost from the interviewed sample when their families moved or refused to be interviewed. Thus, sample loss diminished the number of children in the interviewed sample who had multiple separations before entering care.

The children in the total sample had been in care for many years. Thirty-four (41%) entered foster homes as infants. An additional thirty children

(31%) entered care when under the age of three; twenty-five were placed in foster homes while five were placed in institutions.

The placement histories of the children in the total sample did not reflect the multiple moves often associated with foster care. About a quarter of the children were first placed in their current home. Another quarter had only one prior placement, usually in a short-term emergency foster home. Only nine children (11%) had four or more placements. Of these nine, four experienced two or three foster homes and had also been returned to either their biological parents and/or a relative. Five children had very poor experiences with the child welfare system. While one does not want to minimize the impact for these children, it is only six percent of the total sample. One child had four foster homes (which could not handle his behavior) before being adopted. Another had five homes, and when the sixth family (in our sample) did not adopt him, he was moved to a seventh. Another child had nine placements, moving with regularity between foster homes and institutions. Another child in this group lived in three foster homes prior to seven years in this home, then was in three institutions in an 18 month span, and then returned to this foster home. Of these five children, only one was adopted.

Most former placements had been in foster homes, but some children had experienced institutional care. Four children spent an average of almost one year in a children's home during their first two years, and a fifth child spent fifteen months in a nursing home. Two children had spent three or four months in institutions during their time in foster care (and one of these an additional year in a hospital) and one child had spent eight months in a hospital at age two. Six children were hospitalized as young infants for treatment necessitated by abuse or neglect, and four children spent their first two or three months in the hospital.

If one wished to speculate about the impact of institutional care on the development of the child's capacity to form and sustain close relationships, these are interesting children. Of the ten children who spent early months in a hospital, eight, including all six who had been abused or neglected, were later adopted. Were particularly good foster homes found for these traumatized infants, or did they call forth unusually intense responses from their foster parents? Neither the five children who spent parts of their first two years in institutions, nor the child who spent eight months in the hospital as a two year old, were adopted. Was their capacity to relate somehow impaired by this early institutional experience? The two children institutionalized when older, one of whom spent a year and three months in a psychiatric hospital and three institutions, the other of whom spent two periods of two to three months in instituions, were also not adopted, but institutionalization for them seems more a reflection of troubled behavior than a possible causal factor.

Age at Placement in This Home

Within the total sample, age at placement in this foster home was related to adoption (t = 2.42, df = 80, p = .02). Those who were later adopted were placed in this home at the average age of three years; those not adopted were, on the average, two years older.

Eighteen adopted children were placed in this home as infants, as were only five children who were not adopted. These children are an interesting group. Of the twenty-two children for whom data were available, eleven apparently had uneventful infant years; of these, six were adopted and five were not. The remaining eleven children placed as babies were very ill or very difficult to care for. They were seriously allergic and hard to feed, or suffered the residual effects of severe abuse or neglect, or had illnesses and respiratory problems requiring extensive diagnostic work, hospitalizations and surgery. The mothers spoke of being fearful of taking on the care of such sick infants and feeling that they should have remained in the hospital longer. All eleven of these infants, both black (n = 4) and white (n = 7), were adopted. One sees demonstrated the strength of the bond that is formed as a sick infant is nursed, nurtured, and begins to prosper.

The children in those families who were interviewed had also spent a great deal of their lives in the current foster home. Of those who were adopted, fourteen were under a year old when placed in this home; fully 85 percent were under the age of six. Seventeen of the twenty eight children who were not adopted, 60 percent, were also under six when they entered this home (p < .05).

Table 4.9 displays the interaction of what appears to be two major factors leading to the decision to adopt. About one-third of the children in the total sample were placed in their current foster home as infants. Of these, all but one child in a white home and two-thirds of the children in black homes were adopted. Roughly the same proportion of children were placed between two and five years of age, and at six years or older. In each of these age groups, about two-thirds of the children in white homes and one quarter of the chldren in black homes were adopted. Thus, white families consistently adopted a higher proportion of the children in their care, but this proportion was greatest when the children were young at the time of placement in the home. Again, it should be remembered that white families tended to be in higher socio-economic categories than their black counterparts in the sample.

Table 4.9
Adoption Decision by Race of Foster Mother and
Age at Placement in This Home

Adoption Decision							Race										
	White						Black						Hispanic				
	0-1		2-5		6+		0-1		2-5		6+		0-1		2-5		6+	
	n	%	n	%	n	%	n	%	n	%	n	%	n	%	n	%	n	%
Adopt	13	93	11	69	10	67	8	67	3	23	2	25	1	100	1	50	–	–
Not Adopt	1	7	5	31	5	33	4	33	10	77	6	75	–	–	1	50	1	100
Total	14	100	16	100	15	100	12	100	13	100	8	100	1	100	2	100	1	100

Children who were older at the time of placement in this foster home tended to have had more prior placements, having had more years for misadventures. As is shown in Table 4.10, of the thirty-seven children in the total sample with two or more placements before this one, twenty-five (68%) were three or older when placed in this foster home. Though a higher proportion of the children who were not adopted (55% vs. 38%) had two or more placements, the difference was not statistically significant. According to theory, each successive placement diminishes a child's capacity to form close relationships. One wonders whether the relationship of age at placement in this home and subsequent adoption may not be partially explained by the additional placements which the children who were older at placement had experienced.

Table 4.10 also shows that the total sample contained forty-one children who were under three years old when placed in the studied foster home. Eighteen of these children were placed directly from the biological home, from the hospital after birth, or from the hospital after a stay for treatment of the effects of abuse or neglect. Additionally there were eleven children who were placed in these homes when still under three after a stay in an institution or an emergency foster home. These twenty-nine children have had relatively good continuity of care. Twenty-one of them (72%) were adopted. At the other extreme were the nine children with four or more placements prior to this placement. Only three of them were adopted.

Table 4.10
Age Entered This Foster Home and Number of Prior
Placements by Adoptive Status

Age and Number of Prior Placements	Adoptive Status			
	Adopted		Not Adopted	
	n	*%*	*n*	*%*
Under 3 years				
None	13	45	5	42
One	8	28	3	25
Two or more	8	28	4	33
Total	29	100	12	100
3 < 6 years				
None	2	25	–	–
One	2	25	3	33
Two or more	4	50	6	67
Total	8	100	9	100
6 years and over				
None	2	17	2	17
One	3	25	2	17
Two or more	7	58	8	67
Total	12	100	12	100
Grand Total	49	100	33	100

Time in This Home

Length of time in this foster home was associated with continued foster care within the total sample. The children who were not adopted had been, on average, just over ten years in their present foster home. Those who were adopted had been in their current foster home, on average, seven and one-half years ($t = 3.15$, df $= 80$, p $< .002$).

It appears that sample loss was concentrated among children who, on average, had not been in this foster home as long as the children in the interviewed sample. The adopted children in the interviewed group had been an average of seven years in this foster home. Those who were not adopted had been there only slightly longer; an average of about eight years. Thus, for the interviewed group, the relationship between length of time in this foster home and the adoption decision was not significant.

Special Needs at Placement

Both the workers and the families were asked whether the children had special needs at the time they were placed in this home. The results of these inquiries were remarkably similar, and few differences were reported between the adopting and non-adopting samples.

The workers reported that special needs were present at placement for two-thirds of the children who were eventually adopted and three-quarters of the children who continued to be fostered. Most common were emotional problems (n = 39), which were seen in the same proportion of adopted and non-adopted children. Educational and behavioral problems at the time of placement were somewhat more prevelant among the non-adopted children, while physical problems were somewhat more common among the adopted children. However, no more than 20 percent of the full sample were judged to have problems in these areas, and the differences between the groups were not significant.

When asked to judge the severity of the special needs of all the children at the time of placement based on the workers' reports, the coders believed that about 40 percent had mild or moderate problems, and one-quarter were thought to have severe problems which would require daily care and effort. Again, based on these judgments, there were no differences between the adopted and non-adopted children.

Similar questions were asked of the families who were interviewed. Seventy percent of the adopting families and sixty-four percent of the non-adopting families felt that their children had special needs when they were placed. In contrast to the workers' reports, many more parents reported that their children had physical problems; half of the adopting parents and one quarter of the non-adopting parents reported such problems. This probably reflects the greater knowledge of the parents, and the difference between the two groups is probably reflective of the seriously ill babies who were placed in homes that eventually adopted.

Special Needs at the Time of Adoption Discussion

At the time adoption was discussed, the picture of the children's special needs had changed. Workers reported that almost half of the children in the total sample who were eventually adopted were problem-free. This was true for only one-quarter of the non-adopted children in the total sample (p < .10).
Within the interviewed sample, there was a statistically significant

association between the identification of special needs and the decision to adopt. When the parents were asked if, at the time of the adoption decision, they thought their child had special needs, twenty-seven said "no" and thirty-five answered "yes." As is evident in Table 4.11, three quarters of those who decided not to adopt identified difficulties, as did only 41 percent of those who adopted (p < .01).

Table 4.11
Special Needs of Children At Time of Adoption Discussions
By Adoption Decision

Special Needs	Total Sample				Interviewed Sample			
	Adoption Decision				Adoption Decision			
	Adopt		Not Adopt		Adopt		Not Adopt	
	n	%	n	%	n	%	n	%
No	22	47	9	28	20	59	7	25
Yes	25	53	23	72	14	41	21	75
Total	47	100	32	100	34	100	28	100

The differences between the worker and parent reports are probably due to both differences in perceptions and sample loss. It will be recalled that the adopted children whose families were not interviewed tended to be older; they were more likely than younger children to be displaying behavior problems.

Summarizing information supplied by the workers, coders made a judgment as to the severity of the special needs shown by the total sample of children at the time the decision about adoption was made. As shown in Table 4.12, only 18 percent of the adopted children but 32 percent of the children whose parents decided to continue to foster had severe problems which required daily time and effort. When none or mild problems were compared with moderate or severe problems, the difference between the groups was statistically significant (p < .05).

Physical Problems. Workers and parents did not differ greatly in evaluating the physical problems of children. Fifteen of the children in the total sample had serious physical handicaps and five were in poor health. Nine of the seriously handicapped children were adopted while six were not. Probably the most seriously handicapped child was confined to a wheelchair with cerebral palsy, was epileptic, and had both kidney and eye problems which had

Table 4.12
Coders Assessment of Special Needs of Children at Time
of the Adoption Decision by Adoptive Status

Special Needs	Adoptive Status			
	Adopted		Not Adopted	
	n	%	*n*	%
None Noted	22	48	9	32
Mild-Needs Minimal Special Care	3	7	–	–
Moderate-Special Effort Required	12	27	10	36
Severe-Daily Time/Effort Required	8	18	9	32
Total	45	100	28	100

necessitated repeated surgery. Another child had been burned over 80 percent of her body and was very scarred. She continued to have orthopedic problems and problems with motor coordination. More common were visual, hearing and speech problems, coordination problems due to retardation, and asthma and allergy problems which were severe enough to limit the child's activities.

Ten children were identified by their parents as needing specialized and extensive medical care. Two of these children were limited by severe handicaps and three were characterized as moderately handicapped. Four had serious health problems (three were adopted) and eight moderate health problems (four were adopted). (Some handicapped children also had health problems, and not all twelve children with health problems were characterized as needing special medical care.) Thus, neither the reports of the workers nor of the families seem to indicate that health problems were a serious barrier to adoption.

Intellectual Difficulties. Twenty-five children in the total sample were thought to have "below average" intelligence—somewhere in their records were IQ scores between seventy and ninety. An additional three had tested at below seventy. These below average children represent a wide variety of children, particularly because behavior problems often complicated their performance. The late adolescent reading at the fourth grade level was not uncommon among them. Half of the children who were not adopted (n = 16) had below average intelligence, as did only one quarter (n = 12) of those who were (p. < .01).

Parents were much more optimistic about the intellectual potential of their children than the professional assessments would warrant, particularly among those who adopted. Table 4.13 displays a comparison of parental assessment and professional assessment of intelligence. Note that adopting parents judged 59 percent of their children to be of above average potential, while workers so evaluated only 15 percent of the same children. Agreement was much closer on those children who were not adopted.

Table 4.13
Parental and Professional Assessment of
Intellectual Capacity by Adoptive Status

	Adoptive Status			
	Adopted		Not Adopted	
Parental Assessment				
	n	%	*n*	%
Above Average	19	59	7	26
Average	10	31	12	44
Below Average	3	9	8	30
Total	32	100	27	100
*Professional Assessment**				
	n	%	*n*	%
Above Average	5	15	6	22
Average	23	68	9	33
Below Average	6	18	12	44
Total	34	100	27	100

*Only those families who were later interviewed are included in this table.

Whichever assessment is used, it remains true that those children who were judged to be more intelligent were more likely to be adopted. Nineteen of the adopting parents assessed their children to have above average intelligence, as did only seven of those who did not adopt; eight children who were not adopted were considered to be below average as were only three who were adopted ($X^2 = 7.62$, df $= 2$, p $< .01$). Apparently, whatever the reality may be, the belief that a child has intellectual potential appears to be a factor in the decision to adopt.

Of the twenty-eight adopted children and twenty-seven foster children within the interviewed sample who were in school, twenty (71%) adopted children and only thirteen (48%) foster children were at their proper grade level at the time of the interview. Parents were asked for specific information on the children's last grades in reading and math. Surprisingly, both adoptive and foster parents were vague. They gave non-specific answers, could not find report cards, etc. Only nine parents could report either the last reading or math grade, and only about a quarter knew whether the child was at grade level in these specific subjects. This vagueness is interesting, but the data on school performance is sparse. Whether the fact that more than two-thirds of the adopted children and only half of the foster children were at their proper grade level is a function of better intellectual capacity, reflects differences in status within the homes and the greater security of adoption, or is impacted by differences in overt behavioral problems, cannot be determined.

Behavior Problems. Twenty-eight children in the total sample were reported to have serious behavior problems, and again a higher proportion of the children who were not adopted were so categorized. Of those who were adopted, thirty-nine (78%) were thought to be free of such difficulties, as was true for only sixteen (48%) of those who were not adopted (p < .01).

Differences between adopted and fostered children were evident in the parental description of behavior problems, as well. Eighteen of the sixty-two children in this sample, 29 percent, were characterized by their parents as having moderate or serious behavior problems, and ten were thought to have minor problems. As is displayed in Table 4.14, of the thirty-three children thought to be free of problems, three quarters were adopted; of the eighteen children thought to have more serious problems, fourteen continued to be fostered. These differences were statistically significant (p < .001) if one compares those with none or mild problems with those classified as having moderate or severe problems.

Behavior problems were, for the most part, difficulties with acting out behavior. Children were disobedient at home, hit teachers and peers, truanted, fought, could not concentrate or complete tasks, and/or were hyperactive. A few had stolen, run away or exhibited violent and threatening behavior toward adults and other children. Only three or four children were noted by workers to be withdrawn or unable to communicate. One might suspect that there were more of these children, but that they did not have as great an impact on their social worker's life as did the acting out children.

Most of the children involved in disturbed behavior were described by their workers as having exhibited a balance of problems and successes. They

Table 4.14
Parents' Description of Behavior Problems
by Adoption Decision

Problems	Adoption Decision			
	Adopt		Not Adopt	
	n	%	*n*	%
None	25	76	8	29
Mild—handled within home	4	12	6	21
Moderate—consistent misbehavior in school/community/home	3	9	7	25
Serious—self destructive, aggressive substance abuse, fire setting, etc. School discipline and/or police involved.	1	3	7	25
Total	33	100	28	100

probably provided enough gratification to their foster parents so that they were able to remain in the foster home. One child had been expelled eighteen times from school, but at home was helpful and cooperative and only a "bit immature." Another child was hyperactive and a "handful"—and very intelligent and interesting to be around. Another child, who was withdrawn and at times self destructive, had responded to the foster parents' care with good advances in physical development and health. Interestingly, workers and parents were in fairly close agreement in evaluating behavior problems, and the types of problems described.

The Families Not Interviewed

It is gratifying to note that most of the relationships found in these data were present in both the reports of the worker for the full sample and in the reports of the family for the smaller sample. However, some differences between these sources and samples were noted, and it is wise to look at the sample of families who were not interviewed to begin to ponder why they occurred.

The ten adoptive families who refused to be interviewed are interesting in that they all had adopted older children. The youngest of these children was seven years old, and the average age was eleven and one-half years. With the exception of one infant, the children were between four and seven at placement, and had been in their homes an average of six and a-half years. Eight of the ten were boys. Half of the children were known to have serious physical or behavioral problems. Otherwise these families seemed much like the larger group who adopted. Seven were white, all but two parents were in their late thirties or early forties, and most had between two and four children; a mix of adopted, foster, and biological children. Thus, in this group there was an over-representation of young parents who had adopted older boys, many with problems. Perhaps the reason they refused to be interviewed was that their adoptions were not totally satisfactory.

The five foster families who refused to be interviewed did not appear to be markedly different from the larger group, though they also resembled those adopting parents who refused to be interviewed. They too had older children in their homes; the youngest child was thirteen and the average age was fourteen and a-half. The children had been in their homes an average of ten and one-half years. The parents were in their late forties or early fifties, and there were no single parents in the group. Three of these children were boys, and three had serious physical or behavioral problems.

The Family With Two Sample Children

One family in this sample adopted one child in their care and refused to adopt the other. This was an older black family with three biological children grown and out of the home. They missed having children and eleven years ago began to care for foster children. Of the fifty children they cared for, only two remained more than a few months. Interestingly, the characteristics of these two children mirror those of the "typical" adopted and foster children in the sample.

One child was placed when two weeks old. It soon became evident that he was not well and demanded much care and attention. Continued testing eventually revealed a malfunctioning adrenal gland; he will need medication and face hospitalizations throughout his life. Though he was a bright toddler and responsive, the agency was not successful in finding an adoptive home for him. When the agency asked if they would be interested in adopting, the foster parents agreed immediately—he needed a home, they were attached to him, and they did not want to lose him.

The other child was ten years old at placement, the only older child the family had fostered. They agreed to take him because his need was great, but have been continually frustrated by his inability to conform to their family. "After they are five years old, their characters are shaped," said the father. The youngster, now sixteen years old, is retarded and has serious behavior problems. He and the family seem to have withdrawn from each other, with considerable anger. The family decided, because of his behavior problems and his inability to "fit" with their family, not to adopt. They do intend, however, to remain his foster family until he is grown.

Summary

The parents who decided to adopt the children in their care and the children who were adopted thus differed in many respects from those families who continued to foster and their children. In many ways it was surprising to find such differences in factors which existed independently of the interaction of parents and children.

One might expect that younger parents would adopt younger children, who had been younger at placement. Differences in socio-economic status and race between adopting and non-adopting families were somewhat surprising given the availability of subsidy. The finding that length of time in the home was negatively associated with adoption was surprising, and may be an artifact of the older age of the fostered children.

The family's original intentions to adopt, and a previous history of adoption, were related to the adoption of the sample child. Those families that originally intended to foster were more likely to refuse to adopt. However, original motivations for fostering seemed very similar for both groups.

There was little in the history of the children, other than race and the age at placement in this foster home, that was related to adoption. The circumstances that led to care and the multiple replacements some children experienced make one aware of the possibilities for emotional damage in their lives. However, it was the extent and severity of the child's special needs at the time of the adoption decision that seemed more strongly associated with the decision. Emotional problems, intelligence, and the parents' perception of intelligence appeared to be particularly strong indicators. Children with more serious emotional problems, or perceived as being less intelligent, were less likely to be adopted.

The data examined in the chapter are, for the most part, overt, easily obtained information, and the power of such factors as predictors may be useful. More interesting are the processes of interaction among family members and between family and agency which will be examined in the following chapters.

CHAPTER 5

Becoming a Family

Daniel was four years old, and had lived in seven different homes before he came to the foster family. From the first meeting they were delighted with him—he was "so cute." They could not imagine his own family letting someone else care for him. It was hard the first few months—the foster mother remembers wondering "What did I get into?" and "Can I cope?" But somehow the placement "made them more of a family." Parents and older siblings would plan together how to deal with Daniel's nightmares, his temper tantrums, his periods of withdrawn behavior. And gradually he began to become more and more a part of the family.

One day when Daniel had been in the home about three years, the worker brought up the idea of adoption. They were tempted. "He would stay—there would be no one else involved; just us, making the decisions. We could give him our name, just like the other kids." But Daniel's difficulties were unusual enough that they were unsure what the future held, and what the financial commitments would be. And "he had a home—whether or not he was legally adopted."

Almost all of the families in the study had become cohesive family units. The adoptive families were willing to make a permanent commitment to their children and to take full responsibility for their care. And, they were ready to see themselves as independent family units with minimal agency support and involvement. However, almost all of the families who continued to foster had also developed the balance of needs and gratifications necessary to become functioning families. They were all, at the time adoption was discussed, stable placements which the agency or the foster parents (or both) thought suitable for adoption. Their situations are often similar to that of Daniel's family, discussed at the beginning of the chapter. Most of the foster children will probably grow up in these homes and know no other. Others will retain meaningful contact. Thus, one would not expect to find gross differences in the process of becoming a family between the two groups, but rather subtle distinctions.

In this chapter the interactions between the children and their foster parents, as they join together to become a family, will be explored. The "match" of child and family, the impact of their initial meetings, their early experiences, and their responses to each other over time were all factors which were expected to be part of the process of becoming a family. The description of these events will focus on what the parents themselves told us, with only an occasional look at professional decision making, for family development is a subtle process and it seems the best informants for a study of this nature are those who were directly involved.

The Match of the Child and Family

The match between a child and a family is a delicate matter. No one knows exactly what factors are important, or whether they are the same for all families. One of the more important elements of a match would seem to be whether the stated preferences of a family, whatever they might be, are met in the placement. The reader will remember that families who later adopted tended to express to the worker somewhat more specific preferences than those who did not adopt. However, the differences between the groups were not great. Nine adopting families reported that all of their preferences were met. Four reported that some of their preferences were met. But twelve families who did not adopt gave the same answers. Only four families said that none of their preferences had been met, and none of these adopted.

How did the children appear to "fit" into these families in terms of descriptive factors? There were few patterns. Only eight children were of a different sex than any other children in the home. Since only four of them were adopted, it is apparent that "balance" within the families was not the aim of this group of parents.

Of the fifty-seven children who were not the only children in their family, twenty-two, a little over a third, were the youngest children in the home. Nineteen were "middle" children and sixteen were the oldest children in the home. There was some indication that oldest children were adopted less often—nine of the sixteen oldest children remained as foster children—but these children were also older in years.

All but four children were the same race as at least one of their parents; only two were the only children of their race in the home. Fifteen adopted children (44%) were the only adopted children in the home. Ten foster children (36%) were the only foster children. In all of the remaining families there was at least one other family member of the study child's status.

Expectations

The foster parents were asked if, at the time this child was placed, they expected a long-term placement. There were almost no differences in the responses of the two groups. Thirty-eight families (61%) expected the placement to be long-term, six (10%) were unsure, and seventeen (27%) expected the child to remain for only a short time.

However, there were differences in thinking about adoption. At the time of placement, or very close to it, nineteen families thought they would like to adopt the child; the rest did not consider this possibility until much later. Of these nineteen families, sixteen adopted. A much smaller percentage of those who considered adoption later in the placement actually adopted, and the difference between the groups was statistically significant (p $<$ .001). Thus, it seems that the original intent to adopt, first expressed when foster care was considered, was continued as the child progressed in the home.

The Placement Process

Little is known about the preparation of the children for placement. So many of the placements occurred so long ago that this material was no longer remembered at the time of the interview. Seventeen of the children were under one year of age, and no information was available regarding what was done to help the remaining forty-five children with their transition to a new home. However, from the material available on the pace of placement, it was evident that fewer than half of these older children could have had a visit with their new foster parents prior to placement. One senses that the work done to help these children mourn the loss of a family, and deal with the associated feelings, must have occurred, if at all, after the placement.

Visits prior to placement may have had more of an impact on subsequent attachment than is evident from a first look at these data. As can be seen in Table 5.1, thirteen of the children who were older when placed and were later adopted had pre-placement visits, as did only seven of those not adopted. Of the forty-two children without visits, half were adopted. But, it must be remembered that fourteen of the adopted children were placed when under age one and that this was true for only three children who were fostered. These very young children probably did not have pre-placement visits. When they are extracted from the total, the difference between those later adopted and those who continued to be fostered is statistically significant when compared on the presence of pre-placement visits ($p < .02$). Thus the one bit of evidence that there is about preparation of children for placement indicates that it may be important in later attachment.

Table 5.1

*Age of Child at Placement and Pre-Placement Visits
by Adoption Decision*

	Adoption Decision			
Pre-Placement Visits	*Adopt*		*Not Adopt*	
	n	*%*	*n*	*%*
Child Under One at Placement— Probably No Visit	14	41	3	11
Child Over One at Placement— Visit	13	38	7	25
Child Over One at Placement: No Visit	7	21	18	64
Total	34	100	28	100

Asked to describe their initial reactions when they first saw the child, parents produced some of the most emotionally moving data of the study. Whether parents later adopted or not, their first meeting with the child had been a vivid moment in their lives and was easily recaptured during the interview. For about half of the families this had been a time of pleasure and joy. For another one-third, emotions of sympathy and concern for the child were mixed with a desire to nurture. Said one parent, "She was a baby covered with burns, very tiny in size. I took her in my arms. It was a good feeling." A father commented he "thought he would be like Ivan the Terrible, only he was just a little boy who needed a home." Another family described how the child came to lunch. "The whole family was present. She made up to the dog . . . She said 'Hi, bye, and peanut butter' . . . I was excited and delighted. This would be our little girl."

The response of the foster mother to the first meeting with the child may be an indicator of the direction in which the relationship will move. Most mothers (70%) described themselves as happy, perhaps excited, liking and accepting the child. As is displayed in Table 5.2, this was true for more than four-fifths of the mothers who later adopted, and just over half of those who did not. A higher proportion of the mothers who did not adopt described themselves as feeling sorry for their children, shocked by their treatment, or uneasy, concerned or tense. When the numbers with these complex emotions are compared with the numbers expressing simple pleasure, the difference was statistically significant ($p < .05$). Patterns for foster fathers were similar for both adopting and fostering parents, with more than a third expressing happiness and pleasure in the child.

Table 5.2
Mother's Initial Reaction by Adoption Decision

	Adoption Decision			
	Adopt		Not Adopt	
Initial Reaction				
	n	%	*n*	%
Happy, liked child	26	81	13	54
Sorry for child, shocked	3	9	6	25
Unhappy, Concerned, Tense	3	9	5	21
Total	32	100	24	100

Childrens' responses to the first meeting were also varied, but were not associated with later adoption. Seventeen, of course, were infants. Three comments of the mothers describe the varying reactions of these babies: "She was unable to hold her head up, or move her arms and legs, but she was responsive and tried to smile," said one. Another described her child as, "Nice and frisky." A third "cried a lot."

Twenty-five children, 55 percent of the older children, were described as quiet and withdrawn, taking time before accepting affection and seeming frightened. Reported one mother, "He was quiet, stared, and didn't know how to hold on." A second "couldn't hug." A third parent, showing good insight, stated "He'd been through a difficult time, and he needed time to adjust."

Finally there were children who seemed immediately responsive and happy, but the response of one perceptive foster parent illustrates the emotional tone of this "easy" adjustment: "He was happy and talkative; he had his guard up and didn't come in sad; he seemed to fit right in the family."

Thus, despite the fast pace and lack of visits in many of these placements, the initial response of parents to the children seemed to be one of pleasure mixed with understanding and sympathy for the child. The mother's relatively uncomplicated happiness at first meeting the child may be the reaction most favorable to a later decision to adopt. Children also seemed to respond appropriately at the beginning of placement, generally meeting the expectations of the parents. According to the parents, half of the children made their adjustment to the life of the family within a week or two.

The Child in the Family

The initial pleasure experienced by the parents was not always sustained, and changes in feelings inevitably colored the decision about adoption. Adopting parents tended to sustain their initial positive reaction to the child (26%) or become more positive (68%). However, for 25 percent of the parents who did not adopt, their initial reaction had become more negative over time.

Table 5.3 shows the parents' description of the effect of the child's placement on the family, and presents an even more dramatic picture of the differences between those who adopted and those who did not. One-quarter of those who continued to foster described the effect of the child on the family as negative; one third gave either guarded responses or reported that the placement had no effect. In contrast, 79 percent of those who adopted said the placement had a positive effect on the family. The difference was statistically significant (p < .01) when one compared those with positive responses with others in the sample.

Table 5.3
*Parents Assessment of the Effects of the Child's Placement
on the Family by Adoption Decision*

	Adoption Decision			
	Adopt		*Not Adopt*	
Effects of Placement				
	n	*%*	*n*	*%*
Positive	27	79	11	42
Mixed or Neutral	4	12	9	35
Negative	3	9	6	23
Total	34	100	26	100

Other factors which have been identified by theorists as being important to the attachment process are the perceived similarity of parents and children; parental identification with and "standing up" for the child; a parental sense of entitlement to the child; and the presence of mutual rapport between parents and children. In these data, those who adopted and those who did not differed on some of these factors.

When asked if they thought their child was similar to themselves or to any other family member, almost 80 percent of those who adopted, and only about half of those who did not, said "yes." The difference, displayed in Table 5.4, was statistically significant (p <.05). Similar proportions of foster parents and adoptive parents perceived similarities in mannerisms and temperment. However, many more adopting parents perceived the child to be like the family in physical appearance and interests.

Table 5.4
Perceived Similarity Between Child and Family
by Adoption Decision

	Adoption Decision			
	Adopt		*Not Adopt*	
Perceived Similarity	*n*	*%*	*n*	*%*
Yes	27	79	15	56
No	7	21	12	44
Total	34	100	27	100

In an attempt to find out whether the children were viewed positively, the parents were asked if they thought their children were enjoyable. Almost everyone said "on the whole, yes." Asking whether the child seemed different from other children proved more discriminating. Some said the child was different in a positive sense—more sensitive, more intelligent, etc. Others saw negative differences—slower, more disobedient, harder to live with. As Table 5.5 shows, those who adopted were more likely to see the child as like other children (51%) or different in a positive sense (27%), while those who did not adopt saw the children as like other children (44%) or different in a negative way (44%). This difference was also statistically significant ($X^2 = 4.62$, df = 2, p <.10).

Table 5.5
Perceived Difference Between This Child and Other
Children by Adoption Decision

	Adoption Decision			
	Adopt		Not Adopt	
Perceived Difference				
	n	%	*n*	%
No	17	52	12	44
Yes—Positive	9	27	3	11
Yes—Negative	7	21	12	44
Total	33	100	27	100

Interviewers tried to encourage parents to talk about episodes in which they had had to be aggressive in defense of their children. Thirty-three parents were able to recall such episodes, sixteen of whom eventually adopted and fifteen of whom continued to foster. These differences are not marked. Foster parents were most likely to be active on behalf of the child with the schools (n = 7) or with other children (n = 6). More adopting parents (n = 7) had "protected" the child against the agency or during termination proceedings.

Questions about whether others viewed them as "real" parents to this child seemed curious to our respondents, and fifty answered "of course." The question should probably have been more subtle.

At the end of the interview, the interviewers rated the families on the understanding of the children shown by parents; the affection shown by the parents toward the children and the children toward the parents; and the rapport between the parents and the children. The results are interesting. There were very few negative ratings. On all scales, those who later adopted had very positive ratings; the assessment of those who fostered was more moderate. In interpreting these results, however, a note of caution should be interjected. It is quite possible that our interviewers, all of whom had worked in child welfare, saw the adopting families more favorably simply because they had adopted. Even with tapes of interviews, there was no way to assess the reliability of these judgments. Though these ratings must be interpreted with caution, they present a consistent picture, in the theoretically expected direction, of some of the elements of attachment which occurred during the child's time in the home.

In considering rapport between father and child, shown in Table 5.6, it is evident that 86 percent of those who adopted were thought to have a very close, sharing, understanding, relationship most of the time. The largest number of foster fathers, 63 percent, were judged to have a much more moderate degree of rapport. Among the mothers the pattern was the same. Both these differences are statistically significant (p <.001 for mothers and for fathers).

Table 5.6

Interviewer Ratings of Rapport Between Parents and Child by Adoption Decision

Rapport	Adoption Decision			
	Adopt		Not Adopt	
Between Child and Mother				
	n	*%*	*n*	*%*
Very close, sharing, understanding	29	88	8	30
Moderate rapport	4	12	19	70
Superficial	–	–	–	–
Total	33	100	27	100
Between Child and Father				
	n	*%*	*n*	*%*
Very close, sharing, understanding	24	86	3	19
Moderate rapport	3	11	10	63
Superficial	1	4	3	19
Total	28	100	16	100

Regarding the understanding of the children shown by their parents, interviewers rated 79 percent of the adopting mothers and 78 percent of the adopting fathers in the two most positive categories, indicating that they showed a good sense of the child's capacities and feelings. Only eight foster mothers (29%) and four foster fathers (19%) were so rated (p <.01). Most of the foster parents—thirteen mothers (46%) and eight fathers (38%)—were considered to have a generally good grasp of everyday situations, but to miss subtle aspects of the child's feelings. Six foster mothers and two adoptive mothers were considered to generally fail to recognize the child's viewpoints, capacities and limitations.

Patterns of affection displayed by the parents toward the children were judged in a similar way. A higher proportion of adoptive than foster fathers were judged expressive in their affection. Most fathers, twenty-four, were judged as showing quiet warmth and fondness. Three foster fathers seemed openly annoyed and bothered by the child. Almost all of the mothers were judged to have displayed positive affection toward the child, with a higher proportion of adoptive mothers again being judged as demonstrative in expressing affection. Four foster mothers and two adoptive mothers were considered "aloof and distant." One foster mother was seen as negative.

According to these ratings, the patterns in which the children reciprocated this affection were sharply different between adopted and fostered children. As is shown in Table 5.7, thirteen adopted children and only one foster child were characterized as being loving and expressive of their affection toward the father. Twice as many adopted children than foster children were thought to express quiet affection. Of the children who were thought to be aloof, irritating or hostile to the father, seven were fostered and four adopted.

Patterns of affection toward mothers were judged similarly, with differences between adoptive and foster mothers even more sharply drawn. Nineteen adopted children were thought to be expressively affectionate while only three children who continued to be fostered were so rated. Ten foster children were judged to be aloof and two were judged hostile. Only two adopted children appeared to have distant relationships with their mothers, and none were hostile. These differences were statistically significant and, even when one allows for the different ages of the children and the different patterns that come with age, seem important ($X^2 = 8.96$, df = 2, p < .02 toward fathers; $X^2 = 15.89$, df = 2, p < .001 toward mothers).

The role of the child in displaying affection is particularly interesting to note, and at this point it is well to recall from the preceding chapter that the children who were adopted were younger and fewer had experienced institutional care or multiple placements. One has an image of their growing up in demonstrative homes, being able to respond, and becoming more rewarding children to have around. A positive interactional cycle appears to have formed.

Thus, it is evident that, at least as parents look back on their experiences, some of the elements often noted in the attachment of children and parents were present to a greater degree in those families who moved toward adoption. Parents who adopted more often saw their children as like themselves and viewed them positively in relation to other children. They seemed to have close rapport with their children, and their children appeared to be openly affectionate. Their commitment to the children as family

Table 5.7
Ratings of Affection of Child Towards Parents
by Adoptive Status

Child's Affection	Adoptive Status			
	Adopted		Not Adopted	
Toward Mother				
	n	%	*n*	%
Loving, Expressive	19	56	3	12
Quiet Warmth, Fondness	13	38	11	46
Aloof, Distant or Hostile	2	6	10	42
Total	34	100	24	100
Toward Father				
	n	%	*n*	%
Loving, Expressive	13	45	1	7
Quiet Warmth, Fondness	12	41	6	43
Aloof, Distant or Hostile	4	14	7	50
Total	29	100	14	100

members was strong, and their initial positive feelings had either been sustained or grown stronger.

Changes in the Children

In the average of seven or so years between their placement as foster children and the families' decision about adoption, the children had, of course, also grown, matured, and changed. Through some mix of what they brought to the placement and what the placement offered them, the two groups of children appear to have changed in rather different ways. This is displayed in Table 5.8.

In general, the problems of those children who were later adopted had decreased. Based on information from the workers' interviews, the coders thought that of the twenty-six children in adoptive homes about whom they could make a judgment, eleven had never had problems, and the difficulties of twelve had decreased or disappeared. Among the twenty-four foster children about whom judgments were made, they categorized only five as never having problems, and thought that while the difficulties of eight had decreased, two were the same and nine had worsened. Comparing the children whose problems were thought to have improved with those whose problems were thought to have had remained the same or worsened, the difference between the groups is statistically significant (p < .05 for interviewed parents; p < .01 for total sample).

Table 5.8
Coders' Evaluation of Changes in Children's Behavior
Between Placement and Adoption Decision by Adoptive Status

Problem Status	Adoptive Status			
	Adopted		Not Adopted	
Interviewed Sample				
	n	%	n	%
No Problems Ever	11	42	5	21
Improved	12	46	8	33
Same/Old Problems				
Replaced With New	2	8	2	8
Worse	1	5	9	38
Total	26	100	24	100
Total Sample				
	n	%	n	%
No Problems Ever	18	46	5	20
Improved	17	44	8	32
Same/Old Problems				
Replaced With New	3	8	3	12
Worse	1	3	9	36
Total	39	100	25	100

Parents described specific difficulties when they talked about changes in the children since placement. It became evident that the changes in problems referred to by workers were chiefly changes in behavior. In this area, only two parents who adopted reported worsening or new difficulties, while six foster parents thought their children's behavior had become worse. In judging responsiveness of the child to family members, the same pattern prevailed. Ten adopting parents and only five foster parents reported improvement. However, social skills, personal habits, and physical health were generally thought to have improved for both groups.

A few of the responses of parents illustrate the types of improvement they saw:

—At first he refused to eat and would hide food; he got better, but stayed a light eater.

—He is much more confident now. He doesn't have to compete with everyone to be best.

—He listens now and kisses me goodbye, a show of affection that took a long time coming.

—He used to cower when you told him "no." Now he has occasional temper tantrums.

Obviously problems remain, but parents who see a positive direction of change are apparently more likely to adopt. And, the information from the workers gave some indication that these are real changes in behavior, not just changes in the parents' perceptions.

Contact With the Biological Family

It might be expected that the presence of the biological parents in the life of the child while in the foster home would disrupt the process of family integration. The children might retain their identity with their family of origin. For the foster parents, another set of parents might continually remind them that they could not completely absorb these children into their families; there would be no chance to pretend that they were their "own." One might therefore expect little contact between adopting and biological families; more with families who continue to foster. This, however, was not the case.

There was a surprising amount of contact between the children who were later adopted and their biological families. Twenty-six of these adopted children had visits with biological parents after placement, and in twenty-one instances the adopting parents had met the biological parents. Among the children who continued to be fostered, only nine had contact with their biological parents after this placement, and eight fostering parents had met the biological parents. In addition, one foster family and child were in contact with a grandmother, and one with an aunt. And the situation of tiny, badly neglected twins should be noted. Though their parents and adult relatives never visited the foster home, a thirteen year old sister, who had cared for them and was probably responsible for their survival, visited regularly.

Contacts, of course, varied greatly in frequency. Table 5.9 displays that while two-thirds of the fostering parents had never met the biological parents, this was true for only about one-third of the adopting parents (p < .01). But many of the adopting parents had met the biological parents only once or twice, or only in passing when they took children to visit. About a quarter of each group had extensive contact.

Table 5.9
Contact With Biological Family by Adoption Decision

	Adoption Decision			
Contact With Biological Family	Adopt		Not Adopt	
	n	%	n	%
Never Met Parents or Any Family Member	13*	38	18	64
Have Met Adult Extended Family Member	–	–	2	7
Minimal Contacts (Met in hallway, had one or two discussions)	11**	32	2	7
Extensive Contacts (met several times, relationship apparently formed but contacts now ended)	5	15	5	18
Extensive Contacts Which Continue	55	15	1	4
Total	34	100	28	100

*Includes two cases in which both foster parent and biological parent were at the agency at the same time but the foster mother refused to meet the biological mother.
**Includes two cases in which biological parent asked foster parent to adopt after intensive discussion.

Extensive, even continuing, contact with the biological parents, seemed to have different meaning to these two groups of parents. Of the six foster parents who knew the biological parents well, two saw their interest in their children as a reason not to adopt; and three older boys refused adoption, at least, in part, because of parental contact. The ten adopting parents who had extensive contacts with biological parents reacted in a number of ways. In three instances, anger at the biological parents' behavior seemed to motivate them to push for adoption. In three other instances the relationship between the two sets of parents became so trusting that the biological mother asked this family to adopt. In the remaining four cases the family simply liked the biological family and felt that a rational plan had been made for the child. If one can generalize from these responses, it would seem that the decision to adopt may be influenced either by a resentment at visits and concern about the child that motivates the family to "secure" the placement through adoption or an understanding of the parents as persons, and of the stresses they are under, which allows the adopting families to accept their children's heritages. As might be expected, there was some tendency for the more extensive contacts to develop into the more understanding and positive relationships, though this was not always so.

The timing of the contacts with the biological family appeared to vary between the two groups of parents. While there was a significant difference between the adopting and non-adopting families regarding any contact with the biological parents, this difference was not apparent during the first year of the child's placement in the home. About one-third of the families had contact with the biological parents during this period of time, and both the workers and families reported that the differences in contact were not significantly different between the adopting and non-adopting groups.

However, this was not the case during the year adoption was discussed. Over 90 percent of the non-adopting group reported having no contact with biological parents during this period. This was true for only 58 percent of the adopting families, a difference that was statistically significant ($p < .01$). Thus, it appears that the families who continued to foster experienced decreasing contact with the biological family over time.

As foster and adoptive parents described their own contacts with biological parents, it was apparent that they varied greatly in emotional quality. Overall, adopting parents expressed negative feelings about all or some of the contacts with biological parents significantly more often than non-adopting parents ($p < .01$). Nine adoptive parents expressed resentment ("We had to rearrange our lives to suit the mother's convenience for visits"), uneasiness ("I don't like her a whole lot. She doesn't always show for visits and starts turmoil"), or anxiety ("I was afraid she might harm the baby, or might not like the way I had her dressed"). Only two foster parents reacted in this way. On the other hand, eight adopting parents and five foster parents characterized the visits as "OK" though some of these had had early problems. "The first visit was horrible; I didn't know what to expect. Everyone's feelings got easier as there were more visits," said one mother. The remaining adoptive parents described visits as being an essentially neutral experience ("We weren't really involved") or in mixed terms ("Their mother is OK, but the father tries to be overbearing and has abused his visiting privileges").

Five of the adopting families continue to be in contact with the biological parents even though the adoption is finalized. In four of these instances visits had occurred regularly since the child's placement. In these five cases, a relationship has formed, the parties appear to like each other, and they have planned together for the child. Workers, seemingly, have played little role in these relationships or in the planning process. For example, one biological mother had planned, with the agency, to take her baby home. The foster parents were horrified because they thought she could not meet the needs of this ill and delicate baby. The mother and foster parents talked, over time, and she decided to surrender the baby on the condition that they adopt. She continues to visit and "leans" on them as one might rely on parents. According to the adoptive parents they like the mother, she does not interfere, and they feel secure that the child will remain with them. The social worker in this case was characterized by the family as knowing little about the child and not being helpful; the worker says she worries about the relationship between the two families.

According to the parents' reports, the immediate reactions of the older children who had contact with their biological parents were different for the adopted and non-adopted groups. Among the older adopted children parents tended to report that the children were upset by the visits (n = 6) or had mixed feelings about them (n = 4). Two young adopted children were reported unaffected by the visits. For only two primary school aged adopted children were contacts reported to be enjoyable—"She missed her mother" said one adoptive mother. In contrast, for six children who continued to be fostered, visits with parents, grandparents, or aunts, which had been extensive, were characterized as predominantly positive. For only one foster child were visits reported to be upsetting.

Thus, a high proportion of the adopting parents had cared for children who had visits with their biological parents early in placement and who, if old enough, were upset by these visits. These parents are, of course, strongly identified with their children. The anger that some of them expressed toward the biological parents is expectable: "We grew angry at his disinterest in the children; we told him off several times" said one family. But, the understanding developed by many of these adoptive parents is also remarkable: "She needs help herself; she has no idea how to care for children. I felt sorry for her," said one adopting mother about a young biological mother.

What were the long term effects of these contacts between biological parents and children? The best data are the parents' description, but one must remember that the parents' own needs may color their reports, and that the workers agreed with the parental assessment in only a little more than half of the cases. (Workers tended to speculate about underlying causes of behavior and to identify more problems as "caused" by separation.) Nevertheless, when parents were asked if their children were currently having difficulties which they thought might be related to their feelings about the biological home, four foster parents and eight adoptive parents identified such problems. Additionally, eight foster parents and six adoptive parents reported that such problems were present earlier in the placement but were now resolved. Given the difficult lives of many of these children, one "feels" that these difficulties may have been under-reported.

Foster and adoptive parents reported that they used the same methods to help their children resolve their ties to their biological family. Ten foster parents and nine adoptive parents said they provided love and comfort, discussed the biological family, and tried to help the child accept the new home. Unfortunately, fifteen adoptive parents and five foster parents reported that their children were too young at placement to have ties to their biological families. Six adoptive and four foster parents said they were doing nothing to help the children with feelings about the past. One cannot help but be concerned about the denial implicit in such responses. However, it may also indicate a strong commitment to the children and a desire to absorb them into their new families.

About one-quarter of the children were placed with siblings; eleven of these children were later adopted and nine were not. Eighteen children remained in contact with siblings placed in different foster homes; twelve of these were adopted. These contacts required active encouragement and assistance from the parents, often involving visits to other homes or having siblings spend time at their home.

In conclusion, it is apparent that though a higher proportion of adopting families had contacts with biological families, especially during the year adoption was discussed, these contacts did not impede the adoption. Indeed, some adoptive parents were quite active in facilitating contact with siblings. For adopting parents, the contact with the biological parents may have provided them with additional information about their child and their biological families; information which may have been used to more readily meet the child's needs, and which may have added to their sense of "knowing" about the child's background and heredity. For many, the heritage of the biological family seems to have been accepted. And for some adoptive parents, contacts with the biological parents and concern about the problems it created for them and their children undoubtedly provided an incentive to move toward adoption.

Beginning to Decide About Adoption

At the beginning of the discussion of adoption, twenty-seven families reported that they approached the social worker with the idea, while thirty-two families reported that they were approached by the agency. For twenty-four of the families, the idea developed without outside stimulus; for fourteen it was triggered by change in the status of the biological parents, and for twelve it was triggered by an agency procedure (such as the transfer of the child to an adoption unit) which signaled that a change in status was planned for the child. This "triggering" event was similar for roughly the same proportions of adopting and non-adopting families.

However, at least as reported by the family, who approached whom about adoption was clearly related to the adoption decision. As shown in Table 5.10, about 40 percent of the adopting parents were approached by the agency compared to 70 percent of the non-adopting families. Only forty percent of those approached by the agency later adopted while 70 percent of those who approached the agency pursued this course (p <.02). Workers remember the initiation of this discussion somewhat differently, as is discussed in Chapter 6.

Table 5.10

Initiation of Adoption Discussion by Adoption Decision

| | Adoption Decision | | | |
| | Adopt | | Non-Adopt | |
Initiation	n	%	n	%
Agency	13	39	19	70
Foster Parents	19	58	8	30
Mutual	1	3	–	–
Total	33	100	27	100

Adopting families were asked if, at the time the discussion was initiated, they thought adoption would be possible. Of those families who adopted, twenty-one (61%) thought that it might be. Typical responses were:

—She was free to be adopted, we were afraid someone else would take her.

—Because of the case background the mother never showed a positive response to changing.

—We had a place for her and our finances were OK. We gave her good care
too.

Eight of those parents who doubted that adoption would be possible
thought that legal ties to the biological family would not be resolved. Others
worried about more concrete factors such as their age or finances. Only two
families indicated that they thought their status as "temporary" foster parents
would prohibit their adopting.

As might be expected, the overwhelming reaction of the adopting parents
was one of pleasure when the possibility of adoption was first raised. "The
caseworker gave us hope. We really wanted the adoption" was a typical
response. Seventeen families had reactions similar to this. Five families expressed irritation with agency procedure or with the idea that their qualifications had to be reviewed. These families made clear, however, that they
wanted to adopt the children, and most of them actively encouraged the
worker to start adoption proceedings.

Only three adopting families expressed initial hesitation. One father was
unsure about his feelings, but his wife was strongly attached to the child and
afraid they would lose him if they did not adopt. Another mother was hesitant
because the adoption of another child was not yet complete; there is some indication she felt overwhelmed by this rapidly growing family. The third
mother initially refused because she did not want to be tied down with a
young child but wanted "a job and some freedom." She changed her mind
when it became evident the child was about to be moved to another adoptive
home.

When adoption was first discussed with the parents who continued to
foster, their reactions were less positive. While eighteen foster families had, at
some time, indicated interest in adoption, only eight of these families approached the agency to ask about it, and only nine families responded
positively to the initial discussion. However, only three of these families immediately ruled adoption out, due either to their age and/or illness.

The other ten foster families had simply never thought of adoption,
though the children had been in their homes an average of eight and one half
years. During these years only three of these homes had cared for other foster
children. For most, a stable family with one or two foster children seemed to
have formed. When the social worker raised the possibility of adoption, apparently to the surprise and irritation of these parents, they apparently felt
that a stable situation was being upset because of the agency's quest for "permanency" for all children. Most irritated was the foster mother whose twelve-
year-old child, for whom she had cared since infancy, was shown to a prospec-

tive adoptive family—a rather abrupt way for the agency to call the possibility of adoption to her attention.

Of those families who continued to foster, seventeen initially saw adoption as important for the child. However, not all thought adoption in their home was suitable. Typical were the responses:

—Yes it was important to the child—because this was home to him and he didn't want to leave. But it was best he go to a young, active family.

—Yes, she could stay—there would be no one else involved, just them making the decision. I could give her my name, security—just like other kids.

—Yes, differences in names can be upsetting and you start seeing the child differently.

Of the six foster families who thought adoption was not important, three replied in the manner of the respondent who said "he has a home—whether or not he is legally adopted." Two others mentioned the child's close ties to biological family and thought adoption would be confusing. Only one family mentioned that the child was "set in his ways" and "had bad habits." Thus the initial attitude of this group of foster parents toward adoption was, for the most part, positive, and they considered it for their families.

The Decision About Adoption

For those families who decided to adopt, the decision was usually fairly readily made and the reasons compelling and evident. Asked their main reason for adopting, seventeen families mentioned legal security for the family so that the child could not be moved, thirteen families mentioned the attachment of the child and the family to each other, and twelve families cited security and permanence for the child. Some families gave more than one of these responses, and a few added other reasons including that they had always planned to adopt.

—We wanted him to stay with us. We had become very attached and would never let him go.

—We wanted the permanence and stability of adoption; she had already had too much confusion in her life.

The foster parents were asked what their main reason was "for thinking it was best just to leave things as they were." They gave a variety of reasons and showed much less uniformity in their responses than those who adopted. There were twelve families who focused on reasons having to do with their family situation. Five foster parents emphasized their age. "She couldn't ever take care of herself, and I'd be too old to care for her." Three families were stopped by illness in the family. Particularly poignant was the family in which the father's terminal illness had first been identified during the physical examination which was part of the adoption application. Three families thought their financial situation was such that they could not support another child. Adoption subsidies were discussed with all three of these families, but one father was fearful that after they had adopted the state would "back out" of the subsidy agreement, one family misunderstood and thought subsidies were not available for "healthy kids," and one family decided that the subsidy would not be large enough once the child moved into the more expensive years of adolescence. Finally, one mother said she didn't think it would be wise because she was a widow: "It's different raising a child alone. It's better with two parents."

In four additional situations the family decided not to adopt because of the children's continued contact with their biological families—a father, a grandmother, or aunts and uncles. All four families seemed to feel that adoption should entail a transfer of loyalties to their family and that this would not be possible. Said one: "there is no problem with a foster home and the grandmother's continued contact, but if he were adopted he would feel caught between the two." Additionally, at least one of these families thought that adoption was unimportant and was being discussed only as a part of the agency's procedures.

Eleven families were concerned about their childrens' future and were hesitant about assuming responsibility for them. Two children had serious medical problems, two might well need education in special schools, and eight had serious behavior problems. "We loved him and wanted to help him, but we realized the state wouldn't help out (after an adoption). They were very vague. We couldn't handle his hyperactivity—he needed more than we could provide" was the way one family expressed the common concern of these families. Interestingly, all but four of these children remain in their foster homes and the families seem firmly committed to their continued care as long as they do not have total responsibility and have the continuing support of the agency.

Four adolescent boys refused to be adopted. In all four instances the worker had initiated the idea of adoption when the boys had been in the home for many years. At first two of these boys were eager for adoption; one had even asked about it. Then they became concerned about keeping their last names and, when they were assured that they would remain with the family anyway, decided against adoption. Another boy was sixteen and still in contact with his biological father, though he already used the foster family's name. The idea of adoption, which had seemed like a "natural transition" to the foster family, caused him considerable confusion and unhappiness. The family "decided to let it go . . . we didn't want him to be upset." The fourth simply was firm that he did not want adoption.

As mentioned previously, eighteen of these foster families had, at one time, been interested in adoption. Four, described in the preceding paragraph, would have adopted had their children not decided against it. For five families it was evident that time and circumstances had altered their earlier interest—they had cared for several foster children, had grown older, and illness was, for some, now a problem. The very difficult behavior of their children caused six of these families to hesitate. One family felt unable to take on the rather frightening medical responsibilities of a handicapped child, and another hesitated to take on a life-time commitment to a retarded girl. Two families decided that their children's continued contact with their biological families would interfere with adoption.

As reported earlier, ten families had simply never thought of adoption before it was raised by the worker. Their children ranged in age from five to eighteen and had all been in the homes at least five years. These parents were surprised by being asked to consider adoption; some were angered. Five of these families decided not to adopt because of the needs of the children for special school placements and counseling services; some of these were also worried about their ages and financial problems. Two single women in the group were worried about raising a child without the support of the agency; the children in question were ten and thirteen years of age and had behavior problems and learning disabilities. They too were concerned about finances. One family did not adopt because of the mother's heart condition, though the father, at least, was reported to want this. And, finally, two families thought adoption inappropriate because of the biological family. In one of these instances, the child was in contact with his mother; in the other with a grandmother. In both cases the foster parents thought this appropriate for fostering, but saw adoption as "taking the child away" and "setting up a conflict."

It might be expected that the group of foster families who had once wanted to adopt would resemble the adopting families more than the other foster families in the sample. As can be seen in Table 5.11 this was generally not the case. In terms of parental characteristics and the elements important to attachment, the two groups of foster parents look quite similar. In terms of child characteristics, the children in the foster families who never considered adoption look more like the adopted children than the other foster children, except that a high proportion had behavior problems. Thus, the two groups of parents who continued to foster were quite similar, except that those who initially thought of adopting had children with more serious problems and were less likely to have met the biological family.

Table 5.11
Characteristics of Families and Children by
Consideration of Adoption

Characteristics	Adoption Consideration					
	Actually Adopted		Once Wanted To Adopt		Never Anticipated Adoption	
	n	*%*	*n*	*%*	*n*	*%*
Parents						
Mother Over 45	11	32	14	78	6	60
Mother White	20	59	6	33	2	20
Mother Single Parent	2	6	5	28	2	20
Child						
Placed as Infant	14	41	–	–	4	40
Placed Over Age Five	5	15	9	50	1	10
Average or Above IQ	31	91	11	61	8	80
Severe Behavior Problem	4	12	10	56	4	40
Bonding						
Perceived Likeness	27	79	10	56	5	50
Child's Problems Improved	12	35	6	33	2	20
Placement Affected Family Positively	27	79	8	44	4	40
Foster Parents Met Biological Parents	21	62	3	17	5	50

Wondering how much ambivalence there had been about these decisions, the adopting families were asked if they had had any hesitations about adoption, and the foster families were asked if they had been tempted to adopt. Again, the greater clarity of the decision to adopt stood out; only four adopting families reported any hesitation. One mother was reluctant to commit herself to the care of a young child and one father wasn't sure he could feel toward an adopted child as he did toward his biological children.

Only eight foster families were not tempted to adopt at some time. Seventeen of the families mentioned being attached to their children, loving them, wanting them to stay, and feeling adoption would have been good for them. But, for the variety of reasons specified earlier, they decided that adoption was not wise. The "temptations" these families enumerated were of course, the reasons the adopting parents gave for their decision.

The lower degree of ambivalence among those who adopted was also evident in their report of how long it took to make a final decision about adoption. As Table 5.12 shows, twenty-seven adopting parents, 93 percent of those who reported on this variable, knew their decision immediately; two families took up to 6 months. In contrast, only four foster families decided immediately not to adopt, three families took over a year, and four were still undecided at the time of the interview. These differences were statistically significant when one compared those who made immediate decisions with others in the sample (p < .001).

Table 5.12
Length of Time Taken to Make Adoption
Decision by Adoption Decision

Length of Time	Adoption Decision			
	Adopt		Not Adopt	
	n	%	*n*	%
Immediate	27	93	4	18
One Week to 6 Months	2	7	7	32
Six Months to a Year	–	–	4	18
Over One Year	–	–	3	14
No Decision Yet Made	–	–	4	18
Total	29	100	22	100

Workers saw the families who adopted more positively. They had no hesitations or concerns about the family's capacity to care for the child in more than half of these cases. This was true for only a third of the families who continued to foster. Most commonly mentioned were concerns about the family's ability to handle the child's difficult behavior (n = 8) or special needs (n = 5). Workers mentioned concerns about age or health for five families who adopted and only four who continued to foster, which is interesting considering the demographic differences between the two groups. Workers said they were comfortable with the decisions of all but two families who adopted, which probably reflects both their feelings about the families and their own satisfaction in achieving a permanency for the child. They expressed similar comfort with the decisions of fifteen foster families, were unhappy with the decisions of seven, and gave ambiguous answers about the remainder.

About a quarter of the children in each group had asked to be adopted, usually asking in terms of "being able to stay forever." Names were reported to be important for some children, and seemed to be a concrete indication of belonging and permanence. Some adopted children expressed anxiety about the time necessary for the adoption to take place, and when told it was final were relieved and happy. One little boy, when he understood, exclaimed "I'll never have to move anymore!"

Only about half of the children were involved in discussion of the adoption decision. Ten were thought to be too young. Nine children had discussions with their worker and twenty five with their families. Some of these discussions were repeated and intense as the child sorted out the issues involved. As would be expected, more adopted children (n = 12) had an uncomplicated happy reaction to the discussion, though foster parents thought seven of their children had reacted well. The parents reported that these discussions caused little upset. Only seven foster children had ever asked to be adopted and, at least as the foster parents perceived the situation, the assurance that they could remain in the home was sufficient for most.

Foster parents tended to think that their children were not troubled by their continued status as foster children: "That never came up. I never discussed it. He was treated as my child and belonged to me," said one foster mother. Even when foster parents were aware of the possibility of some problem, they tended not to know how the child felt. Said one, "I really don't think he likes it; I wouldn't! But he knows we love him and treat him no differently than we do our own." Thus, many of the foster parents attempted to meet their childrens' need for security by perceiving them as members of the family.

The Child and Family Since the Decision

Despite their difficulty in arriving at a decision, all but two foster parents felt comfortable with it at the time of the interview. Only four thought their foster children were unhappy with their status, though thirteen reported that they really did not know how the child felt. Half of the foster parents expected the children to grow up in their homes; three more children, now in institutional care, may return at some point. Seven children, all younger, had been moved to adoptive or pre-adoptive foster homes. Apparently all of their foster parents were comfortable with this planning. Except for the seven younger children who were moved to adoptive homes, there was no evidence that discussion of adoption caused any long lasting disruption in these foster homes.

All but six adopted children, all younger, were said to know that they were adopted; only one family did not plan to tell the child. Asked what they thought might be important for the children to know about their adoption, these families stressed the importance of the child's understanding the circumtances which led to their adoption and their biological heritage. These are not the responses commonly reported in earlier studies of infant adoption. One wonders whether this reflects the amount of information about the biological parents these families had, a growing awareness of the needs of an adopted child, the contact and relationship some of these children had with their biological parents, the preparation these parents received from their workers, or some combination of these elements.

The parents were asked if they had perceived any changes in the child since their decision was made. Seventeen adoptive parents and only two foster parents saw positive change. All of the adopted children who were over the age of two when placed in this home were reported to have improved behavior after the adoption decision. These are the children who might remember other homes. Sixteen adopted children and twenty-one foster children were thought to have remained about the same. Negative changes were reported for two foster children and one foster child showed both some improvement and some deterioration. Negative changes were not reported for any adopted children. The reader will remember that the children who were not adopted were reported to have many more problems, and to have had an increasing number of problems since placement. The reports of these parents may reflect a continuation of these problems, modified by a desire to justify their decision not to adopt.

How were the children adjusting after all these decisions had been made? The parents were asked to make an assessment on a five point scale, displayed in Table 5.13. As was so often true in these judgment items, a high proportion of the adopted children were judged to be in the best category. Twenty-five, almost three quarters, were said to be making an excellent adjustment. Only five foster children were placed in this category. Thirteen foster children were thought to be making an adequate adjustment with a hopeful outlook. However one assesses this tendency to place foster families in the good-but-not-best category, it is nevertheless clear that eight foster children and only one adopted child were thought to have problems in adjustment. Corresponding with this assessment, four foster parents expected their children to have problems in becoming self-supporting, one expected serious school problems, six expected behavioral or emotional problems, and one recognized the child would always need constant care and expected a combination of many difficulties. Only three adopting parents expected any such problems. Given the descriptions of the children, these expectations seem to be generally realistic. The expectation of "usual" problems or none, when compared with expectation of serious problems, was statistically significant ($p < .0001$) between the two groups.

Also shown in Table 5.13 is the fact that the workers, while a bit less extreme, made assessments which folowed the same pattern, tending to add reliability to the parental assessment. Differences in worker ratings between the two groups, when compared on excellent and other ratings, were also statistically significant ($p < .001$).

Finally, at the end of a long interview, these parents were asked whether they thought an adoptive home was the same as a foster home. Fifteen adoptive parents (44%) thought it was about the same for the parents, but only six thought it was the same for the child. Sixteen adoptive parents thought the child would feel more secure and more a part of the family in an adoptive home. "The kids will feel more secure when adopted. They had experiences in foster homes, and know their temporary nature and that they can be moved," said one adopting mother. "It doesn't feel any different caring for a foster child or adopting. But the legality makes you feel more secure in the long run. A child needs a permanent home," said another.

Nineteen foster parents, two-thirds of the group, thought adoption and foster care were the same for the parents, and seventeen thought it the same for the child. "It is for us just the same—we treat them like our own child," was a typical reponse. Only five foster parents thought a child would feel more secure in an adoptive home. It is impossible to know whether this was a justification for the decision to remain foster parents or whether it was one of the reasons which lay behind the decision.

After the disturbance of the decision making about adoption, most of

Table 5.13

*Parent and Worker Assessment of the Children's Adjustment Since the
Adoption Decision by Adoptive Status*

Assessment	*Adoptive Status*			
	Adopted		*Not Adopted*	
By Parents				
	n	*%*	*n*	*%*
Child is making an excellent adjustment in all spheres of life—the outlook for future adjustment is *excellent*	25	74	5	19
Child is making an adequate adjustment— Strengths outweigh weaknesses—the outlook for future adjustment is *hopeful*	8	24	13	50
Child is making a mixed adjustment— problems faced are serious and the outlook for his future adjustment is *guarded*	1	3	6	23
Child is making an extremely poor adjustment—the outlook for his future is *unpromising*	–	–	2	8
Total	34	100	26	100
By Workers				
	n	*%*	*n*	*%*
Excellent	20	59	7	26
Good	13	38	11	41
Fair	1	3	8	30
Poor	–	–	1	4
Total	34	100	27	100

these homes, both adoptive and foster, seemed to have settled back into stability. With the excpeption of reported behavioral improvement among some adopted children, the children's adjustment seemed to be proceeding as it had since placement. The parents seemed content with their decision. In those twelve instances where children were no longer in the home, the foster parents seemed to feel that the move had been a proper one. Many remain in contact with the children. For most of the foster families a long term placement was continuing. One senses that in all of these families, no matter what the decision, there had been clarification of plans for the child. Perhaps through this process there was also some added security in all of the homes.

A Note on Changes in the Family

The reader will remember that twelve children were no longer living in their foster homes at the time of this study. All twelve of these families were in the interviewed sample. On those factors associated with family formation which have been examined, these families appeared no different from the foster families whose children are still in the home. The difference seems to lie in characteristics of the children.

Five of these children were twelve years old or older and, because of serious acting-out behavior problems, four were moved to group or residential care; a sixteen-year-old girl was moved to another foster home due to similar behavior problems. In a sense these five children had not left their foster homes, for they still remained in contact, sometimes came "home" for holidays, and the foster parents continued to see themselves as family for the child.

The other seven children had been moved to adoptive homes or pre-adoptive foster homes. They ranged in age from three to thirteen at the time they moved—the thirteen-year-old was adopted by an aunt. For four of these children the move represented the agency's policy of moving children to permanent homes rather than a break-down of their foster home placement. Three of the children were moved to adoptive homes when it became evident that these foster parents could no longer cope with their fairly serious behavior problems. Only in these three situations was there evidence of a failure on the part of the foster family and the child to form a stable unit.

Summary

In this chapter the development of the families of sixty-two children have been traced; thirty-four children who were adopted, sixteen children who remain in long-term foster care, five children who are no longer in these homes but who continue as "children" to these families, and seven children for whom the placement has ended. All of these were relatively stable and cohesive family units at the time of the adoption discussion. This chapter has examined factors which might be expected to be related to the formation of family attachments and other factors in the family situation which might impact the adoption decision. Do close family bonds override other factors? Or are there some circumstances that make adoption virtually impossible? The attitudes and the facts are so intertwined that these questions cannot be answered.

The families who adopted originally expected to have long-term placements in their homes. Shortly after the placement they began to think about adopting this child. They had expressed more preferences to workers, and workers thought that the preferences were better met. They followed through on their interest in adoption by approaching the worker and asking about the possibility.

Little is known about the placement process. Initial reactions to the child were vividly recalled by the parents, and an uncomplicated reaction of happiness and acceptance of the child appears to be a good indicator that an adoption will eventually take place if this becomes possible. Most children were perceived to have a positive reaction to the placement and to settle in quickly. Those older children who had pre-placement visits were more likely to be adopted later. Perhaps this preparation increased their responsiveness.

Some factors which were theoretically postulated to be important to family attachment were present among a greater proportion of adopting families. Adopting parents perceived greater similarity between their children and other family members, and perceived their children as being similar to or better than other children. Though there were problems in measurement, raters perceived more reciprocated affection and better rapport between adopted children and their parents.

Problems improved over the course of the placement for the children who were eventually adopted. The problems of many of those children who continue to be fostered appeared to grow more severe. Adopting families tended to describe the effect of the placement on the family as positive, while foster families tended to see a more negative impact. These factors, combined with poorer rapport between parents and children, seemed to have led to a circle of negative interaction, increased difficulty and distance, and the decision not to adopt. Unanswerable at this time is the question of the relative importance of the problems the children already had at entry and what the placement offered them.

Adopting parents had greater contact with their children's biological parents, especially during the year adoption was discussed. This seems to result in either a greater understanding of the children or an increased resentment of their parents' involvement. Either result appears to call forth nurturing on the part of the parents and to spur the decision to adopt.

In looking at the decision process there appears to be a greater clarity among those who decide to adopt. It takes them less time to make the decision, the reasons for the decisons are less complicated and more cohesive, and less ambivalence is reported. In this discussion the commitment of all of the parents to their children is evident, and there is considerable anguish among those who decide they cannot adopt either because of family circumstances, the child's ties to a biological family, or concern about the future capacities of the child. Despite the stress of the decision, most parents reported that family life has continued with few changes for them and their children.

CHAPTER 6
The Agency Experience

We knew our worker well. We saw her weekly for six months, then monthly for over two years after the placement before adoption was discussed. She was a happy person and very intuitive. We liked her very much and felt free to share problems. Short visits would turn into two hours.

— —An adoptive mother

We hardly knew the worker at all—we saw him about three times in two years. My husband never met him. I didn't like him because he didn't seem to have our youngster's interest at heart. One day he just came out and asked us if we wanted to adopt . . .

— —A foster mother

So two foster mothers reported their experiences with their agency workers. These differing experiences represent two patterns of interaction which foster parents report having had with the agencies that supervised their children's placements.

In attempting to differentiate foster parents who adopted from those who did not, the research explored whether these two groups differed in their experience with the agencies that supervised their placements and with the workers that served them. Information from the interviews with both the families and the workers were used to explore this question. It was anticipated that children and families who received sound agency help might have been more likely to form the attachments necessary for an adoption to occur.

This chapter is divided into two major sections. The first discusses variables which are not specific to the particular child under study, but germain to the families' overall agency experiences. The second details aspects of service which might have directly impacted the sample child. Data in this latter section are, by design, more complete so that further insight into the factors which lead to different outcomes for specific children can be gained. In presenting these findings, similarities and differences between the two data sources are noted so that the reader can judge the reliability of the information presented.

The Agency Experience in General

Cumulative agency experience can affect a family's expectatons with a specific child. It seems reasonable to expect that families would be less likely to accept a child as a permanent member of the family if, in the past, many children had come and gone, or the family had been admonished to keep their distance from children placed with them, or agency workers had not known the family well or were not available to them in times of crisis. It is to these issues that attention is now directed.

History as Foster Parents

Information from both the parents and the workers indicated that many of these families had been foster parents for extended periods of time. About half of the sixty two interviewed families had been fostering for more than ten years; 40 percent had been foster parents with their current agency for at least that length of time. Only one-quarter of the families had been fostering for five years or fewer at the time of the study.

The data suggest that the foster parents who eventually adopted had fostered for shorter periods of time. About one-third of the adopting couples reported that they had served their current agency as foster parents for ten years or longer. This was true for 57 percent of the non-adopting couples (p < .05). This difference remains constant when one compares the *total* years of fostering experience of the two groups; 38 percent of the adopting families and 64 percent of the non-adopting families reported a total of ten years or more of fostering experience (p < .07).

This differential experience as foster parents was reflected in the number of workers with whom the family had interacted during their tenure with the agency. While only one family in each group had been assigned to only one worker, and nine families in each group had had eight or more workers, 45 percent of the families who adopted had experiences with three or fewer workers compared to only 22 percent of the non-adopting group (p < .06).

Given the differences between the two groups regarding length of service and the number of workers, it is surprising that the adopting families had not cared for fewer children than the non-adopting families. While the adopting families reported that they were somewhat more likely to have cared for one or more children for brief periods of time (up to two months), about as likely to have cared for one or more children for moderate periods of time (two months to one year) and somewhat less likely to have cared for three or more children for extended periods of time (more than one year) than their non-adopting counterparts, none of these differences were statistically significant.

Reports from the workers confirmed that the adopting and non-adopting families had cared for about the same number of children. Approximately 40 percent of the total sample had cared for four or more children; 36 percent of the adopting group and 47 percent of the non-adopting group. Three adopting families and four non-adopting families had cared for fifty or more children. Only 23 percent of the total sample (21% of the adopters and 27% of the non-adoptors) had fostered only one child. These patterns were the same for the sixty-two families who were interviewed.

Preparation for Foster Parenthood

The interviewers attempted to gather information regarding the families' experiences with the agency prior to the placement of any children in the home. Unfortunately, many of the families could not recall this information. While this might have been anticipated had the extent of these parents' involvement with the agency been known, it was disappointing that only about 40 percent of the families could recall their early experiences.

Examination of the twenty-five families who reported on these items revealed no differences between the adopting and non-adopting families on either the number of visits the workers made to the families' home, or the number of contacts between worker and family at the agency, prior to the placement of the first child. Nor were there differences between the two groups regarding receipt of formal training as foster parents.

What is disheartening is that little preparation for foster parenthood seems to have occurred across these groups. Almost 60 percent of the families stated that the worker visited their home only once, and that they met with the worker fewer than three times in the office, prior to their first placement. Only 30 percent of the families received any formal agency training at this time.

Given this lack of preparation, it is not surprising that, in retrospect, 43 percent of the interviewed families did not feel that they "knew what they were getting into" at the time they became foster parents. Many of these families expected more consistency and support from the agency or worker. They also mentioned that they did not feel prepared to care for the types of children placed with them.

The following excerpts from the written recordings of the interviewer makes this point clearly. From the adoptive parents:

> Didn't expect so many workers coming in and out . . . they all had different ideas about how to care for children. This can be confusing and cause distress and awkwardness in the relationship.

> We signed up for emergency care and ended up with long-term. We were surprised about the rules around foster care, medical care, etc.

> Three days after placement cancer was discovered (in the child). Didn't expect that. Mother noticed it right away and has lots of feelings about past foster family not noticing it.

> Agency was inept and lost records. Child unassigned to workers. Was supposed to be temporary. . . . Got no information on child. . . .

From the non-adopting parents:

> Mother had high expectations of having a "perfect child in a perfect situation." She did not think about the problems in advance. Almost as if she approached [foster care] in a "dream world."

> The agency staff wasn't honest with the foster parents. . . . When L. had problems foster mother and the worker sent her to a psychiatrist. . . . Foster mother was upset because they had more questions of her instead of the child.

> I didn't expect the children to be in such bad shape—many were neglected. I don't understand how parents can do that to their children.

> Didn't realize I'd get so attached to the kids. Hadn't realized that dealing with bio-mom would be a problem.

Even the families who thought that they knew what they were getting into mentioned difficulties in coping with these problems. In all, only fourteen of the interviewed families stated that nothing was really different than they expected. These families were equally divided between the adopting and non-adopting groups.

Experiences With Workers

Almost three-quarters of the families in the study reported that they had just about the right amount of contact with their workers over the years. Most of the remaining families would have liked more interaction. These findings were consistent across the adopting and non-adopting groups.

However, the quality of the relationships between the adopting families and their workers and the non-adopting families and their workers seemed to have been different. It will be recalled that the non-adopting families had experiences with a greater number of workers than the adopting families. Yet, when asked "How many [of the workers] knew you and your family well," there were no differences between the groups. About one-quarter of each group felt that only one worker knew their family well. An additional one-quarter of the families felt this way about two workers. Thus, the data suggest that the adopting families believed that a greater *proportion* of the workers with whom they had contact knew them well.

While knowing a family "well" is general, and subject to a wide variety of interpretations, these findings gained credibility when the families were asked whether they had "felt free to talk with their workers." Fully 90 percent of the adopting families responded to this question with an unqualified positive response. Just fewer than 70 percent of the non-adopting families responded in this way, a statistically significant difference (Fishers $p = .02$). Thus, a larger proportion of adopting families seemed to have trusted their workers and to have looked to them for guidance in a more unqualified manner.

About equal proportions of adopting and non-adopting families felt that their workers were helpful in supporting their roles as foster parents; about two-fifths felt their workers were very supportive and 25 percent thought them generally supportive. However, the data suggest that the two groups differed in their perceptions of their role. Seventy percent of the parents who continued to foster saw themselves "just like the child's parents" or as surrogate parents to the children. This was true for only 43 percent of the adopting families, who were more likely to see themselves as temporary parents, parents with something "missing," or as conscious "helpers" to the child ($p < .07$). Thus, while the two groups experienced similar amounts of support in their roles, the perceived their roles differently—the adopting families more often felt that they were, in some way, different than the child's parents.

The Agency Experience Regarding The Specific Child

While the general experience of a family may influence their perceptions of the agency and the children they care for, it seems logical to assume that their interactions with the agency regarding a specific child would be more directly related to their adoption decision. The remainder of this chapter explores these relationships.

The Placement

As reported previously, the majority of the families expected that the sample child would remain in their home for an extended period of time. Despite the fact that many of these families had cared for children on a short-term basis in the past, the workers confirmed this impression and reported that just fewer than one-quarter of the families expected the placement of this child to be short-term. This figure was consistent between the interviewed and total samples, and no significant differences were found between the adopting and non-adopting groups.

Nor were there significant differences between the groups as to the conditions under which the child was placed. According to both the adopting and non-adopting families, just under half of the children (44%) were placed under crisis conditions; often a phone call to the family was followed quickly by the placement of the child. This high proportion of crisis placements was confirmed by the workers who reported that 37 percent of the children in the interviewed sample and 40 percent of the children in the total sample were placed under such conditions. The following excerpts from the interviews with the adopting families were typical of these crisis placements:

> We received call at 5:00 P.M. and she was picked up from court at 11:00 A.M. the next day.

> Day's notice given. No plans beforehand. We didn't even have a crib.

> We picked the baby up from the agency on a moment's notice. We had two days to plan for clothes and bottles.

> The worker brought her directly from court. We were notified one day in advance. We don't feel we have the luxury of pre-placement visits. We have two slots in our license for special needs kids.

The reports of the non-adopting foster parents who had children placed in crisis situations were not dissimilar. As the distinction between adoptive and foster homes fades, as has been the trend in recent years, this high percentage of emergency placements is particularly troubling.

As discussed earlier, a number of families in the study had preferences as to the type of child they wished placed. However, on this variable, there was an inconsistency between the workers and families. While about half of the families (46%) reported that they had no preferences, the workers reported this for fewer than one-fourth of both the total and interviewed sample. Whether these differences are due to the families seeing themselves as more flexible, in retrospect, than they actually were, or are due to workers seeing more inflexibility than was actually present within the families, cannot be determined from these data. However, this lack of congruity may have implications for the placement of children and the agencies' attempt to match families and children.

The meeting of preferences did not seem to be dominant in the workers' thinking at the time of the placements. Only twelve children, half of whom were later adopted, were placed because the worker thought they would "fit in" with the family. As is shown in Table 6.1, for eighteen children this was their first foster home, chosen because of availability, a potential for long-term care, and perhaps other factors. An additional four children were moved to this home from another foster home because a long-term placement was possible. For nineteen children a prior foster home placement had broken down, either because of the child's behavior or because of loss of the home due to the death, illness, etc. of foster parents. Of the twenty-two children for whom this was a first planned long-term placement, seventeen were adopted; of the nineteen children for whom this was a later placement, only seven were adopted. The difference was statistically significant (p < .02).

Table 6.1
Placement Planning by Adoption Decision

Planning	Adoption Decision			
	Adopt		Not Adopt	
	n	%	n	%
First Home: Available, Long Term Possible	13	54	5	29
Moved from Temporary Home as Long Term Possible	4	17	–	–
Moved Due to Behavior Problem	5	21	5	29
Moved Due to Death, Illness, etc. of Foster Parents	2	8	7	41
Total	24	100	17	100

The Adoption Decision

When the families were compared on the timing of their adoption decisions, a consistent pattern of the adopting families taking more timely and deliberate actions, and initiating such actions rather than waiting for agency personnel to do so emerged. For the most part, the adopting parents first thought about adoption shortly after the child's placement. Over half first thought about adopting at the time the child was placed or shortly thereafter. Of the remaining families in the adopting group, half first thought about this possibility after the child had been in their home for a while, but within the first year of placement. Thus, for the adopting families who did not anticipate adoption from the beginning, this possibility often occurred within a relatively short period of time after the child's placement.

In contrast, adoption was not thought about or raised within the non-adopting families until much later in the child's placement. In over three-fourths of these families the issue was not considered until the child had been in the home for at least one year; often it was much later than this. In fewer than one-eighth of these families was adoption thought about at the time of the placement or within three months of it. The difference on this variable between the two groups was highly significant (p < .001).

The adopting families reported that they not only thought about adoption earlier, but that they also discussed it earlier with their workers. About half of these families reported the occurrence of adoption discussions during the first year of the child's placement. In contrast, only one-quarter of the non-adopting families reported such discussions within this time frame (p < .05). More dramatically, while one quarter of the adopting families reported that they had discussions about adoption within three months of the child's placement, this was reported by only two of the non-adopting families.

The workers' recollections of when adoption was first discussed was somewhat different from the families'. While the workers also reported that discussion about adoption occurred during the first year of placement for about half of the adopting families, they recalled this to be the case for about 40 percent of the total and one third of the interviewed non-adopting families. Thus, the workers reported early adoption discussions with the non-adopting families more frequently than the families themselves, and did not report that the timing of this discussion was significantly different between the two groups.

The reason for this difference in perception between the families and the workers is a matter for speculation. Perhaps "serious" discussion about adoption with the families who continued to foster did not occur until later, and what the workers reported was that they raised this possibility early in the placement. Perhaps parents, who did not want to adopt, did not "hear" their workers until later discussions. Perhaps there is some other explanation.

A similar difference in perception occurred between the workers and the families regarding the issue of who first raised the subject of adoption. As discussed in Chapter 5, 45 percent of all families reported that they approached the agency about adopting; and adopting families reported this significantly (p. <.02) more often than the non-adopting families (58% vs. 30%). In contrast, the workers reported that fewer than forty percent of the families approached them about adoption and that the difference between the adopting and non-adopting families was not statistically significant. Their reports indicated that 30 percent of the non-adopting families in both the total and interviewed samples approached the agency, but that only 48 percent of the total adoptive sample and 45 percent of the interviewed adoptive sample made the initial approach.

While there is some incongruence between the families' and workers' perception as to who initiated the adoption discussion and when it first occurred, there was no difference between the data sources when they reported the timing of the adoption decision. The workers and families agreed that the families who eventually adopted made this decision in a more timely and immediate way. As reported in Chapter 5, 90 percent of the adopting families said that they made their decision almost immediately after the initiation of the adoption discussion; fewer than one-quarter of the non-adopting families reached their decision this quickly (p <.001). The workers reported that more than three-quarters of the interviewed adopting families, but fewer than 20 percent of the interviewed non-adopting families, reached their decision within this brief time frame (p <.001). The same pattern was reported for the entire sample of eighty-three families (p <.001).

These differences in decision making occurred even though the majority of both groups believed that the discussion about adoption had occurred at about the "right time." All but nine of the adopting families and ten of the non-adopting families thought that the timing of the adoption discussion was appropriate. Of these nineteen families, fifteen felt that the discussion had occurred "too late" in their relationship with the child. Yet this was not a differentiating factor, for this was reported by eight of the adopting families and seven of the non-adopting families.

When asked who was involved in the initial discussion about adoption, the data were remarkably consistent, both between the adopting and non-adopting groups, and between the reports of the families and the workers. These results are presented in Table 6.2. The data presented for the worker is based on the information for the interviewed sample. (The data for the total sample show only slight deviations). The data displayed are the percentage of cases in which the identified individual was involved in the initial discussion about adoption.

Table 6.2
Persons Involved in Adoption Discussion by Informant and Adoption Decision of the Family

Person Involved	Informant							
	Family				Worker			
Family member	Adopt		Not-Adopt		Adopt		Not-Adopt	
	n	%	n	%	n	%	n	%
Foster Mother	33	97	26	96	30	91	26	96
Foster Father	23	68	14	50	23	70	14	52
Child	2	6	3	11	3	9	4	15
Biological Children of Family	1	3	1	4	2	6	2	7
Other Foster Children in Family	1	3	–	–	–	–	1	4
Agency Personnel								
Foster Care Worker	29	85	20	71	25	76	21	78
*Adoption Worker	2	5	6	21	3	9	7	26
Other Agency Worker	3	9	3	11	2	6	1	4

*The "adoption worker" designation refers to a worker whose sole function is to facilitate adoptions. She is thus probably a new worker for a foster family.

A number of ideas emerge from the data presented in this table. First, as one might expect, the initial discussion about adoption was most likely to include the foster mother and the foster care worker who had been working with the family. Foster fathers were included to a lesser degree in these initial discussions, although they were included in the majority of cases. Children, including the child about whom the decision was being made, were, for the most part, excluded from these discussions despite their current age. Agency personnel, other than the foster care worker, tended not to be included in the initial adoption discussion.

Second, the data are consistent between the worker and the families. This reliability lends support to the above information and one has the sense that, indeed, it was primarily the mother and the foster care worker who were initially involved in the discussion of adoption.

Finally, few differences were present between the adopters and the non-adopters when one looked at who was initially involved in this discussion. Only the inclusion of father and adoption workers in the initial discussion of adoption appeared to be at all discriminating between the groups. Fathers were somewhat more likely to be involved in initial discussions in the adopting families. However, the difference between the groups was not statistically significant, and is probably accounted for by the larger proportion of two-parent families present in the adopting sample.

Adoption workers, newly assigned to the families, were involved in more initial discussions with non-adopting families than with adopting families. This difference was statistically significant (Fishers $p = .02$ for family data; Fishers $p = .08$ for worker data). The reader will note that three quarters of the families who had an adoption worker involved in their initial adoption discussions did not adopt.

The finding seems to suggest that the introduction of a new "actor" at the time of the initial discussion about adoption does not enhance the likelihood that an adoption will occur. There are a number of possible explanations for this. First, a new adoption worker will not know the family well. They may not know the interpersonal dynamics of the family or the best way to help them come to a decision. Further, the family may be hesitant to discuss their concerns about adoption with a new worker. Thus, issues critical to making a decision to adopt may not be raised and therefore cannot be resolved. Finally, if the family was not aware of the plan to involve an adoption worker or to transfer their case to an adoption unit, they may feel pressure to make a decision for which they had not been properly prepared and may feel betrayed by the agency. If, in fact, the agency transferred the case in order to force an adoption decision, it seems clear from these data that such pressure was not productive.

The Worker-Family Relationship

Research in a number of areas of child welfare has documented the importance of good family-worker relationships if desired goals are to be reached[1], and this project collected data from both the family and the worker in this area. Unfortunately, because of the amount of specificity required in answering the questions, the families' responses regarding the amount of contact they had with workers, both before adoption was mentioned and during the adoption discussion, was so incomplete as to render the data unreliable. Therefore it is not reported here. The only question to which an adequate response rate was obtained was whether the family thought the worker with whom they discussed adoption "knew them well." Ninety percent of the adoptive families, but only 70 percent of the non-adoptive families (p < .10) felt this to be true.

Fortunately, the data from the workers was quite complete in this area. Significant differences between the adopting and non-adopting families were evident on a number of variables concerned with the amount and nature of the contact between the worker and the family, both prior to and during the adoption discussion. In general, workers had the opportunity to know the adopting families better than the non-adopting families.

Given worker turnover, it is not surprising that only seven of the families who were eventually interviewed were known to their workers for more than five years; two adopting and five non-adopting families. Of the remaining fifty-four families, more than 70 percent of the adopting families had known their worker between two and five years. This was true for only 43 percent of the non-adopting families, a statistically significant difference (p < .05). In terms of the total sample, fourteen families had known their workers more than five years; seven in both the adopting and non-adopting groups. Of the remaining families in the total sample, 74 percent of the adopting families but only half of the non-adopting families knew their workers for between two and five years. Thus, other than the increase in the "over five year" group, these figures are quite similar to those reported for the interviewed sample and are also statistically significant.

The workers of the adopting group also appeared to have had more intense contact with both the families and the children during the period adoption was discussed. These relationships are detailed in Tables 6.3 and 6.4.

These tables show similar patterns of contact between worker and family and worker and child during the period adoption was discussed. Within the interviewed sample, similar proportions of the adopting and non-adopting families, and adopted and non-adopted children, appeared to have had intensive contact (more than twice per month) with their worker. However, adopting families and their adopted children appear to have had more regular contact (once a month or "as needed") than their counterparts in the non-adopting group, who were more likely to have contact with their worker less than once

Table 6.3
Contacts With Parents During Adoption
Discussion by Adoption Decision

Frequency of Contact	Adoption Decision			
	Adopt		Not Adopt	
	n	%	n	%
At least every other week	6	18	5	21
Once per month	13	39	7	29
Less than once per month	4	12	9	37
Regularly; as needed	10	30	3	13
Total	33	100	24	100

Table 6.4
Contacts With Children During Adoption
Discussion by Adoptive Status

Frequency of Contact	Adoptive Status			
	Adopted		Not Adopted	
	n	%	n	%
At least every other week	5	15	4	15
Once per month	10	29	3	11
Less than once per month	9	26	16	59
Regularly; as needed	10	29	4	15
Total	34	100	27	100

per month ($X^2 = 6.32$, df = 3, p < .10 for parents; $X^2 = 7.71$, df = 3, p < .05 for children). These relationships were even stronger, when one looked at the data for the total sample of eighty-three families.

Not only did the two groups have differential contact with their workers, but the quality of the relationship was also reported to be different. The workers reported at least adequate relationships with significantly more adopted than non-adopted children ($X^2 = 7.51$, df = 2, p < .02). Good relationships were reported with the adopting families somewhat more often than with the non-adopting families, although this difference was not statistically significant. These findings are displayed in Tables 6.5 and 6.6, which report the data for the interviewed sample. The data for the total sample were quite similar.

Table 6.5
Worker's Report of Relationship With
Child by Adoptive Status

Relationship With Child	Adoptive Status			
	Adopted		Not Adopted	
	n	%	n	%
Good to Excellent	12	41	12	46
Adequate	12	41	3	12
Difficult/Strained/Superficial	5	17	11	42
Total	29	100	26	100

Table 6.6
Worker's Report of Relationship With
Family by Adoption Decision

Relationship With Child	Adoption Decision			
	Adopt		Not Adopt	
	n	%	n	%
Good to Excellent	18	55	10	36
Adequate or Worse	15	45	18	64
Total	33	100	28	100

Information

Whether a family had information about the child, and whether they discussed issues germain to adoption with their worker, can be important to their adoption deliberations. It can be hypothesized that the greater the family's knowledge the more likely they are to have discussed and resolved issues about the child's heritage and past. Also, with such information, they may be better able to respond to the child's individual needs. In addition, comprehensive discussions about adoption and related issues can lead to fuller family deliberations and, perhaps, less apprehension about the decision which is reached.

The data indicate that the adopting families had more information than the non-adopting families about their children and their backgrounds prior to their adoption discussion. The adopting families also appear to have had somewhat more comprehensive discussions with their workers about adoption and related issues. Table 6.7 summarizes this information. The data about the children prior to the adoption discussion was gathered from the workers; that about adoption issues from the families. The workers' data reflects information about the full sample of families. It is however, quite congruent with the data for the smaller sample of interviewed families.

Table 6.7

*Information Given Prior to Adoption Discussion
and Areas Discussed during Adoption Discussion by Adoption Decision*

Areas Discussed	Adoption Decision				
Prior to Adoption Discussion *	*Adopt*		*Not Adopt*		*Sig.*
	n	*%*	*n*	*%*	
Reason Child Entered Care (n = 76)	41	85	18	64	.031[1]
Living Experience With Biological Family (n = 70)	27	61	9	35	.031[1]
Information About Medical Problems/Handicaps (n = 75)	33	70	14	50	.082[2]
Information About Emotional/ Behavioral Problems (n = 73)	34	74	18	70	n.s.
Reason Entered This Foster Home (n = 68)	28	67	13	50	n.s.
During Adoption Discussion **					
Family Related					
Motivations for Adoption (n = 55)	26	76	15	71	n.s.
Financial Status (n = 60)	30	91	21	78	n.s.
Health (n = 59)	27	82	21	81	n.s.
Reaction of Family Members (n = 59)	22	68	21	81	n.s.
Marital Relationship (n = 52)	21	68	12	57	n.s.
Sources of Emotional Support (n = 60)	21	64	21	78	n.s.
Continue as Foster Parents (n = 60)	23	68	10	38	.02
Handling Child's Questions About Past (n = 61)	18	53	10	37	n.s.
Handling Child's Questions About Care (n = 59)	20	68	14	52	n.s.
Anticipated Problems With Child Over Time (n = 60)	17	50	14	54	n.s.
Possibility Adoption Will Not Work Out (n = 60)	14	42	14	52	n.s.

(Table 6.7 Continued)

	Adopt		Not Adopt		Sig.
	n	%	*n*	%	
Child Related					
Child's Feelings About Adoption (n = 54)	19	68	19	73	n.s.
Child's Past History (n = 60)	28	85	12	44	.001
Child's Current Functioning (n = 58)	28	88	23	88	n.s.
Services Child Might Need (n = 59)	20	63	22	81	.10
Contact With Biological Family (n = 58)	20	63	10	38	.07
Child's Future Potential (n = 57)	17	53	15	60	n.s.
Possibility of Child's "Searching" (n = 58)	17	53	10	38	n.s.
Agency Related					
Legal Process (n = 61)	32	94	16	59	.001
Subsidy (n = 59)	27	82	20	77	n.s.

*Figures presented reflect the number and percentage of families whom the workers report had a "good deal" of information in this area.

**Figures presented reflect the number and percentage of parents reporting that the specific area had been discussed.

[1]Significance level maintained when calculation is performed eliminating cases where no family interview was completed.

[2]Significance level raises above .10 when calculation is performed eliminating cases where no family interview was completed.

As a group, the adopting families knew more about their children's backgrounds prior to the adoption discussion than the non-adopting families. Workers reported that a significantly higher percentage of the adopting parents had "a good deal" of information regarding why their children entered care, their living situations and experiences with their biological parents, and their medical problems or handicaps. Further, they reported that a somewhat greater proportion of adopting parents also had information about their children's emotional/behavioral problems and the reason they entered this foster home, although these relationships did not reach statistical significance.

To a lesser extent, it also appears that at the time adoption was being considered the adopting parents had somewhat more comprehensive discussions with their workers. A significantly larger proportion of adopting families reported having discussions with their workers in four areas: whether the family would continue as foster parents after adoption; continuation of contact with the child's biological parents; the legal processes involved in adoption; and the child's past history. Differences in the first three of these areas might have been expected, since these are issues of greater concern to adopting families. The last area of difference, discussion about the child's past history, could not have been anticipated. While the reasons that these discussions occurred more frequently with adopting parents cannot be speculated upon, one can speculate about the effects of such discussions. Through the process of casting the child's past into the discussion of adoption, some of these parents may have realized the progress their child had made; some may have come to understand their child better; and some may have been better able to accept their child as being "separate but a part" of their family. Any of these effects can strengthen a parent's already existing commitment.

Non-adopting parents were significantly more likely to have discussed only one area with their worker—the services which the child might continue to need. This relationship is not strong, but does indicate the more "damaged" condition of the non-adopted children. In this regard, it is interesting to note that it was primarily in areas which reflected concern about the child's condition and future that more non-adopting parents reported discussions with their workers. While the differences were not statistically significant, more non-adopting parents reported that they had discussion about the possible reaction of other family members to an adoption; the sources of external emotional support that the family might have to draw upon; the anticipated problems that the child might present over time; the possibility that the adoption might not work out; and the child's future potential. While these realistic discussions must take place with the families of children who present more problems, concentration of discussion in these areas may focus the more hesitant families' attention in these areas, and reinforce their reluctance to adopt a child.

Before leaving this discussion one additional point should be made. It will be noted that for a large minority of families, whether adopting or non-adopting, areas thought to be important in adoption considerations were never discussed with the worker. More than one third of the families did not have discussions about how to handle their children's questions about foster care or their past; the possible problems their children might encounter over time; their children's future potential; the possibility that the adoption might disrupt; or that their children might need to "search" for their biological parents in the future. These are issues which are germain to the adoption of older children and the absence of discussion about them appears to be contrary to good practice.

Involvement in Foster Care Processes

Up until this point, the discussion of service variables has focused on the interactions between the workers and the families which might be related to the adoption decision. However, foster care is broader than the parent-child-agency relationship. Other people and systems are often involved in the course of services. Biological parents may have continuing contact with their children. If adoption is eventually planned, the courts may be called upon to terminate parental rights. The nature and extent of the parents' involvements in these other aspects of service is now explored.

Biological Parents. Information was gathered from both the workers and the parents regarding the extent of contact between the biological parents and the foster parents at a number of points in time. The data obtained are consistent between these groups, adding to the reliability of these findings.

Both the workers and the families reported that just under one-half (about 45%) of the families had contact with the child's biological family at some point during the placement. However, as previously reported, this contact was not equally distributed between the adopting and non-adopting parents. Workers reported that within the full sample of eighty-three families, 57 percent of those who adopted but only 26 percent of those who continued to foster had any such contact (p < .01). Within the smaller group of families interviewed, 52 percent of the adopting families but only 30 percent of the non-adopting families had such contact (p < .10). These latter figures are remarkably similar to the reports of the families themselves; 60 percent of the adopting families reported contact with the biological families compared to 30 percent of the non-adopting families (p < .05). Details of these contacts and when they took place are reported in Chapter V.

Termination of Parental Rights. Twelve of the eighty-three children in the sample had not had their parental rights terminated by the court. They remained in the sample because their workers had offered their foster parents the opportunity to adopt. Apparently the workers were confident that termination could be accomplished. Obviously, none of these twelve children had been adopted. Court proceedings were underway and termination was expected shortly for three. For the remaining nine children, further action in this direction was not reported by the worker at the time of the interview.

The workers cited a number of reasons for the delay of termination proceedings. Termination of parental rights was not being pursued for four children because their foster parents were not willing to adopt. For three children, problems in obtaining relinquishment or in working with the biological parents toward this goal was cited as the reason. An additional two children did not want to be adopted and therefore termination was not being pursued. In the remaining three cases, either problems with the agency, with the court, or both, were the reasons for the delay.

When one looks at the characteristics of the children whose parental rights were not terminated by the reason cited by the worker for this, some interesting differences appear. The two children who chose not to be adopted and the four children whose foster parents chose not to adopt were all over twelve years old and in their current foster homes for at least eight years. Those children who chose not to be adopted were basically problem free, while those whose foster parents did not want to adopt all had serious problems—either physical, emotional or intellectual. For all, the long term plan was to remain in this foster home.

The six children who were not free for adoption because of court or agency reasons, or because of problems in obtaining cooperation from their biological parents, had a different profile. All were under twelve (three were five) and all but two had been in their current foster home for less than four years. All were of minority backgrounds and all but one was problem free.

While one might argue that because of age and handicapping conditions, as well as the child's desire, termination of parental rights should not have been pursued for the first group of children, this cannot be argued for the second group. Clearly, more vigorous actions must be taken on their behalf, since these are children who would probably benefit from adoption and for whom adoptive homes can be found. And, there was some indication that this was being done—all three children whose termination proceedings were still ongoing were in this latter group.

Thus, there were seventy-one children in the total sample and fifty children in the interviewed sample whose parental rights had been terminated. Analysis of the data by how parental rights were terminated showed an interesting difference between the children who were eventually adopted and those who were not. A significantly larger number of children who were eventually adopted had their parental rights terminated by voluntary surrender or by voluntary surrender followed by court action. Sixty percent of the adopted children in both the total and interviewed sample had parents who voluntarily surrendered; 71 percent of the non-adopted children had court action only (p < .02 for total sample; p < .05 for interviewed sample).

Not only did the two groups differ in the manner in which parental rights were severed, but they also differed in the timing of this action. Among the total sample of biological parents who had voluntarily relinquished their parental rights, 60 percent had done so within the three years preceding the interview. All of their children were eventually adopted. None of the biological parents of children who continued to be fostered had voluntarily surrendered their parental rights within this time frame (Fishers p < .001). This same pattern occurred among the children whose biological parents' rights had been terminated by court action. Among this group, 92 percent of the adopted children but only 40 percent of the non-adopted children had this action taken within the three years preceding the interview (p < .001). These patterns were the same among the smaller group of children whose families were interviewed.

These findings should not suggest that termination of parental rights for the adopted children (which was more likely to occur outside of court and within the last three years) was accomplished with less difficulty than for the non-adopted legally freed children. In fact, quite the opposite was reported by the workers. They indicated that there were difficulties in the termination process for slightly more than half of the adopted children but for fewer than 20 percent of the non-adopted children. These differences were significant for both the total sample (p < .01) and the interviewed sample (p < .01). The nature of these difficulties varied, but within the total sample, most of the problems occurred in finding biological parents or in their resisting the termination of their rights (n = 18). Problems were also reported in moving cases through the court (n = 9), in the use of the termination statutes (n = 4) and in agency procedures (n = 4).

From the data just discussed an interesting pattern emerges. For the non-adopted children, termination of parental rights was more likely to have occurred through the courts with relatively little difficulty, many years before an adoption discussion. What this seems to suggest is that, in the past, termination of parental rights was attempted only on relatively "easy" cases, and that after it occurred little was done to find an adoptive family for the child. However, with the recent emphasis on permanency planning, workers appear to be attempting and obtaining more voluntary surrenders. They also seem to be pursuing termination of parental rights on more "difficult" cases. This work appears to be followed by more immediate and successful efforts to convert foster homes to adoptive homes. This suggests that attempts to facilitate the adoption of children by their foster parents are more likely to succeed when there is deliberate, ongoing planning for this purpose. It seems to be less successful when a shift in plans, from long-term foster care to adoption, is dictated by a philosophical shift in the child caring system, and "catch-up" work has to be done. This augers well for the future!

If, in fact, more deliberate, ongoing planning is currently occurring, it seems quite understandable that the foster parents who eventually adopted were significantly more likely to be involved in the process of terminating parental rights. Almost half of the adopting parents reported some involvement in this process—either prodding the agency, attending and/or testifying at court hearings, or seeing and discussing this issue with the biological mother. This was reported by only 6 percent of the non-adopting parents (p

<.01). These same percentages were reported by the workers for both the total sample (p <.001) and the interviewed sample (p <.01).

Adoption Subsidy

The availability of an adoption subsidy can be an important consideration to some foster families as they deliberate about adoption. For a low income family, the board payment they receive for the care of a foster child often becomes part of their family budget; its discontinuance would make it difficult for them to maintain financial stability. For a foster family caring for a child with medical, developmental, emotional, or educational problems, the receipt of supplemental income might be critical to their ability to obtain needed resources. Thus, the absence of a subsidy, or a family's belief that their subsidy will not always be available, can be an impediment to consummating an adoption.

About two-thirds of the families in the sample reported that they either received or were offered an adoption subsidy. Most of these subsidies were for basic child care, but six families received or were offered help for specific purposes including the costs of their child's medical treatment, special education, or treatment for emotional problems. The twenty-one families who did not receive or were not offered subsidies were evenly divided between the adopting and non-adopting groups. This number seems high given the length of time these children had been in care, the many children in the sample with handicapping conditions, and the low incomes reported by many non-adopting families. The reasons that they did not receive or were not offered subsidies are unknown, but amelioration of this situation might lead to a greater number of foster parent adoptions.

It appears that subsidy was an important consideration in the deliberations of sixteen of the adopting families. Nine of these families reported that they would have adopted without the subsidy but that a non-subsidized adoption would have caused them serious financial difficulties. The other seven families reported that they could not adopt without it. For the remaining adopting families subsidy was not as critical—they were either so attached to the child that nothing could have stopped the adoption or they were financially secure.

The importance of subsidy to some adopting families was confirmed in the worker data. When asked what the most important factors were in the specific families' decisions to adopt, workers cited subsidy for about 20 percent of the families in both the total and interviewed sample. Thus, the receipt of a subsidy played an important role in the decisions of at least a minority of the adopting families.

Subsidies seemed even more important to the non-adopting group. Of the twenty-two families for whom data were available, only two stated that they would not have wanted a subsidy had they adopted. This was probably related both to the lower incomes of these families and the degree of impairment of their children. These data raise an even greater concern about the ten families in this group who were not offered a subsidy at the time adoption was discussed.

About 15 percent of the families stated that they had some hesitations about subsidy. While the proportion of adopting and non-adopting families was not significantly different, the types of hesitations voiced did reflect differences between these groups. Only non-adopting families had concerns about whether the subsidy would be sufficient; whether it would last until the child was grown; or whether it would meet all of the child's needs. On the other hand, only adopting families voiced hesitations concerning what "others might think" (the welfare connotations sometimes associated with receiving an adoption subsidy) or the child's reaction to learning about it.

Service After the Decision

While adopting families may have had more intensive contacts with their worker during the adoption discussion, this intensity of contact was not continued after the adoption decision was made. In fact, in this post-decision phase, adopting families appeared to have somewhat fewer contacts with their worker than their non-adopting counterparts, although these differences were not statistically significant. Workers reported having no contact with almost 40 percent of the total sample and 28 percent of the interviewed sample of the adopting families since the adoption decision. (The discrepancy between the total and interviewed sample probably occurred because some of the adopters moved to distant places and therefore both contact with their workers and completion of the research interview were not possible). No contact since the adoption decision was reported for fewer than 20 percent of the non-adopting families in both samples.

Thirty-two percent of the interviewed adopting families reported having no contact with the agency since their adoption was finalized. While it is heartening to note that many of the adopting families continued to have contact with the agency since finalization, the reader is cautioned not to interpret this finding to mean that full "post-adoption services" were provided. Of the twenty-two adoptive families who had such contact, almost half reported that it concerned other foster children in the home. Only eleven adopting families had follow-up contacts concerning the study child's physical problems, emotional adjustment, or adoption subsidy.

Most of the families who did not adopt continue to receive service at the same level and about the same issues that they had prior to the adoption discussion. Four-fifths of these families felt that their contact at the time of the interview was adequate; only 20 percent would have liked more help from the agency. The non-adopting families who had not had agency contact since the close of adoption discussions were, for the most part, families in which the child had been replaced.

It is not surprising that the non-adopting families were significantly more likely to see the need for continuing agency services than the families who adopted. Only about one-third of the non-adopting families wished no services from the agency, compared to two thirds of those who adopted (p <.02). And, while the non-adopting families desired *ongoing* support, counseling, or additional foster children, the adopting families desired help only "when needed" or about concrete problems such as financial support or medical treatment.

Interestingly, the workers saw a greater need for continuing agency service for both the adopting and non-adopting group than the families themselves. While the perceived need for service remained significantly different between the two groups, workers thought about 60 percent of the adopting parents and more than 80 percent of the non-adopting parents (in both the total and the interviewed sample) needed continuing service (p <.05 for total sample; p <.10 for interviewed sample). They also perceived many more adopting families needing ongoing support/counseling/therapy services for either themselves or the child.

Interviewers' Judgments of Agency Service

The data from the interviews with both the workers and the families suggest that, in some important areas, adopting families had more positive experiences with the agency-worker system than their non-adopting counterparts. These differences were reflected in the reports of the research interviewers who made judgments after each of these interviews.

After their contact with the worker, the interviewer rated the quality of help received by the family in considering adoption, the workers' knowledge of the family and their fostering experience, and the quality of services re-

ceived by the child. Tables 6.8 and 6.9 report some of the findings regarding
these variables.

Table 6.8
*Interviewer's Judgment After the Worker Interview of the Quality
of Help Received by Family in Considering
Adoption by Adoption Decision*

Quality of Help	Adoption Decision			
	Adopt		Not Adopt	
	n	%	n	%
Excellent	17	36	1	3
Good	16	34	12	37
Adequate	9	19	11	34
Poor	5	11	8	25
Total	47	100	32	100

Table 6.9
*Interviewer's Judgment After the Worker Interview of the Worker's Knowledge
of the Foster Family by Adoption Decision*

Worker's Knowledge	Adoption Decision			
	Adopt		Not Adopt	
	n	%	n	%
Very Knowledgeable	26	52	9	27
Adequate Knowledge	12	24	14	42
Less Than Adequate/Poor	12	24	10	30
Total	50	100	33	100

These data indicate that the interviewers judged the adopting parents to
have received a better quality of help ($X^2 = 13.31$, df = 3, p < .01) from
workers who were more knowledgeable about them ($X^2 = 5.34$, df = 2, p
< .07) than the non-adopting families. What should be noted, however, is
that the difference between the two groups was not all that substantial in the
"poor" category, especially on the variable measuring the worker's knowledge

of the family. The differential judgments occurred in the most favorable categories; adopting families were judged to have received "excellent" service and their workers were judged to be "very knowledgeable" more frequently than the non-adopting families.

These differences in the judgment did not appear when the interviewers judged the quality of the service provided by the worker to the child. Almost half of the children were judged to have received highly appropriate services, another 30 percent to have received generally appropriate services, and about 20 percent to have received less than appropriate services. No differences were apparent between the adopted and non-adopted children.

The interviewers' impression that the adopting families had received better service in considering adoption was repeated after the interviews with the families. However, the pattern was somewhat different for these judgments. As can be seen in Table 6.10 almost 40 percent of the non-adopting group was judged to have received "poor" services, compared to only 15 percent of the adopting group. Thus, the significant difference between the two groups on these ratings was due to differential ratings in both the most positive and negative categories ($X^2 = 4.60$, df = 2, p < .10).

Table 6.10
Interviewer Judgment After Family Interview of the Quality
of Help Received by Family in Considering Adoption
by Adoption Decision

Quality of Help	Adoption Decision			
	Adopt		Not Adopt	
	n	%	n	%
Excellent/Good	19	58	11	39
Adequate	9	27	6	21
Poor	5	15	11	39
Total	33	100	28	100

A total of thirty-one families were judged to have received only adequate or poor service—fourteen adopting and seventeen non-adopting families. For these families the interviewers were asked to specify what factors led them to this judgment, and some of the reasons differentiated the adopters from the non-adopters at significant levels. Services for the non-adopters were more often judged to be only adequate or poor because of a lack of contact or interest on the part of worker (Fishers p = .006); because they did not receive support around problems or during periods of crisis (Fishers p = .10); or because they received inconsistent services (Fishers p = .06). On the other hand, adopters were more often judged to have received only adequate or poor services because they encountered delays in the adoption process (Fishers p = .10).

Summary

From the data presented in this chapter a number of important points can be made. First, when information was available from both the workers and the families on the same variable it tended to be congruent. This enhances the reliability of the data and lends credence to the information presented.

Second, for these data, the information reported by the workers was very similar for the full sample and the interviewed sample of families. This is heartening, since one can conclude that the sample loss did not significantly alter the relationships discovered. In fact, one might speculate that had interviews been available from all of the families eligible for the study, the relationships which did appear in the family data might have been even stronger due to the increased sample size.

Third, there were important differences between the adopting and non-adopting groups in a number of service areas. In general, the adopting group had been foster parents for less time, had fewer workers and knew more of their workers well, and felt freer to talk with their workers. They were also more likely to feel that something was "missing" in their relationship with their foster children.

The adopting families also appeared to have received better service regarding the sample child. They were more likely to have had substantial contact on a more regular basis with their workers, to have had more complete background information about their children, to have had somewhat more comprehensive discussions with their workers about adoption and to feel that their workers knew them well. They were also more likely to know the children's biological parents and to be involved in the termination process. These experiences appear to be motivators that encourage the foster parents to resolve their "temporary" status.

In addition, the adopting families appeared to be more motivated to adopt from the beginning. They were more likely to have had earlier discussions about adoption, to have approached the agency about adoption and to have made more timely decisions than their non-adopting counterparts.

Finally, one must note some of the deficiences in the service delivery system present for both adopting and non-adopting foster parents. Significant numbers of foster parents had little preparation for foster parenthood, had children placed under crisis circumstances, did not discuss factors thought to be important to the adoption decision, and were not offered subsidy. Twelve of the children were not legally freed for adoption. If foster parent adoptions are to be accomplished, attention must be paid to these factors and their assumed negative consequences. If this is not done, children who could be adopted might remain in foster care and incur the risks that have been identified with this service.

CHAPTER 7

Refining The Distinction Between Adopting and Non-Adopting Foster Parents

Bruce (whose situation was reported in Chapter 1), is loved in his foster home and there "to stay" . . . the foster parents do not see that adoption will make any real difference. . . . They will continue as foster parents. For Sam (also discussed in Chapter I) and his foster parents it was "love at first sight". . . . They "knew they could care for him better than anyone else". . . . There was no hesitation about adoption. The three previous chapters have shown that there are a large number of variables which distinguish adopting from non-adopting foster parents. These differences occurred in all four areas under study—family characteristics, child characteristics, family-child interaction, and agency service. The question which this chapter will address is: "Of all the variables found to significantly differentiate adopting from non-adopting families which are the most useful in distinguishing between the two groups?"

In order to answer this question, the data were subjected to a series of discriminant analyses.[1] This statistical technique allows the researcher to answer the following questions:

1. Is discrimination between the groups on the basis of some set of characteristics possible?

2. How well does the set of characteristics discriminate?

3. Which characteristics are the most powerful discriminators?[2]

Through this technique one is able to simultaneously relate a series of independent variables (discriminators) to a single dependent variable in order to

143

determine the strongest predictors of group membership and their power to discriminate between the two groups.

The discriminant analyses were conducted in two stages. First, all of the variables found to significantly differentiate between the adopting and non-adopting groups in the bivariate analysis were classified as belonging to one of the four domains under study—family characteristics, child characteristics, family-child interaction, or agency service. The breakdown of significant variables into these four groups is presented in Figure 7.1. Then, each group of variables was separately entered into a discriminant analysis. In this way the best discriminating variables within each domain could be determined and the classificatory power of the specific group of variables could be ascertained.

With this accomplished the second stage of the multivariate analysis was undertaken. This involved entering all of the variables which appeared as important discriminators in the separate analyses into a final discriminant analysis. In this way the relative strength of the important variables from each of the four domains could be determined and a complete picture of the variables which best discriminate adopters from non-adopters could be obtained.

Before presenting the findings of these analyses a note of caution is needed. As with all multi-variate techniques, there are a number of assumptions which underlie the use of discriminant analysis. Due to the nature of the data, some of these assumptions could not be met in these analyses.* Thus, while the results of the discriminant analyses are reported here for the sake of organizing and clarifying the findings of the study, the reader is cautioned that these results *must be seen as tentative* and are subject to confirmation through replication of the study.

---

*One assumption of discriminant analysis is that the independent variables are measured at the interval level. Since many of the variables in this study were measured at the nominal level, dichotomous "dummy" variables had to be created. This procedure is often used in the social sciences.[3] However, this creates a problem in significance testing, and thus in the use of the stepwise procedure, since tests of significance in this procedure depend on the assumption of multi-variate normality and equal variance—convariance matrices for the independent variables in the two groups. Normality cannot be attained with dichtomous variables. In addition, if the groups are really different, the convariance matrices will not be equal.

An additional, and perhaps more important problem in the use of discriminant analyses with these data is that a large number of independent variables were available for analysis on a relatively small number of cases. Under these circumstances this procedure capitalizes on purely random variations (due to sampling and measurement error) in the data and thus a large number of cases can be correctly classified.[4]

Figure 7.1

Classification of Significant Variables
According to Study Domain

Family Characteristics

From Worker Interview

Age of Foster Mother
Race of Foster Mother
Education of Foster Mother
Age of Foster Father
Education of Foster Father
Occupation of Foster Father
Family Income
Number of Children Placed With Family
Whether Family Wanted to Adopt When Applied to be
    Foster Parents
Preferences for Type of Child Met

From Family Interview

Years as Foster Parents
Years With Agency
Number of Adopted Children in Home
Number of Foster Children in Home
Number of Children in Home Under 3 years old
Number of Children in Home 3–6 years old
Number of Children in Home 6–9 years old
Number of Children in Home 9–12 years old
Number of Children in Home 12–15 years old
Number of Children in Home over 15 years old
Involvement in Community Organizations
Involvement in Foster or Adoptive Parent Organizations
Preference for Infants
Whether Preferences for Type of Child Met
When Family First Thought of Adoption
Length of Time to Make Final Adoption Decision

Child Characteristics

From Worker Interview

Age at Initial Placement

Age at Placement in This Home
Current Age
Number of Placements Prior to This Home
Reason for Placement in This Home
Intelligence
Emotional Problems
Coders Judgment—Severity of Emotional Problems at Time Adoption was Discussed
Coders Judgment—Change in Child's Behavior Between Placement and Adoption Discussion

From Family Interview
Race
Presence of Behavior Problems
Intelligence
Family Felt Child Had Special Needs When Adoption Discussed

Family-Child Interaction

From Family Interview
Mother's Feelings at First Meeting With Child
Effects of Child's Placement on Family
Perceived Similarity to Other Family Members
Whether Child Is Perceived Differently Than Other Children
Interviewer Judgment—Affection of Child Toward Mother
Interviewer Judgment—Affection of Child Toward Father
Interviewer Judgment—Rapport Between Child and Mother
Interviewer Judgment—Rapport Between Child and Father
Interviewer Judgment—Understanding of Child Shown by Mother
Interviewer Judgment—Understanding of Child Shown by Father

Service Variables

From Worker Interview
When Child Surrendered Voluntarily
When Child Surrendered by Court Action
When Case Assigned to Worker

Amount of Contact With Parents During Adoption Discussion

Amount of Contact With Child During Adoption Discussion

Worker's Relationship With Child

Family Preferences for Type of Child Met

Family Had Information About Reason Child Entered Care Prior to Adoption Discussion

Family Had Information About Child's Living Experience With Biological Parents Prior to Adoption Discussion

Foster Parents Met Biological Parents

Frequency of Contact With Biological Parents During Year Adoption Discussed

Family Involved in Termination Proceedings

Difficulties in Legal Termination Present

From Family Interview

Total Number of Workers

Family Believed Worker Who Discussed Adoption Knew Them Well

Family Perception of Foster Parent Role

Family Preferences for Type of Child Met

Contact With Biological Parents During Year Adoption Discussed

Length of Time Until Adoption Discussed

Who Approached Whom About Adoption

Adoption Worker Involved in Initial Adoption Discussion

Discussion of Child's Past History During Adoption Deliberation

Discussion of Special Helps Child Might Need During Adoption Deliberation

Discussion of Legal Processes During Adoption Deliberation

Current Contact With Biological Parents

Contact With Biological Parents Perceived as Positive or Negative

Family Involved in Termination Proceedings

Family Characteristics

It can be seen in Figure 7.1 that twenty-six family characteristics were entered into the first discriminant analysis. These variables captured a number of domains including family composition, socio-economic characteristics, experience as foster parents, adoption decision making and community involvement. Of these twenty-six variables, twelve were found to be important discriminators. These are displayed in Table 7.1 in the order of their discriminatory power.

Table 7.1

Family Variables Discriminating Between Adopting and Non-Adopting Group

Variable	Standardized Canonical Discriminant Function Coefficient
Number of Adopted Children	.947
Foster Father Age	-.690
Family Wanted to Adopt When Applied (Worker Report)	.639
When First Thought of Adopting This Child (Family Report)	-.621
Foster Mother Education	.536
Foster Father Education	.513
Length of Time Until Final Adoption Decision	-.497
Years as Foster Parents With Agency	-.349
Family Income	.343
Number of Children Over 15 Years Old	.307
Preference for Infant	.305
Involvement in Foster or Adoptive Parent Organization	.200

These twelve variables correctly classified 93.6 percent of the families. That is, based on the information from these twelve variables, all but four of the sixty-two families in the interviewed sample could be correctly classified as adopting or non-adopting. Two adopting and two non-adopting families would have been incorrectly classified based on these variables.

In the analysis of family characteristics, the single most important discriminator between the adopting and non-adopting families was whether the family had adopted in the past. Thus, the notion of childlessness as a major motivator for adoption must be rejected within this sample. The presence of other adopted children within the family was a strong indicator of the family's intent with the child under study.

This finding suggests that some parents who eventually adopted may have been motivated to foster for different reasons than other foster parents in the study. Having previously adopted, they may continue to foster with the hope that the opportunity to adopt will eventually present itself again. Thus, some of the adopting parents may be using foster care as a "back door" to adoption; they may realize that foster parenting is a promising road open to them in their pursuit of an additional child.

This speculation gains credence when one notices that three variables which can be seen as measures of adoption motivation also discriminate the adopting from the non-adopting families. Reports of the worker that the family thought about adoption at the point they applied to be foster parents, reports by the family that they thought about adopting this child at the time of placement or shortly thereafter, and the families' making their decisions shortly after the opportunity to adopt was presented, all discriminated the adopting families from others in the study. From these findings it appears that many of the families who eventually adopted had hoped to adopt from the start and responded quickly when this opportunity presented itself.

If this is the case, it is not surprising that the family's preference for an infant also appeared as a discriminator in this analysis. Families motivated by the thought of adopting, rather than temporarily caring for a child, would, understandably, want to care for a child with whom they believed they could form close attachments. The perception that this is more likely to occur and more readily accomplished with a young child is quite common. However, the fact that the two variables measuring whether family preferences were actually met did not appear as discriminators seems to indicate that the initial motivation to adopt takes precedence over the preferences for a specific type of child when parents are faced with an adoption decision.

Age of the foster parents (mother's and father's ages are closely related) is also a predictor of whether a family will adopt and, while distinct, is probably related to two other less important discriminators within this analysis—number of children over the age of fifteen present in the home and the number of years the parents had fostered for the agency. Older parents, who may be nearing the end of their intense parenting responsibilities, are probably less likely to want to take total responsibility for raising another child and are therefore less likely to adopt. Further, parents already in the midst of raising an older adolescent may be more intensely aware of the potential problems in this process, and may display greater hesitance in making a total commitment to another child without the continuing support of the agency. Additionally, lessened energy and perhaps health problems may accompany advancing age.

Older parents are also more likely to have been foster parents for their agency for longer periods of time than their younger counterparts. This variable is obviously redundant with the variable measuring total time as foster parents and thus the latter was not included in the list of discriminating variables. Further, long-time foster parents are more likely to have come to foster parenting with the understanding that they should not get too "close" to their child and that adoption would never be possible. These understandings were reinforced by agencies as little as ten years ago.[5] Thus, the idea of adopting a foster child might be more alien to these long-time foster parents than to their younger, less experienced counterparts. They are more likely to have been socialized as "true" foster parents.

Socio-economic status of the family also seems to be an important discriminator between adopters and non-adopters. Three measures of this—mother's education, father's education, and family income—all appeared as predictors of adoption, and are probably redundant with the other measures of socio-economic status originally included in the analysis. The appearance of measures of socio-economic status in this analysis is understandable—families with low incomes, often due to poor education, would understandably be more reluctant to make a permanent commitment to a child, even with the availability of subsidy. What is interesting in this anaylsis is that race is not a discriminator between adopters and non-adopters when these associated socio-economic factors are controlled.

Thus, if the interpretation of the data from this analysis of family characteristics is correct, four areas within this domain seem to emerge as the primary discriminators between adopting and non-adopting families. These are previous experience with adoption, an ongoing motivation to adopt, age and its possible relationship to the desire to take full responsibility for parenting, and socio-economic status.

Child Characteristics

Thirteen child characteristics were entered into the second discriminant analysis. Six, displayed in Table 7.2, were found to be discriminators between children who were adopted and those who were not. Based on these six characteristics, 79 percent of the children were correctly classified. Those incorrectly classified were about evenly divided between adoptees (n = 6) and non-adoptees (n = 7).

The strongest discriminator between the adopted and non-adopted children was race. Black children in the sample were less likely to be adopted than white children. Since these black children were placed in black homes,

Table 7.2
Child Variables Discriminating Between
Adopting and Non-Adopting Group

Variable	Standardized Canonical Discriminant Function Coefficient
Race	−.615
Reason For Placement in This Home	.529
Intelligence (Parents' Report)	.449
Family Felt Child had "Special Needs" When Adoption Discussed	−.369
Age at Placement in This Home	−.352
Presence of Behavior Problems	−.259

this may well be a reflection of the poorer economic circumstances of the black families within the sample (see previous analysis). Thus, the economic circumstances of the black families within the sample probably diminished their foster children's chances of being adopted. The implications of this finding will be discussed in the concluding chapter.

The next strongest discriminator in the analysis was the reason for the child's placement in this home. Its presence in this analysis confirms the importance of the bi-variate relationship previously reported. Children placed in their current home in a planful way, either as a first placement, a move from a short-term home, or because adoption was a possibility, were more likely to be adopted than children who were moved from another home due to their behavioral problems or because the foster parents, for whatever reason, could not continue to care for them. Thus, there is confirmation in this analysis that less damaged children—children less likely to be showing behavior problems or to have suffered difficult separations—were more likely to be adopted. This makes sense, for such children are probably easier to form bonds with and more likely to allow new attachments to develop.

Interestingly, this factor takes precedence over the direct measure of the number of previous placements the child had experienced, which did not prove to be an important discriminator in this analysis. Thus, replacement is probably only a part of a total picture; one must consider the reason for the replacement in differentiating those who were adopted from those who were not.

Three other variables, all concerned with the condition of the child at the time adoption was discussed, were found to discriminate between the two groups of children. These were intelligence, whether the child was perceived to have special needs, and the presence of behavior problems.

It will be recalled from the bi-variate analysis that both the worker and the family estimated the child's intelligence. While their estimates differed, better intellectual capacity was associated with the childs' being adopted. Rather than confound the analysis with two estimations of the same variable, only the family's estimate of the child's intelligence was entered into this analysis,[6] and this was found to discriminate between the two groups.

The family's perception that the child had "special needs" in its broad sense, and the specific presence of behavior problems, also discriminated between the groups; in both cases more "normal" children were more likely to be adopted. While behavior problems and limited intelligence may be part of the child's "special needs," these concepts are distinct enough so that they all appear in the analysis. However, these three variables may be redundant with judgments of the child's emotional problems, and may be the reason that this variable does not appear as a discriminator.

The variables just discussed are reports of the family. Interestingly it is these family reports which appeared as discriminators, rather than either the workers' reports of problems in these areas or the coders' judgment based on information provided by the worker (See Figure 7.1). Thus, family perceptions of behavior and potential, which may be more "subjective," were more powerful. The workers more "objective" perceptions which were, in many ways, redundant with the parents' reports, did not add any additional discriminating power to the analysis.

Age at placement *in this home* was the final discriminator in the analysis of child characteristics. This variable takes precedence over two other age variables—age the child entered foster care and the child's current age—and thus is a better variable for predicting the adoption decision. When one thinks about this finding it seems to lend support to the importance of early attachment between parent and child. Children who entered their foster homes early are less likely to have had prior meaningful relationships or to have experienced replacement. They may be more capable of forming close relationships with substitute parents. Parents, too, may relate more "naturally" to a very young child. This early attachment appears to be sustained until an adoption can take place.

From this analysis and the interpretation of the findings, four factors seem to be important discriminators between children who are adopted and children who are not. First, the difference in age and socio-economic status between black and white foster families seems to hinder the black child's chances of adoption. Second, children who move through the foster care system in a planful way seem to have a better chance of adoption when the opportunity arises. Third, the parents' perceptions that the child has special needs at the time adoption is considered appear to be deterrent to adoption. Finally, children placed in their foster homes at early ages are more likely to be adopted, regardless of the time which elapses between the placement and the consideration of adoption.

Parent-Child Interaction

The discriminant analysis performed on the parent-child interaction variables initially contained ten items. Four of these were reports of the parents, while the remaining six were interviewer judgments of interactional factors.[7] Of these ten variables, six appeared as discriminators and are displayed in Table 7.3. Based on these variables, 81 percent of the sample were correctly classified. Six families in both the adopting and non-adopting families would have been misclassified based on these variables alone.

Table 7.3
Parent-Child Interaction Variables
Discriminating Between Adopting and Non-Adopting Groups

Variable	Standardized Canonical Discriminant Function Coefficient
Interviewer Judgment—Affection of Child Toward Mother	.419
Effects of Child's Placement on Family	.412
Interviewer Judgment—Rapport Between Mother and Child	.369
Mother's Feelings at First Meeting With Child	.311
Interviewer Judgment—Understanding of Child Shown by Mother	.274
Perceived Similarity to Other Family Members	.256

The appearance of all three interviewers' judgments concerning the relationship of the child and the mother in this analysis is interesting for two reasons. First, it means that these judgments were not redundant with each other—that the interviewers were able to discriminate between the various dimensions and to differentially rate the families on each. Second, it demonstrates that the child's relationship with the mother along the various dimensions are more powerful discriminators than the judgments of the relationship with the father along the same dimensions.

The reason that the judgments of the mother-child interaction were better discriminators than the judgments of the father-child interaction is a matter for speculation. It may be that the two sets of judgments were redundant, and that the judgments of father-child interactions simply did not add any discriminating power to the analysis. On the other hand, it may be that the mothers tended to have greater interaction with their children, and that this interaction was more important to process of family formation. This latter explanation is most likely to be valid for young children who are home for most of the day.

What is most interesting about these data is that the most powerful discriminator within this domain is the judgment of the affection shown *by the child toward the mother.* Children who were eventually adopted were, according to the interviewers, better able to display affection. This variable highlights the interactional nature of parent-child relationships.[8] Children who are able to display affection are more likely to encourage positive reactions from their parents. Parents with such children are likely to feel rewarded for their efforts and to engage in behaviors which encourage this cycle of positive interactions. This may well lead to greater rapport between the mother and child (the next most important judgment discriminator) and may be a motivator for parents to attempt to understand their children's behavior better. Thus, while these three areas appear to be discrete, they are probably intertwined with each other.

The presence of positive interactions within the adoptive families seems to be confirmed by data received directly from the families. Parents who eventually adopted were more likely to feel that the child affected their family in a positive way. They were also more likely to perceive greater similarities between themselves and their children. (The one family report that does not appear as an important discriminator, perceived similarity between this child and other children, may be redundant with this measure.) Whether these children were, in fact, similar to their parents is a matter of conjecture. It is the perception that the child has had a positive effect on the family and is like other family members, rather than the objective reality, which was entered into this analysis and proved to be discriminating.

These perceptions of the adopting families may be colored by the fact that they were more likely to have been motivated to adopt from the beginning. They therefore may have a greater "need" to perceive their children as similar to themselves and their children's effects on the family as positive. Because of this initial motivation, these parents may have been more positive in their initial reaction to the child, another discriminator in the analysis. Parents who reacted in positive ways initially, rather than being hesitant, shocked, concerned, tense, or by feeling sorry for the child, were more likely to adopt.

From this analysis it seems clear that the quality of the interaction betwen parents and children discriminates adopting from non-adopting families. However, there is no way of determining whose input into the interaction is more important. Clearly, the child plays a major role, for the two most important discriminators within this analysis are the child's ability to show affection and the child's effect on the family. However, who initiates the positive interactional cycle is not clear. Thus, there is a need for more detailed research in this area, and a need to study this interactional process using measures which are less subjective and more valid.

Agency Service Variables

Twenty-eight measures of agency service were entered into the final discriminant analysis in this first phase of multi-variate analysis.[9] Nineteen of these measures proved to be discriminators between the two groups. This is a very large number of discriminators. These nineteen measures correctly classified all but one of the sixty-two families in the study and are displayed in Table 7.4.

By far, the best discriminator among these variables was whether the parents report having contact with the biological family during the year adoption was discussed. This variable, while different, is logically connected with four other discriminators in the analysis—the worker's report of whether the foster parents had ever met the biological parents, the family's perception of contact with biological parents as negative, their involvement in termination procedures, and the foster parents' perception of their role. The strength of these variables is somewhat surprising, given the other variables in the analysis. It seems to add credence, as posited in a previous chapter, to the conclusion that contact with the biological parents, especially during the year adoption was discussed, acts as a strong motivator for foster parents to move toward adoption. The involvement of biological parents may either pose a threat to the foster parent-child relationship and to the attachments which

Table 7.4

Service Variables Discriminating Between
Adopting and Non-Adopting Groups

Variable	Standardized Canonical Discriminant Function Coefficient
Contact With Biological Parents During Year Adoption Discussed (Family Report)	1.075
Family Believed Worker Who Discussed Adoption Knew Them Well	.621
Adoption Worker Involved in Initial Adoption Discussion	−.602
Foster Parents Met Biological Parents (Worker Report)	.569
When Case Assigned to Worker	−.567
Workers' Relationship With Child	.541
Discussion of Child's Past History During Adoption Deliberation	.531
Discussion of Special Helps Child Might Need During Adoption Deliberation	−.500
Total Number of Workers	−.499
Family Had Information About Child's Living Experiences With Biological Family Prior to Adoption Discussion	.468
Length of Time Until Adoption Discussed	−.465
Contact With Biological Parents Perceived as Negative	.350
When Child Surrendered By Court Action	.337
Parents' Involvement in Termination Proceedings (Family Report)	.289
Family Felt Free to Talk With Worker	.270
Amount of Contact With Child During Adoption Discussion	.258
Family Had Information About Reasons Child Entered Care Prior to Adoption Discussion	.233
Family Preferences for Type of Child Met (Family Perception)	.206
Family Perception of Foster Parent Role	.197

may have formed between them, or help the parents to "know" their children better and to resolve their feelings about their past. In either case, this contact alone was strongly related to the decision to adopt.

The motivation to adopt appears to be even stronger when the foster parents perceive the biological parents and/or their relationship with them negatively. This negative perception appears to bring out the family's protective feelings toward the child. The fear that a "bad" biological parent may "reclaim" their child, and the foster parents recognition of the strength of blood ties, may create a situation which is resolved by moving toward adoption.

It is not surprising, then, that the adopting parents were more likely to be involved in termination proceedings. Their greater need to confirm their relationship with the child may lead them to get involved in procedures which allows this confirmation, through adoption, to take place.

How the foster parents perceived their role was also a discriminator, although not a particularly powerful one, in this analysis. Foster parents who saw themselves "just like the child's parents" were less likely to adopt. Parents who felt that something was missing from their relationship or that they had to provide something special for the child were more likely to move toward adoption. Their feelings of not being "full" parents, or of needing to provide something special to the child, are undoubtedly heightened if the biological parents continue to be involved with the child.

Interestingly, once the relationship is resolved through adoption, the need to shelter the child from contact with biological parents appears to diminish. It will be recalled from the bi-variate analysis that adopted children continue to have more contact with their biological families than their non-adopted counterparts after the adoption decision. However, this variable is not a discriminator in this analysis and is probably redundant with reports of previous contact.

Further, it should be noted that it was the parents' reports of contact with the biological parents during the year adoption was discussed, and their report of involvement in termination proceedings, rather than the workers', which were the important discriminators in the analysis. Thus, once again, parents' preceptions appear to take precedence over the workers' preceptions. Once the parents' perceptions are entered into the analysis, the workers' reports of the same variables add no additional discriminating power.

The second most important discriminator was whether the family believed that the worker with whom they discussed adoption knew them well. Families with these feelings were more likely to adopt. This finding highlights the influence that the relationship between the worker and the family might have on the adoption decision, and confirms much research which demonstrates the importance of "relationship" to all social work practice.[10] While knowing a family "well" is a broad term, one might expect this to occur when: 1) there has been a history between the foster parents and the worker; 2) the relationship has been characterized by open communication; and 3) the relationship with other family members is also positive in nature. Indicators of these characteristics within the family-worker relationship also appear as discriminators within the analysis; and adopting families appear to have fared better in all of these areas.

History of relationship was indicated in this analysis by the presence of three variables—whether an adoption worker (who was probably new to the case) was involved in the initial adoption discussion, when the case was assigned to the worker, and the total number of workers to whom the family has had to relate. When continuity of family-worker relationship has been preserved, there is greater possibility of trust developing. While these conditions do not guarantee that the worker will know the family well, and therefore are discreet indicators of service, the chances that a knowledgeable relationship will develop and an adoption will occur are undoubtedly enhanced under these conditions.

Open communication, while obviously a part of being knowledgeable about the family, goes beyond this concept. It means that the family is given information about the child and that the family feels free to discuss their hesitations, concerns and weaknesses with the worker. There are a number of variables which indicated that openness in the family-worker relationship was present to a greater degree in the adopting families. These include whether the family had information about the child's living experiences with the biological family prior to the adoption discussion; whether the family had information about why the child entered care prior to the adoption discussion; whether the child's history was reacpitulated during the adoption discussion; and whether the family "felt free" to talk with their worker.

The fact that discussion of the child's problems during the adoption deliberation also appeared as an important discriminator needs careful examination. It will be recalled that such discussions took place more frequently with non-adopting than with adopting families, and that the non-adopted children had more special needs than their adopted counterparts. Thus, one might expect such discussions to discriminate between the groups. But, this should not be taken as an indicator that openness in discussion mitigates against adoption. Rather, it is probably an indicator of the child's condition and, perhaps, should have been analyzed with the child's characteristics. However, it might indicate that when adoption discussions are underway, care should be taken not to overemphasize the child's problems and continuing needs. And, when discussing this area, concurrent discussions about the availability of resources to meet these needs and discussions about the child's progress should also occur.

The final part of knowing a family "well" may have to do with the nature of the relationship with family members. From the bi-variate analysis it will be recalled that workers did not report differences in the quality of their relationships with families but did report better relationships with the adopted than with the non-adopted children. The fact that this difference in relationship with the child continues as an important discriminator in this analysis highlights the importance of the "quality" issues of relationships.

Positive relationships with children may motivate workers to invest more in their adoption. And, in fact, there are a number of indicators in this analysis which lend support to the conclusion that workers invested more in the adopted children and their families. First, the adopted children were freed more recently for adoption. Second, adopted children were more likely to be freed through the courts. Both of these are indicators of recent and increased efforts on the part of the workers. Further, the presence of the variables showing that adoption was raised earlier with the adopting families, and that contact during the adoption discussion was more intense with them (contact with child and contact with family are probably highly correlated and therefore redundant), all seem to indicate more worker investment, carried out in a planned manner, for the families who eventually adopted.

Interestingly, when all of the service variables are entered into the analysis, who initiated the adoption discussion does not appear as a discriminator. Further, whether the family's initial preferences for a particular type of child were met (family report rather than worker) is only a very weak discriminator.

The Combined Factors

The final analysis performed involved entering the forty-three variables found to be discriminators in the previous four analyses into a final discriminant analysis. Thus one determines their relative importance when all factors are considered, as well as the importance of each of the four sub-areas in differentiating between adopting and non-adopting families. Of these variables, twenty-two were found to be discriminators. These twenty-two variables classified all sixty-two cases correctly and are displayed in Table 7.5.

Family Variables. The most important discriminator in this combined analysis is the variable which was most important in the analysis of family characteristics—the number of previously adopted children present in the home. The presence of this variable in the analysis, as well as the indicator of the family's adoption intentions at the point of application, highlight the importance of initial motivation to adoption outcome. Parents who continue to

Table 7.5
Variables From Four Sub-Analyses Discriminating
Between Adopting and Non-Adopting Groups

Variable	Standardized Canonical Discriminant Function Coefficient
Number of Adopted Children	1.113
Adoption Worker Involved in Initial Adoption Discussion	-.999
Contact With Biological Parents During Year Adoption Discussed	.882
Family Income	.842
Family Felt Free to Talk With Worker	.759
Length of Time Until Adoption Discussed	-.713
Perceived Similarity to Other Family Members	.682
Worker's Relationship to Child	.664
Foster Mother Education	.631
Family Perception of Foster Parent Role	.615
Interviewer's Judgment—Understanding of Child Shown by Mother	.593
Family Had InformationAbout Child's Living Experience With Biological Family Prior to Adoption Discussion	.558
Family Wanted to Adopt When Applied (Worker Report)	.546
Family Felt Child Had Special Needs When Adoption Discussed	-.510
Number of Children Over 15 Years Old	-.486
Age at Placement in the Home	-.434
Total Number of Workers	-.419
Reason for Placement in This Home	.395
Effects of Child's Placement on Family	.351
When Case Assigned to Worker	-.307
Years as Foster Parents With Agency	-.256
Contacts With Biological Parents Perceived as Negative	.238

foster after a previous adoption, and foster parents who see foster care as a "back door" to adoption, appear to follow through on their initial intentions. Weaker indications of motivations which appeared in the analysis of family characteristics (when the family first thought about adopting this child and the amount of time it took the family to make its final decision) do not appear in this larger analysis.

In this final analysis indicators of socio-economic status are the second group of family characteristics which differentiate the adopters from the non-adopters. Income appears to be a stronger discriminator than education (the opposite was true in the analysis of family characteristics alone) although both are present. With the foster mothers' education entered into the analysis, the foster fathers' education adds no additional discriminating power in the larger analysis.

Interestingly, age, which was the second most powerful discriminator in the analysis of family characteristics, does not appear in this analysis. Other factors associated with age—the number of children over age fifteen in the household and the years of foster care experience—are present, but are not particularly strong discriminators. Thus, with other factors controlled, age of the foster parents appears to be less important to the adoption decision than was initially anticipated.

Agency Service. Variables associated with agency service continued as important discriminators between adopting and non-adopting families. In fact, five of the eight strongest discriminators in this overall analysis were from this domain. While in some cases different indicators of the underlying concepts were stronger in this analysis than they appeared in the previous analysis, almost all of the concepts delineated in the previous analysis are present.

The involvement of an adoption worker (probably new to a family) in the initial adoption discussion appears as the most important service discriminator, and the second most important variable in the overall analysis. As mentioned previously, this variable is probably conceptually connected with two other variables which also appear in this overall analysis—the number of workers to whom the family had related and the length of time the family knew the worker with whom they discussed adoption. Thus, the relationship between worker-family continuity and a decision to adopt becomes even more important in this analysis than in the previous analysis of service variables.

The importance of contact with biological parents during the year adoption was discussed is again underscored in this analysis by the presence of this variable as the third most important discriminator. The perception of this contact as negative also appears in this analysis, although as the least important discriminator. The only indicator of biological parent contact that did not appear in this analysis that did appear in the analysis of service variables was whether the foster parents *ever* met the biological parents. Thus, contact during the decision-making period takes precedence over earlier contact, and lends support to the speculations made earlier that this contact may serve as a catalyst to the decision to adopt.

How the parents perceived their role, which was previously posited to be conceptually connected with the involvement of biological parents in the foster parent-child relationship, had greater significance in the overall analysis than it had in the analysis of service factors. Feelings of being different than biological parents, which may be heightened by interactions with workers and biological families, are associated with the decision to adopt and become one of the stronger service discriminators in this overall analysis.

In this analysis, as in the analysis of service variables, an indicator of the quality of the family-worker relationship was an important discriminator. However, the discriminator which appears in this analysis—whether the family felt free to talk with the worker— was only a weak discriminator in the previous analysis. The strong discriminator from the previous analysis which measured the quality of the family-worker relationship (whether the family felt the worker who discussed adoption with them knew them well) did not appear in this analysis. It seems clear, however, that these two variables are tapping information from the same domain and that it is this larger domain, quality of the relationship with the worker, which is important to the adoption decision.

Within this analysis, once the measure of the quality of the worker-family relationship was entered, indicators of "openness" in communication between family and worker appear to be less important than they had in the analysis of service factors alone. Only one variable, whether the family had information about the child's living experience with the biological family, is a discriminator in this analysis. Other variables, including measures of the specific areas discussed during the time adoption was being considered, as well as other measures of information which the parents possessed prior to this discussion, were not included in the list of discriminators. Perhaps in this larger analysis these more specific measures were redundant with the primary measure of the quality of the worker-family relationship.

Another indicator of the quality of the worker-family relationship which continues as a discriminator in the overall analysis is the worker's report of the nature of the relationship with the child. This variable continued to take precedence over the actual amount of contact with the child, which did not appear in this analysis. Thus, there continues to be support for the hypothesis that continuity and quality are more important than quantity in all spheres of family-worker interactions. Consistent and more frequent contacts may be conducive to the development of good relationships, but do not guarantee that they will occur.

Only one variable of worker investment was an important discriminator in this analysis. The parents' report of when the adoption discussion took place had greater importance in this analysis than it did in the analysis of the service variables alone. Other variables thought to be associated with investment (date of surrender, surrender in court and quantity of contact) do not appear as discriminators in this analysis. Thus, in the overall analysis, investment appears to be only a weak indicator, for timing of the adoption discussion may be indicative of other things, including parental motivation and more thoughtful planning on the part of the worker.

Parent-Child Interactions. A curious phenomena occurs when one attempts to analyze the importance of parent-child interactions in the overall analysis. Those parent-child variables which were the weakest discriminators in the analysis of parent-child interaction factors appear as the strongest discriminators among this group of variables in the total analysis. Perceived similarity to family members and the judgment of the understanding of the child shown by the mother were the most important discriminators within this domain. The effects of the child's placement on the family, which was an important discriminator in the previous analysis, appears as the weakest discriminator from this set of variables in the overall analysis. Three of the four most important variables in this domain in the partial analysis (the judgments of affection of the child toward the mother, rapport between mother and child, and the mother's feelings on first meeting the child) do not even appear in this analysis. Thus, while the more limited analysis of parent-child interactions emphasized the importance of the child's role, the overall analysis seems to emphasize the importance of the parents' actions and perceptions in this area. Perhaps this occurrence is a further indicator of the importance of reciprocity within these relationships.

It seems clear, then, that the conclusions generated in the previous section must remain extremely tentative. Clearly, parent-child interaction is important, but the most important elements within this domain remain elusive. Only with better operational definitions and greater precision of measurement can the nature of the relationships within this area be defined and their association with the adoption decision be fully ascertained.

Child Variables. In looking at the overall analysis there are a number of factors about the child variables which the reader should observe. First, these variables appear to be the weakest discriminators in the overall analysis of the twenty-two discriminators; the first child variable to appear has the fourteenth highest standardized discriminant coefficient. Thus, in general, child characteristics are the poorest discriminators between the adopted and non-adopted group when other factors are controlled.

Second, race, the most important variable in child characteristics analysis, does not appear as a discriminator in the overall analysis. Thus, when age and socio-economic status of the parents is controlled, race of the child is a redundant variable.

Finally, in this overall analysis, the presence of general measures of the child's special needs at the time of adoption take precedence over the specific areas of child functioning. Measures of intelligence and behavior problems, present in the more limited analysis, were not present in the overall analysis. This is not surprising as "special needs" undoubtedly cover these specific areas of functioning.

There is some evidence that the ability to form relationships on the part of the child continued as a discriminator in the overall analysis. These included when and why the child was placed in this particular home. Early placement due to non-traumatic circumstances, which would auger well for the capacity to form relationships, was a discriminator, albeit a weak one, in the overall analysis.

Conclusions

From these analyses one can rank order the relative importance of the concepts found to be significantly related to the adoption decision. One must, however, see such a ranking as *very tentative*, since some areas within the study were probed more deeply and measured more reliably and validly than others, and not all of the assumptions of discriminant analysis could be met by the data. With this caveat in mind, based on the overall discriminant analysis, it appears, to these writers, that such a rank ordering might be:

1. The family's prior experience with adoption and continuing motivation to adopt;

2. Continuity and quality of the family's relationship with the worker;

3. Family contact with the biological parent(s), especially when perceived as negative;

4. Socio-economic status of the family;

5. Parent-child interactions including the ability of the child to form relationships;

6. Feelings on the part of the parents that they are different than the child's biological parents;

7. Special needs of the child at the time adoption is discussed;

8. Parents' age.

The implications of these findings for policy and practice will be discussed in the final chapter.

CHAPTER 8

Foster Parent Adoptions That Failed

As if someone had died in the family is the best I can put it. I've had to take many kids down the expressway to the city with their little sack of clothes and take them to the agency office. I came back with tears in my eyes often. Then to have to do that with your own kid. . . .

——An adoptive father

As work with the advisory committee continued on the project's major research questions, it became evident that there was concern about foster parent adoptions which were not successful. Some agency representatives had the impression that a large number of foster families who had completed adoptions eventually returned to the agency and asked for the child's removal. Since the children had spent many years in these homes, and the permanence of the placement had seemed assured by adoption, these requests caused much distress.

In Chapter 1, Laura was described. The case was selected for presentation because it presents many features typical of the girls in this group. The situation of the boys is similar, though the behavior problems differ. Take, for example, the case of Chris.

> Chris was two years old when he was placed, and 14 when he left his adoptive home. The parents were given little information about his background, although they quickly noticed that he was slow developmentally. Throughout his placement they compared him unfavorably to his adopted sister. Initially, however, he seemed to be a happy youngster and made many behavioral changes.
>
> When Chris was eight, the agency approached his foster parents about adopting. They were surprised and hesitant. The foster mother reported, "The worker said that if we did not adopt him, they would be taking him away. She

never considered our feelings. It was forced on us. We felt too old." The
family proceeded to adopt as they did not want to be separated from Chris.

At age ten, Chris became unruly. He was disobedient, truanted from school,
and became involved with gangs. He evidenced confusion about this status,
once saying, "Mama, I love you and Daddy, but why did my mother give me
away? Why did you have to take me? And if I ever catch my daddy, you
know what I'm going to do to him." Family relationships quickly worsened.
The final straw occurred on the day that Chris let gang members into the
home, while the parents were away, and they robbed the house. The family
asked for his replacement. Extensive counseling was helpful, but Chris'
behavior did not improve sufficiently. He was placed in a group home. Now
he telephones daily and comes home for holidays and birthdays. The mother
feels that "Chris will always be close to us."

The data from this project suggested that foster parents adopted because
they were attached to specific children who had been in their home for a long
time and because they wished to make a permanent commitment to them.
The children who were adopted were generally affectionate and responsive to
the care of the family, and the families appeared to be understanding and nurturing. Additionally, families who adopted tended to be self-confident, and
many appeared to want to be independent of the agency. Under these conditions, it seemed that the adoption would continue to be a mutually rewarding
experience for both the parents and the child.

The question of why some adoptions contracted under these conditions
would fail is intriguing. The literature states that adoptive placements of older
children fail when the family is not able to adapt to the child, either because
they are not prepared for the child's disturbance or because they are not
prepared for changes in family patterns. Further, it is suggested that these
adoptions fail because the match of child and family was wrong and attachment did not take place. Another reason advanced is that agency services may
not have continued long enough, or may not have been intensive enough, to
support the family in its adjustment.[1] None of these reasons seems to explain
adoption failure when a family adopts a child who has been in its' care for a
fairly long period of time.

In discussing foster parent adoption breakdown, the advisory board
focused their speculations on the services provided by the agency at the point
of transition from foster home to adoptive home. They thought that the
children might not have received adequate help in coping with the reality and
finality of the loss of their biological parents or to overcome the trauma of
other separations. They speculated that the parents might not have received

adequate assistance in assessing the depth of their commitment to their children or their readiness to assume total responsibility for them. It appeared to them that current practices in the field assumed that the transition from foster to adoptive status was natural and easy, and that agencies made little investment in helping families with this change.

More specifically, they thought that the actual breakdown of the adoption might be attributed to a failure to assess parental commitment (particularly that of the father) or parental adequacy; to situational factors which cause stress; to failure to assess the child's ability to sustain family relationships; and to failure to help the children understand their life situation. Further, it was suggested that unseen or unresolved problems might become acute when the child entered adolescence.

All of these speculations, and the apparent availability of a fairly large sample of foster parent adoptions which failed, led the researchers to apply for and obtain a supplementary grant to study this problem. It seemed that the factors which were associated with the adoption in the main study might be related to the experiences of families who could not sustain an adoption. It appeared that a comparison of the three groups might well illuminate the crucial factors.

Before proceeding to describe the research in this area, a note on terminology must be interjected. Various words, with varying connotations, are used to describe the termination of placements. "Disruption" implies that the child's progress toward a permanent home has been interrupted, but planning is continuing. "Breakdown" connotes more of an ending, and focuses more on the particular placement. "Failure" is a harsh word, and means that there has been a lack of success both in the particular placement and in the planning. Failure is not a popular word. However, given the damage to both the children and the families which seems to occur when a long-term foster/adoptive placement ends prematurely, it seems the most apt word to use in describing this sample.

The Sample and the Incidence of Failure

The first thing learned in studying foster parent adoption failures was that they did not appear to occur as often as many of the agency representatives thought. Each failure apparently has an intense impact on the agency, is extensively discussed and worked over, and consumes a high proportion of available staff energy and time during the period of breakdown.

Because of this it seems that failure is perceived to occur in a larger number of cases than it actually does.

The sample of failed adoptions was drawn totally from the large public agency cooperating with the study—The Illinois Department of Children and Family Services. Only this agency served a large enough number of families to provide a sizable sample, and most adoption failures were returned to them for planning.

The process of drawing this sample was extraordinarily laborious, for there were no central records through which these families could be identified. Additionally, the continuum of experiences as a family moved from foster care to adoption tended to make it difficult to identify points of transition. Therefore, agency administrators and supervisors were asked to list every family they could think of who had:

1. cared for a foster child for at least twelve months;

2. decided to adopt the child, and either finalized the adoption or taken a specific step (filing an adoption petition or completing a subsidy application) indicating intent to adopt; and

3. after at least another six months and within the last three years, asked to have the child replaced and the adoption legally set aside, and persisted in the request, so that the adoption was terminated.

From this source a list of thirty-eight families was developed.

Subsequently, the research associate checked a card file giving basic data on the families and discovered that thirteen families were not eligible for the sample, mainly because the child had not been in the home twelve months as a foster child prior to the adoption. After reading records it was discovered that another six families were not eligible for the sample because the child had originally been placed for adoption and had only technically been a foster child for a short time; these were really new adoptive placements that had disrupted. After interviews with the worker or families, four more cases were eliminated for the above reasons, and three were transferred to our "decision not to adopt" sample because an early interest in adoption had been followed by a long period of hesitation, a declining interest in adoption, and an apparent decision to remain foster parents. In these cases no formal steps had been taken toward adoption. There thus remained twelve families who had fostered a child for at least a year, decided to adopt, and then, at least 6 months later, had the adoption fail.

Twelve families were not enough to enter into the statistical analysis of the main study, and the expected high rate of refusal to participate in the study would have been devastating to any analysis. Fortunately the expectations of a high refusal rate were erroneous. An initial letter explaining the study, sent from the University, elicited only one refusal. This letter was followed by a telephone call to explain the study further, and at this point one additional family decided not to participate. Thus ten families agreed to be interviewed, and they constituted the sample of foster parent adoption failures.

The pursuit of information from the agency records and the workers was, surprisingly, less productive. Information about the child and family were in three scattered records. Summary material about the adoption failure was read for almost all children, and for some, supplemental case records were available.

Workers were also difficult to locate. After much persistence, workers who were, in one way or another, familiar with nine of the twelve cases were located and interviewed.

Unfortunately, the nine families about whom we obtained information from the worker and the ten families interviewed did not totally correspond. Information from the record, worker, and family was available on seven cases; information from the record and family was available on two cases; information from record and worker was available in one case; information from only the family was available in one case; and only record information was available on the final case.

From this description it becomes clear that the agency data about the families was not consistent. Record data came from two sources, each of which was not available for all cases. Interview data did not, in all cases, come from the family worker, and when it did these workers did not always know the family at the same point in time. Because of this, and the fact that analysis of the data in the main study had shown that family reports tended to provide the most meaningful data, the primary data reported in this chapter will be from the ten family interviews which were obtained. Only occasional reference to the agency data will be made.

The Families Interviewed

The families in this sample looked like neither the adoptive nor the foster families in the main sample. In demographic characteristics they were rather like the foster families, but in family composition and history as foster parents they resembled the adopting parents.

There were, in this sample, seven black families and three white families. The average age of the mothers was about fifty, with a range from thirty-four to sixty-two. The average age of fathers was fifty-three, with a range from thirty-five to seventy-one. On the average the mothers were thirty-six years older than the child in the sample. There was one single mother in the sample.

The families were unusual in today's world in that a high proportion of the mothers did not work outside the home; seven categorized themselves as "housewives." The three who worked, two as practical nurses and one as a domestic, had small families of older children. Five fathers worked at unskilled jobs, two owned small businesses, and two were retired. Incomes seemed relatively modest; eight families had gross income between $500 and $1,000 per month. The families in which the wife was working did not have higher incomes.

In six of these families at least one of the parents had a chronic health problem—ulcers, high blood pressure, heart disease, diabetes. This is a much higher proportion than in either of our other samples.

These families had experience with children and were not foster families accustomed to the coming and going of children. The "typical" family had two children in the home in addition to the child in the sample. The range was from one child to five other children. Additionally, five families had grown children who were now out of the home. Eight families contained other adopted children. Only one family currently had foster children, and their adoption was underway. Seven families had fostered children for seven or more years; one had been fostering for twenty-three years. None, however, had cared for children for short periods of time; only four had experienced foster children leaving their homes. The remainder had adopted or were adopting all of the children that they had cared for. These seemed to be families which took children and kept them.

The Children's Histories

Only one of the ten children in this sample was placed in this foster/adoptive home as an infant. The average age at placement for the rest was almost seven, with a range of from two to eleven years. Thus, most of the children arrived in these homes with many experiences, most of them difficult, behind them. Only the child placed as an infant was free of behavior problems at placement. On this variable these children were similar to the group of non-adopted children.

All of the children had some deprivation in their backgrounds. The three children with the "best" histories received care in a benign home or institution before this placement, though not much was known about the actual quality of care they received in their early years. Four children had experienced severe abuse or neglect, but had lived in only one foster home (and perhaps an emergency placement) before this home. Three children had lived in five or six different homes before placement in this home at the age of nine, ten, or eleven. The nine year old had been seriously abused in a previous placement.

Six of these children were placed in this home at the same time as siblings, a higher proportion than in the total sample. Most were placed with one brother or sister, but one was placed at the same time as four other siblings. And, in one case, two years after the placement of two siblings, two more siblings were placed in the foster home. In all of these homes, the siblings had also been adopted and have remained in the home.

Most of the children exhibited problems at the time of placement in this home. However, not all were seen as "difficult" children by their parents. Six parents described the children as being responsive to family members in the early years of their placement. Again, the parents descriptions are vivid:

— He was withdrawn and frightened—he needed to be taught to cuddle. He responded very well to us and seemed to become a happy little boy. (age 2)

— She stole, but she was very responsive to me (the mother). She loved the park. I took her there often, and she played and played. (age 11)

Four parents described more complex and difficult behavior:

— He was quiet and withdrawn, but easy to live with at first. Within a few months it was clear that he was introverted, very complex, rarely talked, lied, and was very cunning. (age 4)

— He had tics, wet his bed and pants. He pretended to be deaf and blind. He could not understand family rules. (age 10)

— He was destructive and hard to handle. (age 7)

— He soiled and smeared feces. He was destructive. He urinated on things around the house. (age 7)

The troubled histories of these children did not seem to be directly reflected in their behavior at placement. While two of the four children who exhibited the most difficult behavior at placement were known to have been severely abused, this was not reported for other children with poor early experiences.

In general, the children were in good health and free of physical handicaps at the time they entered this home.

Becoming A Family

The degree to which a child meets the expectations and preferences of a family, the quality of the initial response of the family and the child to each other, the manner in which issues of the biological family are handled, and the child's responsiveness to the parents, are some of the elements that may be associated with the attachment of a child and a family to each other. In these families, the commitment established was not sufficient to hold the family together. It is interesting to speculate about what might have gone wrong in this process.

Seven families stated that they had definite preferences and expectations about the children they wanted. This was a higher proportion than in our larger samples. They wanted children younger than those placed with them who were "warm," "outgoing," and "smart". Only two families thought their preferences had been met.

Nevertheless, as in both of the other samples, the initial reaction of most parents to the children was enthusiastic: "I was glad to see him. I grabbed him and hugged him—it was like I had known him for a long time," said one mother. "I fell in love with her. She was frightened, and protective of her little sister," said another. These were typical of the reactions of seven sets of parents. Two others were "sorry" and "thought they could help." Only one family was uncertain from the start.

Two families knew the biological parents quite well. The other eight had never met them. Among those eight, six felt thay had inadequate information, particularly about the child's emotional difficulties. The two other families did not express a need for more information, but said that most of what they knew had been related to them by the child and was negative. All eight of these parents seemed to have been in a poor position to help their children with questions about their past.

These children seemed to manifest problems related to the loss of their biological parents. The most exotic expression of these problems occurred in a little boy who had visions of his mother on a white horse. Another little boy cried when he learned he would not see his mother in court when he was adopted. For another child, adoption was the bitter confirmation that his mother would not keep her promise to come and get him, and he too cried. One little girl continues to be angry about being "given away." From this information one gets the impression that little was done to help these children with their feelings. The parents tended to feel that love and care should be enough; and the social workers seemed to have played a small role in these families prior to adoption, when these feelings might have been resolved.

At the time of the adoption, seven of these children were showing some responsiveness to the care of their families. Typical were these descriptions by adoptive parents:

— He began to accept the family structure. He became more self-reliant.

— She was stealing. Yet she was responsive and part of the family.

In three instances the child's behavior was deteriorating at this point. Two of these children were placed with siblings who were making better adjustments. In all three cases the families felt that the agency had pushed them into making a decision.

Thus, of the elements of attachment which were reported in the retrospective interviews with these families, only in their initial reactions to the child and the child's responsiveness to their care did they resemble the larger sample of adopting families. Preferences were generally not met, little information was known about the children, and there was little opportunity to resolve the issues concerning the child's biological heritage.

The Adoption Decision

There is no doubt about the commitment of these parents to adoption; all but one adoption was finalized and that adoption was in process in the court. The average time between the placement and the adoption was about four years, with a range of from one to twelve years. The average age of the children at adoption was ten; only one child was under six years old.

In their motivation for adoption, these families did resemble the sample of adopting foster parents. Seven of them had hoped to adopt before a child was placed. Eight first thought of adopting this child "from the start" or during the first year the child was in the home.

However, half of these parents expressed hesitations about adoption, mostly because of their children's behavior. One family was, at first, only interested in adopting the baby of a group of brothers and sisters. The agency insisted on a decision about adoption in seven of these cases. In this respect these families resembled the larger sample of families who continued to foster, except that, due perhaps to a combination of early intentions and agency pressure, they decided to adopt.

It was difficult to get good information about the social worker's role during the transition from foster care to adoption. Parents felt they had been pressured to adopt and had gotten little information from their workers. Three families seemed to have liked their adoption workers; five expressed anger or hostility toward them. (Two gave no information.) Of course, one must note that these memories may be colored by the abortive adoption experience.

Only four workers who seemed to know what happened during the transition from foster care to adoption were interviewed. From these interviews it appears that minimal discussion of this transition occurred. Discussions during this time seemed to focus on legal procedures and subsidies. Families did get help with the complex problems these children presented from outside sources, but not from the adoption workers.

The Children at the Time of the Placement Failure

The children had in common the age at which they left the adoptive home and the severe nature of their behavior problems. Otherwise there was considerable variability in their characteristics, though certain patterns were evident.

Six of the children were between thirteen and fourteen years old at the time they left their adoptive homes; two were fifteen, one twelve, and one ten years old. Thus, the range in ages was very small. There were five girls and five boys. All were the same race as their adoptive parents.

Eight of the children were exhibiting severe behavior problems at the time of the adoption failure. The girls were angry, hostile, involved in sexual activity, truanting from school or running away from home. The boys were destructive, negative, and/or stealing. The older boys in this sample were in trouble with the police. The two youngsters whose behavior was under better control, one boy and one girl, had been sexually involved with another child in the home. In both cases this had resulted in pregnancies, and continuation of the placement was unthinkable for both sets of parents.

The adoptive parents' description gives the "flavor" of these behavior problems better than any summary:

— She would pull up her clothes in the yard—we couldn't stop her open sexual behavior. She did no work at school. She was so angry and attacking; she turned on us so bad. We were afraid she would hurt us or one of the younger children.

— He seemed a normal little boy. Then, at ten, his anger began to come out. He was unruly, disobedient, and excluded from school because of disruptive behavior. He got involved with gangs and in trouble with the police. Finally he let gang members in to rob our home.

— She heard voices. She could not understand rules and refused to conform. She was disruptive and did no work in school. I grew frightened when she told me the Halloween pumpkin was talking to her.

— He soiled, smeared feces, and was terribly destructive. Most of his negative behavior seemed directed at me (the mother). His behavior grew constantly worse.

— There was a sudden change. She began to stay out at night and to truant from school. Her behavior became quite disturbed. Then she ran away and made a suicide attempt.

Six of these children were described as below average in intelligence; three were in special education classes in school. One parent noted that it was impossible to estimate the child's intelligence because of the extent of her disturbance (the child who heard voices). Only three children were described as average or above. Interestingly, there were discrepancies between the worker's and the parents' estimation of intelligence in only two instances in this sample. In both cases, the worker described the children as being more intelligent than the parents did. Thus, the parents' perception of the children's intelligence—and probably the actual capacity of the children—is quite unlike the larger sample of adopted children.

All of the children were in good health; none had handicaps at the time of the placement failure.

The Parents at the Time of the Placement Failure

Unfortunately the data have little information on the capacities and problems of this group of foster/adoptive parents. Our primary source of information was the parents, but ratings made at the time of the interview seem quite useless, for these judgments are confounded by an assessment of the present situation. The best data available are probably the assessments of the home made by the seven workers who knew the families:

— Both parents' health was very poor and they simply lacked the energy to cope with the child.

— The mother was very rigid and thought she could mold the girls.

— The father was very rigid and unable to accept normal adolescent acting-out. The mother was more understanding, but always deferred to him.

— The mother has no parenting skills and never should have been permitted to foster.

— They did a good job until this episode (pregnancy) but could not accept this and saw their only solution as getting rid of the child.

— the family invested a lot of energy in trying to salvage the adoption, but he was more than they could handle. They had no children or parenting experience prior to taking these four sibs.

— They were emotionally exhausted, guilt-ridden, angry and frustrated. They did not readily make changes. They needed a different set of parenting skills than they had.

And from the subsidy records in two instances in which a worker who knew the family could not be interviewed, came these evaluations:

— There was a poor match. A severely emotionally disturbed child was placed in a rigid and inflexible family. He had to be moved from this hostile environment to a more nurturing and accepting one.

— The parents had serious marital problems and the child became a scapegoat. Unfavorable comparisons with his younger brother were often made. The mother's need to control only made the child rebel more.

For one case, there was no record information and no worker was located.

Thus, one gets a sense of a variety of families and a variety of relatonships with the social worker. One "thread" which seemed to emerge strongly is rigidity. Parents could not accept a child with acting-out behavior; and a parent's need to control family members may have precipitated acting out. The other thread which emerged was a statement of a deficiency in "parenting skills"—one wishes there was better definition of this term.

The Disruption of the Adoption

For the nine cases in which the adoption was completed, the average length of time between the completion of the adoption and the request for the child's removal was more than three years. In one instance the child remained in the adoptive home for two years after his removal was requested; in all other instances the children left within a few months.

In all instances, the child's disruptive behavior was the reason that the families felt they could no longer care for the children. Additionally, all of the families were able to identify a single incident which they saw as the "last straw." These incidents varied greatly, but all were perceived as manifestations of problems which the families expected to continue:

- Two children were discovered to have been sexually involved with adopted siblings.

- Two teen-age daughters accused their adoptive fathers of sexual abuse.

- One teen-ager ran away and made a suicide attempt.

- One child physically attacked her godmother.

- One teen-ager let gang members in to rob his home.

- One child publicly soiled himself at a family funeral.

- One father found he was beating the child.

Disparate as these incidents are, their common theme is an attack on the integrity of the family. When the child's behavior threatened family cohesion or precipitated inappropriate behavior in family members, the adoption began to disrupt.

The behavior problems exhibited by these children were described earlier in the chapter and were, indeed, severe. It is notable that whatever the pattern of change between placement and adoption, the problems had grown worse between adoption and disruption. The behavior at this time was severely disruptive, the children were attacking the family structure, and the parents could see no prospect of improvement.

Prior to deciding to end the placement, six families had extensive help from mental health specialists. In five families, parents and child were seen in weekly or bi-weekly sessions for a year or more; in the sixth family the parent had extensive counseling. Three other families had between three and eight counseling sessions between the time they requested the child's removal and the removal itself. One set of parents refused counseling, though the child was seen. And, of course, all families had contacts with the agency worker after they asked for the child's replacement.

Families were fairly evenly divided in their reponse to their agency worker at this time. Four families found them helpful. "They did what they could," said one; "They tried to maintain her home for her." Three families were ambivalent—"The worker was very businesslike," said one. Three families were openly hostile:

— They only listened to the child.

— They would not move to place the child until I told my wife to tell the worker we would kill him if he stayed.

— they tried to force me to keep her.

Where there was information, it seemed that the workers' opinions mirrored those of the family. "The mother rejected the child, was unreasonable, a nut who took children for the money" said one worker. "I liked them; they did their best and held on for a long time," said another.

The parents were asked if they could describe how the experience of the child's leaving "felt." Almost universally, they expressed the pain and grief:

— It felt terrible. It felt like I was sick inside. The other children looked like they were sick. They said "don't take me; we haven't done anything, don't take us."

— It hurt me. I had done the best I could do. It may not have been much.

— It was stressful. I felt isolated . . . helpless. I was angry at the kids, at myself for not getting through to them, at everyone else because no one understood what we went through. No one wanted to hear what we had to say.

— It was draining; unbearable. I don't think the other kids will ever forget it. They were upset. The whole house was upset.

Parents were asked if they thought anything could have been done to prevent the failure of the placement. Their replies were mixed, and reflect a sort of hopelessness. Two ideas which did emerge were better information about the child's early experiences, and easy availability of respite care services. These answers, of course, must be seen against the background of the extensive counseling services which many of these families had received.

If the impact on the parents was so great, one is even more concerned about the impact on the child. But here the data were poor. Parents, due to their own emotions, were not particularly good informants. And only five workers who had known the child well at the time of the adoption failure were interviewed. Their comments are revealing, but concern only a small number of the children.

> — She is hostile, impossible to read. She tunes out adults and will not open up.

> — I don't know how she feels. Her behavior was totally out of control in the adoptive home, and there are no problems in the new foster home. But she wears a hard facade.

> — The child had a history of rejections, and he recreates rejections with his provocative behavior. This was not a good family for him—he was probably relieved when the placement ended.*

> — The breakdown was devastating—an attachment had been made to the family. He has never been able to separate.

> — He feels lots of guilt and remorse—he lost the home he wanted.

It would have been most difficult, but one does wish that an attempt had been made to gather data directly from these children.

The Children and Their Families Later

Six children were moved to foster homes from these adoptive homes. It was obviously hard for these adoptive parents to see their children go into other families, but some sense of vindication was present as they reported "she ran away from that home too" or "they requested his removal because of his behavior." Three parents noted that the agency should have recognized that the child needed the specialized help of residential treatment.

Four children went directly to group homes. One of these has since moved on to a specialized residential setting where intensive treatment is available. Two of the others apparently will grow up in the group homes. A fifth child, originally moved to a foster home, was in an institution at the time of the interview.

Plans for adoption have been made by the agency for only two of these

---

*This child's subsequent activity is fascinating. After another failed adoptive placement, he went into group care. He then found his biological mother, had face-to-face contact with her, and was devastated when she again rejected him. He then proceeded to find and develop another adoptive home for himself. One wonders if he may not now be ready to make a family commitment.

children. However, one cannot be optimistic about them. The youngest child in the sample, aged ten when he left the home, was placed for adoption after a short stay in a group home. This placement failed. After another stay in the group home he is about to move to another adoptive home. For the second child, age thirteen, preparations were made to introduce him to an adoptive family. This was so upsetting that he made a suicide attempt and the planning was stopped.

An attempt was made to find out about the parents' relationship with the children in the year or two since they had left the home. It was discovered that, though the child was absent and the adoption legally terminated, eight of the ten families maintained some contact. These were older children, and one feels that this adoptive home will be "family" to many of these children as they grow into adult life. They may not be able to live together, but there is some bond.

At the time of the research interview, two children were living independently and were in contact with their former adoptive families through telephoning and visiting. Three children were in foster homes, and two of them remained in close contact with the adoptive family. Of the five children in group facilities, three telephoned and visited. A fourth runs away to see his twin sister, still in the adoptive home. Thus, all contact with the adoptive home had ended for only two children. However, in all eight instances where contact continued, it seemed to be the adolescent who initiated and maintained it.

What was the prognosis for these children? Interviewers and workers consistently commented on the serious nature of the disturbances which many of these children displayed. Those in congregate care were thought to be the most disturbed, as evidenced by the following:

— I fear he will never get his problems resolved.

— He will need periodic psychiatric hospitalization.

— The placement in the group home is suitable as the child cannot handle a family placement.

Those now in foster care or independent living seemed to be functioning better:

— It sounds like she is somehow managing on her own and has an ongoing relationship with her [former adoptive] parents.

— He is in a good foster home, close enough so that he can remain in contact with his adoptive home and their community.

Workers thought most of the children had made a reasonable adjustment to their new situation. Apparently, most have had fairly extensive counseling around the transition. However, given the extensive disruption in the lives of most of these children, one cannot be too optimistic.

Conclusions

This sub-study, while exploratory, and in some ways unsatisfactory, does provide some interesting ideas. One wishes it had been possible to contact a larger sample of families and more workers who had known the families well. Almost all of the data were from the perspective of the parents. Nevertheless, the data open some interesting avenues for speculation.

Situational factors and long term stress may have played a part in these failures. Income was fairly low in eight families. In five, there were chronic health problems. In six homes more than one child was placed at the same time; in one of these two additional children were later placed. In two homes marital problems during the placement were mentioned. In only one home were none of these stress factors present. While situational factors did not dominate in any of these families, they may have played a part in the adoption failure.

In many ways these parents resembled the larger sample of foster parents who decided not to adopt—age, race, income, preferences and expectations which the children placed did not meet, lack of information about the child, and hesitations about adopting when approached by the agency. However, most had no history of fostering and most wanted to adopt either before placement or very early in the placement. Somehow this combination of early commitment to adoption and agency pressure may have led them to overcome their hesitations. They decided to adopt in situations in which other foster parents had decided against it.

It is difficult to form any assessment of the capacity of these parents, for it was their data that was used in the study. All have been successful parents to other children. The interviewers were generally fairly positive in assessing these homes, though they obviously saw many problems with this child. Workers used descriptive words such as "rigid," "controlling," "rejecting," "destructive," even while emphasizing that "they tried" and "stayed with it a long time." Clearly the families did not have the capacity to deal with these children—but these were very difficult children.

Similar to the non-adopted children in the main study, the children in this sample were older at the time of placement in this home and many had experienced previous traumatic separations. They came from deprived and

disturbed backgrounds and almost all were manifesting problems at placement. For most, there was no opportunity to resolve feelings associated with
separation from their biological parents. Some had problems so severe that
their ability to form close family relationships is questionable. Others,
however, responded to their families through their primary school years. It
was only with the coming of adolescence that their behavior deteriorated.
One might speculate that problems resulting from early experiences,
unrecognized and unresolved, became apparent at that time. It is evident
that, at the time of the disruption, all of the children were displaying serious
acting-out behavior which was not improving.

One does not want to speculate too much about agency service, for the
perspective of the workers is missing from these data. However, there seems
to have been little work with families around the transition from foster care to
adoption, and no direct work with children in preparation for adoption. The
ending of the placement seems generally to have received much more attention, with all participants receiving counseling. The families' requests for easy
access to respite care should be noted. Both families and children seemed to
have been deeply upset by the separation, but the families have generally not
had continuing help from the agency.

Thus one can tentatively identify several factors which might be
associated with adoption failure. A background of somewhat stressful circumstances and minimal agency support was present. Neither children nor
parents had help with the transition between foster care and adoption. Most
dominant was the disruptive behavior of the children, which did not change in
response to parental efforts, and which eventually seemed to attack the very
structure of the family. For some reason—the age of the child at placement,
the frustration of the parents' expectations, or some other factors—a bond did
not form which could override this attack and keep the family together.

In many ways these ten families resemble the foster families who chose
not to adopt. For some reason they decided to adopt, possibly due to agency
pressure, possibly because of a temporary improvement in the children's
problems, possibly due to their own initial motivation, or possibly for some
other reason. Perhaps they should not have adopted, for their pain was more
intense than that reported by the foster families in the main study whose
children were moved. One is again led back to the services provided at the
crucial transition point between foster care and adoption.

CHAPTER 9

The Workers, Their Attitudes, and Their Ideas About Foster Parent Adoptions

Some foster parents don't adopt because of fear of the future, not feeling close to the child, not feeling a personal commitment.

Kids who "give something in return" are most likely to be adopted.

Legalizing the relationship [through adoption] is a system need, not the need of the parents. It is not their priority. If they distrust the system, they won't adopt, no matter how committed they are to the child.

All kids are adoptable, given the right match.

The reader will recall that an early stage of the research collected information from the workers about their general perceptions of the factors which differentiated foster parents who adopt from those who do not. A few of their responses are noted above. Also measured were a number of worker attitudes thought to be associated with such adoptions. This information was not only valuable in its own right, but also helped to determine the areas which would be explored with the sample of foster/adoptive parents. It is these worker attitudes and general ideas with which this chapter is concerned.

The Workers

In all, forty-three workers were interviewed as part of this study. Twenty, almost half, were employed by the public sector; the remainder by five voluntary agencies. All but two of those interviewed were female and almost two-thirds (63%) were in line positions.

This was not a group of young, untrained, inexperienced workers. They ranged in age from twenty-six to sixty-one years old; fully half were over the age of thirty-five. Only thirteen workers held only the bachelors degree, and of these, three were B.S.W.'s The remainder held advanced degrees; most in social work. They had been employed in social work for from two to thirty-three years and had an average of almost twelve years of experience. Half had been working in social work for ten years or more. They had been employed by their current agency for an average of eight years at the time of the interview.

Supervisory/administrative positions tended to be held by experienced workers in both the public and the voluntary sector. However, as is so often the case, workers in the public agency were significantly less likely to hold an MSW or other advanced degree. While more than half of the line workers had less than 10 years experience, three quarters of the supervisory/administration positions were held by persons with ten or more years experience in child welfare work (p <.05). Only one worker in the voluntary agencies did not have an MSW or equivalent degree, while twelve of the nineteen workers in the public sector for whom data were available held only a bachelors degree (p <.001).

Two-thirds of the workers were white. Of the remaining, thirteen were black and one was oriental. There were no Hispanic workers in the sample. Non-white workers were significantly more likely to be employed by the public sector. Sixty-five percent of the white workers were employed in the voluntary sector, while 71 percent of the non-white workers were employed by the public agency (p = .02). Thus, within the public sector, half of the workers interviewed were white, and half were not. Within the voluntary sector, five-sixths of the sample was white and only one-sixth black.

The non-white workers in the sample had not attained the same educational levels as their white counterparts. Fewer than half of the non-white workers held graduate degrees while almost 80 percent of the white workers had achieved this level of education (p <.05). Yet, despite the difference in education and some evidence that the non-white workers had less experience in the field, white workers were no more likely to hold supervisory/administrative jobs than non-white workers.

This group of workers was active and involved in social work activities outside of working hours. Over 60 percent had had formal, non-agency training within the last few years. Over half (55%) were members of at least one professional organization. One-third were actively involved with community groups outside of working hours.

Interestingly, access to formal, non-agency training was not more likely to be reported by any particular group. The workers in public agencies were as likely to have obtained such training as the workers in the voluntary sector. So, also, were line workers when compared to supervisors and administrators. Blacks and whites pursued such training in equal proportions, as did bachelors and graduate level workers.

Work Functions

Each of the workers was asked about primary job resposibilities. These results are reported in Table 9.1.

Table 9.1
Work Activities of Sample

	n	%*
Direct Work With Children	31	76
Direct Work With Foster/Adoptive Families	22	54
Direct Work With Biological Families	20	49
Supervision/Administration Within Agency	20	49
Liaison Work With other Agencies/Courts	10	24
Recruitment and Training of Foster Parents	9	22
Other	10	24

*NOTE: Percentages add to more than 100% due to multiple responses.

Analysis of these data revealed that workers in the voluntary sector were involved in a wider range of activities than their colleagues in the public sector. More than two-thirds of the voluntary sector workers reported responsibility for direct work with biological parents and foster/adoptive families as part of their work, compared to only about one-third of the public sector workers (p < .02). Further, there was some indication that voluntary sector workers were more involved in some supervisory activity—66 percent of these workers reported such involvement compared to 40 percent of the public agency workers (p < .10).

Given these differences between public and voluntary agency personnel, it is not surprising that graduate level workers were more involved in both direct work with foster/adoptive families and in supervisory activities, for graduate level workers were more likely to be employed in the voluntary sector. What is surprising is that bachelor level workers were more likely to be involved in the recruitment and training of foster parents. Half of the B.A./B.S.W. workers reported that this was a job function compared to only 10 percent of the better educated workers in the sample (Fishers $p = .01$). This difference occurred despite the fact that there was no difference in the proportion of public and voluntary sector employees who reported this activity as a job function. This finding is somewhat disquieting. As the field embraces the policy of foster parent adoptions, and as the role of the foster parent becomes more complex, should not workers who are better trained in assessment do the critical job of recruiting and training these families?

Experience With Foster Parent Adoptions

Workers were asked to estimate both the number of completed foster parent adoptions with which they had been involved and the number of foster parents with whom they had worked who chose not to adopt. The results of this query are presented in Table 9.2 and reveal that there was a wide range of experience among the workers. Of the workers whose answers to these questions could be quantified, two had no experience completing a foster parent adoption while two had completed as least fifty such adoptions. Similarly, seven of these workers had no experience with foster families who chose not to adopt while three workers had experience with at least fifty such families.

Table 9.2
Experience With Foster Parent Adoptions

	Experience			
	Completed Adoptions		Adoptions Attempted But Not Completed	
Number of Cases	*n*	*%*	*n*	*%*
Less than 3	11	30	19	46
3 - 9	10	27	10	24
10 - 24	8	22	5	12
25 or more	8	22	7	17
Total	37	100	41	100

Interestingly, a higher proportion of workers had experience with foster parents who adopted than with those who did not. Forty four percent of the workers had been involved with at least ten completed foster parent adoptions. Only 29 percent of the workers had been involved with ten or more foster parents who chose not to adopt. Whether the greater experience with successful attempts to convert foster homes to adoptive homes is a function of workers approaching foster parents who they believe will adopt, or due to the fact that the majority of foster parents want to adopt children in their care, cannot be ascertained from these data. What is clear is that workers are likely to encounter "success" in their attempts to convert foster homes to adoptive homes and that, as reported in the literature,[1] many foster parents welcome this opportunity.

Workers in the public sector were likely to have had more experience with foster parent adoptions than workers in the voluntary sector. Eighty percent of the interviewed public agency workers had completed ten or more foster parent adoptions, compared to only 18 percent of the workers in the voluntary sector (p < .001). Similarly, three-quarters of the public sector workers had been involved with three or more foster parents who, when offered, had decided not to adopt compared with only one-third of their voluntary sector counterparts (p < .02).

These findings might have been anticipated given the greater specialization of work tasks and the higher caseloads present in the public sector. As shown in Table 9.3, the data clearly indicate that workers involved with larger numbers of completed foster parent adoptions were also more likely to be involved with greater numbers of foster parents who chose not to adopt (p < .01).

Table 9.3
Involvement in Completed Foster Parent
Adoptions by Involvement in Foster
Parent Adoptions Attempted But Not Completed

	Completed Foster Parent Adoptions			
Foster Parent Adoption Attempted But Not Completed	*Less Than Ten*		*Ten or More*	
	n	*%*	*n*	*%*
Less Than Three	15	71	4	25
Three or More	6	29	12	75
Total	21	100	16	100

Working Conditions

Each worker in the study was asked a series of questions regarding the working conditions and pressures they experienced in their respective agencies. These included a description of the working conditions, caseload size, the amount of "crisis" as opposed to "planned" work, and an assessment as to whether the agency was a "good" place to work. While the majority of workers reported favorably on each of these aspects of their work, a substantial minority appeared to be under pressure.

About 40 percent of the workers reported being less than satisfied with their working conditions. Cited by these workers were problems of work pressure, difficulties and frustrations within the service delivery system and within their own bureaucracies, and demoralization of staff.

Caseloads seemed reasonable for the 58 percent of the workers with responsibility for thirty or fewer cases. An additional seven workers carried between thirty-one and fifty cases, probably stretching their capacity to stay "on top" of developments. Seven workers, over one-fifth of the sample who had caseloads, had responsibility for over fifty cases. It is therefore not surprising that just under one-fifth of the sample believed their caseload to be unmanageable or completely impossible to handle.

Almost two-thirds of the workers reported that their work was, for the most part, planned. An additional 28 percent reported that some crises occurred, but that much of their work was of a planned nature. Only six workers said that most of their work was crisis centered.

Exactly half of the workers believed their agency to be a good place to work. These workers cited a variety of reasons for this including the agencies' commitment to their staff and clients, the quality of services offered, the supervision provided, and the degree of worker autonomy and flexibility afforded by the agency. Those workers who did not feel positively about their agency most frequently cited the poor attitudes towards clients and workers displayed in the agency, the presence of political and/or bureaucratic problems which hampered their work, or the poor physical conditions under which they worked, as the reason for this judgment.

Analysis of these variables revealed what has come to be a predictable pattern within the child welfare system—differences in conditions were related to the auspices of the worker's agency. As can be seen in Table 9.4, workers in the public sector reported that they worked under more difficult circumstances (p $<.01$) and had higher caseloads (p $<.0001$). They were less favorable in their evaluation of the agency (Fishers p $= .02$) than workers in the voluntary sector.

Table 9.4
Work Circumstances by Agency Auspices

Work Circumstances		Auspices		
Working Conditions		Public		Voluntary
	n	%	n	%
Adequate to Excellent	7	39	18	78
Less Than Adequate	11	61	5	22
Total	18	100	23	100
Caseload				
Thirty or Less	2	14	16	89
More Than Thirty	12	86	2	11
Total	14	100	18	100
Evaluation of Agency				
Favorable	12	60	19	95
Mixed or Negative	8	40	1	5
Total	20	100	20	100

Future Career Plans

In order to get a sense of the workers commitment to the field, a series of questions was asked regarding future career plans. Workers were asked if they planned to stay in child welfare and with their current agency. The results were somewhat disquieting given the length of time these workers had already committed to both social work and their current agency.

Only about half of the workers (54%) responded in an unqualified manner that they planned to stay in child welfare. About one-fifth of the workers were unsure of their future plans, and fully one-quarter responded that they expected to leave the field. The response was very similar to the question about remaining at their current agency—half of the sample responded that they were either unsure or did not plan to remain with their agency.

Interestingly, despite the higher caseloads and poorer working conditions in the public sector, these workers were no less likely to expect to remain in child welfare or with their agency than workers in the voluntary sector. Nor did workers with only bachelor degrees appear any less committed to child welfare or their agency than those with professional education. The discriminating variables appeared to be the position of the worker within the agency, the worker's age, and the length of time the worker had been employed in social work. Line workers, less experienced workers, and younger workers were significantly more likely to be contemplating a change of field and of agency.

The Workers' Attitudes

As part of the data collection with the workers, a number of attitudes thought to be related to foster parent adoptions were measured. The aim of collecting this data was to see if there were relationships between worker characteristics and their attitude scores. If, in fact, attitudes are predispositions to action, identifying such relationships might provide the field with strategies for selecting personnel favorably disposed to foster parent adoptions and thus to permanent plans for children who cannot return to their bioligical homes.

Index Construction

In all, seven attitude areas were eventually chosen for study. For each area, Likert-type items, designed either for this study or used in previous research,[2] were used to measure the attitudes. Thus the workers were presented with fifty items to which they were asked to respond along a continuum from "strongly agree" to "strongly disagree." The items were ordered by random assignment, and both positive and negative items were initially used within each attitude area in order to avoid response bias in the instrument. On positive items the response of "strongly agree" was given a score of one and "strongly disagree" was scored as four. These scores were reversed on negative items.

The workers' responses to the items in each of the seven targeted areas were then subjected to analysis for internal reliability.[3] Items which were not reliable were discarded from the indices. The final indices contained between two and seven items, and a total of twenty seven items were used to measure the seven areas of concern. The individual's score on a given index was determined by adding the scores on the individual items and dividing this total by the total number of items in the index. Thus, the possible scores on any index ranged from a low of one to a high of four.

The Specific Attitudes

Termination of Parental Rights. The dimensions of this index ranged from feeling that the child's right to a permanent home should be a paramount consideration for child welfare workers (low score) to feeling that the biological parent-child tie should be disrupted only in extreme circumstances (high score). Three items were used to construct this index:

1a. Too many children suffer because agencies and courts wait too long to terminate parental rights.

1b. The child's rights to a permanent home should take precedence over the parents' right to the guardianship of a child.

1c. Rarely should society be allowed to terminate the right of a mother to the guardianship of her child. *

The item criterion correlations for these items ranged from .39 to .50 and the index attained an Alpha of .63, showing rather good internal consistency for an index of only three items. The mean score for the workers on this scale was 1.50 and the standard deviation for the index was .45, indicating that the workers, as a group, were strong in their belief that permanency for children should take precedence over biological parents' rights.

Of all of the variables measured pertaining to workers in this study, only one differentiated workers with higher scores on the scale from workers with lower scores. Workers who had direct responsibility for work with biological parents had significantly higher scores on this scale than workers who did not ($t = 1.83$, $df = 33$, $p < .08$). Thus, agency personnel involved with biological parents were less extreme in their views regarding terminating parental rights for the sake of achieving permanence for children. However, the mean score on this index for this group was still quite low (1.83), indicating a strong commitment to permanency for children. Their work with biological parents appears to only temper this commitment, and is thus associated with somewhat greater caution in moving toward abridging parental rights. This seems reasonable, as such workers are more likely to be aware of the strengths of biological families.

Subsidized Adoption. This index was designed to measure the range of feelings about adoption subsidy, from believing that subsidy should not be

---

*Throughout this chapter items designated with an asterisk are items in which scoring was reversed.

provided to adoptive parents (high score) to believing that subsidy is an integral part of adoption (low score). Due to the results of the analysis for internal reliability, the three items eventually used in this index all reflect one end of this continuum—the belief that adoption subsidy should be used cautiously, if at all. These items were:

> 2a. If parents need subsidy to adopt a child they probably should not take on the burden.*
>
> 2b. Subsidies should be used only when the child has a known medical problem at the time of adoption.*
>
> 2c. Parents should never be given money to help raise a child that they love and wish to adopt.*

The item-criteria correlations for these items narrowly ranged between .48 and .50. The Alpha for this index was .68, slightly above that for the previous index which also contained three items. The mean score and standard deviation for this index was remarkably similar to the previous index ($\bar{X} = 1.50$, s.d. $= .45$) indicating that the workers, as a group, were strongly in favor of the wide use of subsidy.

Although the mean scores indicated that both black and white workers were committed to the use of subsidy, white workers were more extreme in this commitment ($t = 2.05$, df $= 35$, p $< .05$). So, also, were workers who were directly involved with foster/adoptive families ($t = 2.16$, df $= 33$, p $< .05$). While the latter finding might have been expected, given these workers' direct knowledge of the needs of foster-adoptive families, the former could not have been. Perhaps black workers are more sensitive to the "welfare" connotations of subsidy and are therefore more restrained in the advocacy of its use.

Effects of Foster Care. This index was designed to determine the degree of harm that workers believed children experience if they grow up in foster care. Again, based on the internal reliability analysis, three items were used, and all three reflected the attitude that growing up in foster care was often a damaging experience. These three items were:

> 3a. Foster care is often a very damaging experience for the child since long range emotional needs are often not met through this system.

3b. Children who grow up in foster care are less able to form meaningful relationships than children who are raised in permanent homes.

3c. Only in exceptional cases should children remain in foster care until their majority.

The item criteria correlations for this scale were quite high, ranging from .54 to .60 and the index's internal reliability was quite strong for a three item index (Alpha = .75). The mean and standard deviation for this scale were 2.03 and .67 respectively, indicating that the workers as a group, while agreeing that foster care was damaging, did not do so strongly.

Foster care was seen as more damaging by line workers (t = 2.52, df = 35, p < .02), workers under the age of thirty-five (t = 2.14, df = 35, p < .05), workers who had responsibility for more than thirty cases (t = 1.96, df = 30, p < .06), and by workers who had direct responsibility for working with foster/adoptive parents (t = 1.85, df = 33, p < .07) and with the courts (t = 1.87, df = 33, p < .07). It was seen as less damaging by workers who had caseloads which included biological parents (t = 1.90, df = 33, p < .02). Thus, those who dealt directly with the daily problems of the foster care system, who were pressured in their work, and who were involved in cases where the children were less likely to leave the system for their biological homes, were more likely to believe that foster care was damaging. This, again, seems to make sense. Such workers are less likely to see any potential benefits and positive effects of the foster care system. Further, younger line workers are more likely to have been "schooled" in the philosophy of permanency planning, are rewarded for moving children out of the system, and may justify their difficult decisions and actions by taking a more negative view of foster care.

Adoptability of Children. The dimensions of this index ranged from believing that "all children are adoptable" and that children are not adopted due primarily to problems in the service delivery system (low score) to believing that adoption services should not be extended to some children (high score). The six items in this index had item criteria correlations ranging from .42 to .69 and included:

4a. Children are unadoptable only because social workers and agencies look at them that way.

4b. If enough creativity and effort is extended, an adoptive home can be found for just about any child who needs one.

4c. There are many children in the foster care system who are too damaged to benefit from adoption.*

4d. "No child is unadoptable" is a nice rallying cry, but not realistic for social workers to base their practice on.*

4e. Social agencies label children "hard to place" without exerting enough effort to find homes for them.

4f. Special needs children really need agencies to reach out and find homes for them with much more effort than they are currently doing.

This index showed good internal consistency (Alpha = .80) and the distribution of workers' scores indicated that they were somewhat ambivalent. The mean score was 2.37—about the mid-point of the index.

The analysis of this index clearly showed that workers in the public sector saw systems barriers as much more a hindrance to adoption than workers in the voluntary sector, who were more likely to see the children's characteristics as barriers to adoption. Not only were there significant differences when the data were analyzed on the basis of agency auspices (t = 3.92, df = 35, p < .001), but there were also significant differences based on caseload size (t = 2.61, df = 30, p < .05), educational attainment (t = 4.93, df = 34, p < .001), quality of working conditions (t = 2.75, df = 33, p < .01) and specialization within the caseload. In each of these cases, the group with the characteristic associated with public sector employment (see previous discussion) scored significantly lower on this index, tending to view most children as potentially adoptable. It appears that workers in the voluntary sector are more cautious than their counterparts in the public sector regarding the children they perceive as "adoptable." Or, perhaps these workers are simply more pessimistic about just how much can be accomplished for special needs children needing permanent homes.

Foster Parent Adoptions. This index measured the workers' attitudes about foster parent adoption along a continuum of believing that foster parents make good adoptive parents and should have preference in adopting their foster children (low score) to believing that foster parents and adoptive parents are different and that foster parents should not be encouraged to adopt (high score).

The four items in this index had item criteria correlations ranging from .28 to .48 and obtained an Alpha score of .57, demonstrating somewhat weak internal consistency for the index. The items included were:

5a. If a child is freed for adoption while in foster care his foster parents should have first preference to become his adoptive parents.

5b. Most foster parents should not be encouraged to adopt a child in their care even if the child is legally free.*

5c. There are major differences between foster parents and adoptive parents and the line between the two should not be blurred.*

5d. Foster parents make the best adoptive parents for a child in their care because they know the child so well.

The workers in this study supported the concept of foster parent adoptions, though not as strongly as one might have anticipated. The index had a mean score of 1.91 and a standard deviation of .41.

Interestingly, while workers in the voluntary sector seemed to be more cautious about who might be adoptable, their endorsement of foster parent adoptions as a way of achieving permanence was significantly stronger than that of workers in the public sector. Again, these differences appeared not only in terms of agency auspices (t = 2.88, df = 32, p <.01) but also in terms of the characteristics and job functions associated with employment in the voluntary sector. Workers who were white (t = 1.80, df = 32, p <.08), had graduate training (t = 1.71, df = 31, p <.10), had been involved in less than ten foster parent adoptions (t = 1.84, df = 29, p <.08), were involved with foster/adoptive families (t = 1.73, df = 30, p <.09), and reported good working conditions (t = 2.68, df = 30, p <.01) all scored significantly lower on the foster parent adoption index, and thus appeared more committed to the conversion of foster homes to adoptive homes.

The interpretaton of these data can only remain speculative. It may be that workers in the public sector, who were more likely to have more experience with foster parent adoptions (and, perhaps, their failure), are more acutely aware of the problems involved in the conversion of foster homes to adoptive homes and therefore more cautious in their endorsement of this practice. Perhaps workers in the voluntary sector feel more positively about their foster parents than do workers in the public sector, and are therefore stronger in their endorsement. The possible explanations for these findings are numerous.

Commitment to Child Welfare. The items in this index were designed to measure satisfaction with one's work and a commitment to it. This was the most internally consistent index used in the study. The six items had item criteria correlations ranging from .55 to .83 and the Alpha for the index was .86. The items included were:

6a. If I had to relocate outside of Chicago, I would look for work similar to my current job.

6b. I cannot think of a field of social work I would rather be in than child welfare.

6c. If a position outside of child welfare was offered me at the same salary I am currently making I would take it. *

6d. The demands and frustrations of child welfare work are outweighed by the gratification one gets from providing services to children in need.

6e. Even though my work is tiring, frustrating and sometimes upsetting I really do enjoy it.

6f. There are few times I feel satisfied with the work I am currently doing. *

As reported in the previous section, the workers, as a group, were by no means unanimous in their commitment to the field, and this was reflected in their response to this index. With a low score indicating strong commitment, the mean score for this index was 2.13 and the standard deviation was .59. However, while a number of variables discriminated committed from non-committed workers in terms of their future plans, only one variable, whether the worker expected to stay in child welfare, discriminated the groups based on the attitude data which was oriented toward satisfaction at the present time. As would be expected, workers who anticipated staying in child welfare appeared significantly more committed ($t = 3.56$, $df = 34$, $p < .001$). Youth and the limits of the current job, while they impact future planning, thus do not seem associated with current level of commitment.

Client Versus Procedure Orientation. This index was designed to measure the degree to which workers were concerned with giving service (low score) rather than with the efficient operation or bureaucratic aspects of their agencies (high score). As with previous indices, the items eventually used in the index reflect only one end of this continuum and were client oriented. Two items, with item criterion correlations of .45, were used in the final index, and its Alpha score was .62. These two items were:

7a. A caseworker should act so as to meet the needs of her clients even though a particular act is considered unacceptable to her colleagues.

7b. One cannot really blame clients for lying to get the things they need.

The distribution of scores for workers showed a mean of 2.40 and a standard deviation of .71. This indicates that workers, on the average, fell in the middle of the continuum being measured, and that there was a good deal of variability among workers' scores.

Unlike data reported elsewhere using similar items,[4] workers in the public sector were no more procedure-oriented than voluntary sector workers. Further, none of the worker characteristics measured showed significant differences on this index. The only variable found to be associated with the score on this index was caseload size. Workers with low caseloads appeared to be significantly more client-oriented than workers with heavy caseloads. Perhaps they have the luxury to be.

The Inter-relationship of the Indices

Since the concepts measured were all expected to be related to the phenomena under study, it was anticipated that the indices, while related to each other, would not be redundant. In order to test this, a correlational analysis was performed. These results are presented in Table 9.5.

Table 9.5
Correlation Matrix of Index Scores

	Subsidy	Effects of Foster Care	Adopt-ability	Foster Parent Adoptions	Commit-ment	Client vs. Procedure
Termination of Parental Rights	.33	.32	.13	−.01	.14	−.03
Subsidy		.27	.17	.14	.14	−.09
Effects of Foster Care			.14	.29	.06	−.05
Adoptability				−.21	.18	.00
Foster Parent Adoptions					.31	.19
Commitment						.22

The matrix reveals correlations between the index scores which are, on the whole, quite modest. In no case are the correlations statistically significant nor can more than 10 percent of the variance in one index be explained by the score on another index. Thus, while the concepts are somewhat related, they are clearly sampling attitudes in different domains.

The positive relationships which were found between most of the attitudes were expected. For example, one would anticipate that those workers who saw foster care as more damaging would also be more favorably disposed to termination of parental rights, to adoption subsidy, and to see children as "more" adoptable. What could not have been anticipated was the negative correlation between the adoptability index and the foster parent adoption index—those most favorably disposed toward adoption had greater hesitations about foster parent adoptions. This is probably explained by the number of foster parent adoptions the workers had completed and the sector in which the worker was employed. Workers in the public sector, who have completed more foster parent adoptions, seem to show commitment to adoption but greater hesitancy toward foster parent adoptions.

In fact, all of the differences in attitudes which appeared between the workers seem to stem from their specific work functions and their sector of employment. Workers appear most committed to the groups they serve. These attitudes, however, are tempered by the agency they work for and its philosophy, training, and commitments.

The Workers' Ideas

It will be recalled that the worker interview began by asking a series of general questions concerning foster parent adoptions. These questions gathered the workers' opinions as to why some foster parents adopt and others do not and the differences between those who adopt and those who do not; whether foster parents should be given the first opportunity to adopt and under what circumstances; whether adoption is important to children and if there are children for whom adoption should not be pursued; the important elements of attachment between foster parents and their children; whether there were problems in arranging these adoptions; and why some foster parent adoptions fail. These responses will now be presented and, when possible, comparisons will be made to the data collected regarding the specific children.

The Adoption Decision

When looking at the three broad questions used to tap the workers' general ideas as to why some foster parents adopt and others do not, a number of themes emerged which confirmed the data from the specific families. Dominant among the reasons given for foster parents deciding to adopt was the positive nature of the relationship between the parent and the child and the commitment and attachment of each to the other; parental motivation, including an initial intention to adopt, a previous adoption, and the child's fulfilling some of the emotional needs of the parents; and the parents' ability to cope with the child's special needs or behaviors. The dominant reasons given for parents choosing to continue to foster were the child's behavior (including current problems, concerns about future behavior, the child's effects on family functioning, and the fear of taking total responsibility for the child); the view that foster parenthood was a "profession" that did not entail long-term obligations to a specific child; and the parents' socio-economic circumstances (including finances, age, and health). One worker summarized by saying:

> Two aspects play against each other—the long-term needs of the child and the personality needs of the foster parents. . . . Parents who view themselves as being able to take care of the children's needs are more likely to adopt—the more confidence they have in their abilities, the more likely they are to adopt.

Thus, in their answers to these general questions, workers were able to identify five of the eight areas that the discriminant analysis showed to be important to the adoption decisions: parental motivation; socio-economic status; parent-child interaction; the child's special needs; and parental age. However, three areas which emerged in the discriminant analysis as important to an adoption decision were either not mentioned or assumed to have an opposite effect by the workers. Thus, their knowledge of the factors associated with foster parent adoptions was incomplete; sometimes it was wrong.

No worker mentioned the importance of the service the family received and the quality of relationship with the worker, or the families' feelings of being "different," as impacting the adoption decision. Only a very few workers saw the impact that contact with the biological parents might have on this decision, and all who did saw it as *negatively* affecting the adoption decision. The reader will note that these are the areas over which the worker has the most direct control. Such omissions may be an indicator that the workers did not see their potential impact on the adoption decision. This obviously has practice implications, which will be discussed in the final chapter.

Priority in Adoption

Only one worker felt, unequivocally, that foster parents should always be given the first opportunity to adopt a child for whom they have cared. All of the remaining thirty-seven workers felt that such decisions depended on the situation and should be made on a case-by-case basis. When asked when the foster parents should not be considered for adoptive parenthood, the workers cited a variety of circumstances. Table 9.6 displays the reasons cited by five or more workers. Almost all of these responses could have been anticipated.

Table 9.6
Circumstances When Foster Parents Should Not
Be Considered for Adoptive Parenthood

Reason	*n*	*%**
Foster Parent Age (Old)	19	51
Difficulties Apparent During Placement	14	38
Not a Suitable Home (General Statement)	14	38
Parents Are Not Interested in Adoption	12	32
Parents Did Not Provide Adequate Care During Placement	12	32
Attachment Between Family and Child Did Not Form	11	30
Parents Unable to Cope With Child's Special Needs or Problems	10	27
Foster Parents Health (Poor)	6	16

*Note: Percentages add to more than 100% due to multiple responses.

It seems to make sense not to consider adoption when the placement has not gone well, when the parents cannot provide for the needs of the child, or when attachments between the parent and the child have not formed. However, to assume that adoption may not be suitable simply because the parents are "too old" needs further examination. The content analyses of these responses revealed that workers were concerned about foster parents who were over the age of sixty. One can understand such hesitancy when the child in the home is young; it is less understandable when the child is a teenager. And, one must question an agency policy which uses such homes as long-term foster homes for children unlikely to return to their biological parents if they will not consider them for adoption.

Pursuing Adoption for Children

As might be expected from the analysis of worker attitudes, the majority of the workers believed that adoption was preferable to long-term foster care, primarily because it provided children with a sense of stability and security. However, about one-third of the workers thought that this was not always true, and that the preference for adoption over long-term foster-care depended both on the family's situation and the child's condition.

In response to another question, almost three-quarters of the interviewed workers believed that there were children for whom adoption should not be pursued even if they had not had contact with their biological parents for a long period of time. Of these twenty-eight workers, almost none mentioned a specific *class* of children for whom adoption would not be appropriate. Rather, they mentioned a combination of factors, often including age, emotional problems, ties to biological parents, and the child's interest, which they felt had to be taken into account before considering adoption. Typical of these responses were:

— If its an older child they may not want to be adopted. They may have fantasies of returning to the birth parents.

— For children who have been in care for a long time, whom the foster parents don't want to adopt, the court process is needless since plan would be to have the child in this home anyway.

— Older children may have attachments to bio-family so strong that severing the ties would harm the child.

— With older kids there may be loyalty issues to the original family—where previous, extensive contract left them with some real attachment—and adoption may represent such a conflict that they will undermine the placement. With other kids, the only real barrier to adoption is resources available for them. Worker must listen to child's desire as he gets older—especially in adolescence.

— Some older children—15, 16, 17 year olds—may not want to be adopted. These kids may have contact with sibs elsewhere in the community. Severely handicapped children may need institutional care because of no available family. However this should be the last resort.

Thus, the workers seemed strongly committed to adoption but tempered this commitment with realistic appraisals of the children's abilities to benefit from it. Perhaps they are reflecting a growing awareness that permanency planning cannot be seen as *absolute* policy, but must be tempered based on the needs of the child and the reality of the circumstances. This idea will be further elaborated in the final chapter.

Attachment

Both the review of the literature and the data from the interviews pointed to the importance of attachment between parent and child as an important and necessary pre-condition to a successful adoption. In order to get a better understanding of this process, the workers were asked both an open-ended and a series of closed-ended questons about the elements of attachment which they thought were important to the process of family formation.

Responses to the open-ended question were, perhaps, more revealing, since they were not structured for the workers. These responses stressed the interactional nature of attachment which was posited in previous chapters. Of the elements of attachment most frequently mentioned, three stressed the mutuality of the process: warm, caring parent-child interactions; the ability of the parties to fulfill each other's needs; and the day to day sharing of experiences. Of the remaining elements, the parents nurturing response to the child and the child's ability to respond positively to the parents were most often mentioned. Also mentioned with some frequency were parental acceptance of their children's behavior, and parental willingness to invest in their children and to fight for them.

Interestingly, the workers tended to see attachment as a process which occurred over time and which did not need outside confirmation. The least frequently mentioned elements of attachment were *early* identification between parents and child; an *early* calling forth of a nurturing response on the part of the child; acceptance of the relationship outside of the family system; and a perceived similarity between parent and child. Certainly, the presence of these elements cannot hurt the attachment process, but they may not be necessary to it.

Problems in Arranging Adoptions

Most of the workers reported that their agencies provided substantial help in planning for permanent homes for children. Fully four-fifths stated that their agency provided special training sessions concerned with permanency planning and, for most of these, this training was either frequent (at least every other month) or ongoing. Almost three-quarters of the workers had special manuals or handbooks concerning permanency planning available to them which, for the most part, they found useful and easy to use. All but one worker had access to legal assistance in preparing cases for court, etc.; 85 percent of these found this assistance readily available and easy to use. Finally, most (84%) of the workers had access to consultants and other "experts" who were, for the most part, easily accessible and helpful.

Only four of the workers in this sample had sole responsibility for making permanency decisions for the children on their caseloads. Most shared this responsibility with supervisors, and over one-fourth were members of teams which met periodically to discuss planning for cases. Further, over 40 percent of the workers discussed their decisions with others in the agency, including review boards.

Thus, from these data, one gets the sense that the internal functioning of the cooperating agencies supported the goal of finding permanent homes for children. Training, legal assistance, consultation and shared responsibility were present for most of the workers and were readily accessible. However, permanent plans involving adoption can never be achieved by an agency alone. Courts are always involved and often state subsidy offices must approve a family. In these areas, many of the workers appeared to encounter difficulty.

Thirty-two of the workers had experience in arranging subsidies and 40 percent of these had either encountered difficulties (n = 10) or anticipated problems in the future (n = 3). Most of the problems cited were not problems with approval of a subsidy request or delays in such approvals. Rather, the problems most cited were "bureaucratic" problems; workers felt that the forms were either overwhelming or confusing and the documentation required was, at times, inconvenient, difficult to obtain, and excessive. While one can understand the need for accountability in spending government funds for subsidy, especially given the length of some of these financial commitments, this process, at least from the workers' point of view, appears to need streamlining. Perhaps it is because workers see the process of obtaining subsidy as cumbersome and demanding that they do not discuss it with some families (see Chapter 6). If this is the case, these bureaucratic problems may diminish a child's chance of being adopted.

While arranging subsidies was burdensome for some workers, difficulties with the courts were evident for almost all. Only three workers in the sample reported that their work with the court was problem-free. Almost all of the rest reported multiple problems in their work with this system. The following four statements by workers capture the essence of the problems mentioned.

— Frequent changes in states attorney's office. Inability to contact the states attorney. Details of case not remembered. Failure to send notices to natural parents. Judges don't know cases. Kids are returned to the natural parents in error.

— Adoption screening is difficult because of confusion of responsibility between social work and legal rules. Too much useless time in court with too many continuances without foreknowledge. Court process is confusing and inconsistent around termination. States attorneys need better preparation. Social workers need better understanding of legal rules and realities. Social worker needs access to legal files.

— Backlog of cases, hard to get into court, at least 1 year for termination. Many continuances, too many court dates. Clerical errors in publications, summons [not delivered, misfiled]. Changing states' attorneys with different ideas. Long waits in court, then often ending in errors. Adoption screening—"picky" about details and not letting case go to court. Massive paper work that is often not read. Changing faces produces lack of consistency. Legal differences of opinion among lawyers results in lack of clarity in what to do.

— Problems with the court range from: natural parents show in court and the judge will not default them; servicing and publications not done on the natural parents; large court caseloads; states' attorney has problems individualizing cases. Too easy for kids to get into child welfare system, and too difficult to get them out through permanent planning.

When the responses of the workers who reported difficulties were content analyzed, a number of themes emerged. These are detailed in Table 9.7.

Table 9.7
Problems in Working With Courts

Problem	n	%*
Delays/Continuances/Workings of Court	21	66
Problems With Court Personnel (turnover, unknowledgeable, etc)	17	53
Time Consuming	16	50
Bias in Favor of Biological Parent	12	38
Problems in Publishing for Biological Parents	8	25
Problems in Adoption Screening	8	25

*Note: Percentages add to more than 100% due to multiple responses.

Clearly, workers were most disturbed about bureaucratic problems in working with the court including delays, staff turnover, and court errors. Some questioned the philosophy of the court and believed that their bias toward protecting the biological parents' rights hindered completing adoptions. While clearly these rights must be protected, one does understand the workers' frustration, especially when the child has been in care for an extended period of time.

Given these results, it is not surprising that in response to a general question regarding impediments to adoption, the workers most frequently cited problems with the courts; lack of interagency coordination; and a systematic bias toward biological parents' rights. All three of these would obviously impede adoption in general as well as foster parent adoptions. Further, the perception that these impediments exist may deter workers from attempting to free children for adoption, especially when an adoptive home is not readily available. This may explain the larger-than-anticipated number of non-adopted children who were not free for adoption in the sample.

Adoption Failure

The workers general ideas concerning foster-parent adoption failure closely parallel the data presented in Chapter 8. The workers cited the child's behavior (especially during adolescence) as the primary reason for such failures. Often, they tied these behavior problems to unresolved attachments to biological parents. They did not, however, neglect the possibility that the foster parent's behavior might contribute to the child's acting out. Almost one third of the workers mentioned that adoptions fail due to "unrealistic expectations" on the part of the parents; parents expected the child to behave in proscribed ways and the child was not ready or capable of meeting these expectations. Perhaps this is the rigidity mentioned in the case records.

Also mentioned as a reason for foster parent adoption failure by a substantial minority of the workers was that parents and children were not appropriately prepared for the transition from foster care to adoption. This was the point so often raised by the advisory board as critical to successful adoptions, and highlights, again, that for some families this transition is not as natural as one might expect.

Some workers (about 20%) went beyond inadequate preparation of the family as a reason for adoption failure, and stated that families were sometimes "pushed" into adoptions which they did not desire. This problem seemed to be present in some of the adoption failures which were examined in this research, and have also been mentioned in the literature.[5] "Forced" adoptions appear to be a by-product of an agency's desire to achieve premanency; families with questionable attachments to children or other hesitations about adoption are forced to proceed with them in order to guarantee the integrity of their families. This problem is expressed in the following excerpts from the worker interview:

— Because of the pressure of statistics . . . [and] the desire to remain in the family, work may [be done to] "patch up" a shaky situation.

— Pushing a family who is not interested—agency conveys to foster parents that they have no choice. One-shot interviews [are done] shoving [adoption] down their throat.

Summary

For the most part, the workers interviewed were highly trained and quite experienced. They appeared generally committed to social work, although the younger, less experienced workers appeared unsure of their commitment to child welfare. Differences between workers in the public and voluntary sectors were evident on a number of variables including race, education, work pressures, and job functions. Workers in the voluntary sector appeared less specialized in their work and more likely to work with a number of groups of clients. Workers in the public sector, however, had greater experience with foster parent adoptions.

It does not appear that socio-demographic characteristics are strongly related to worker attitudes. Rather, it appears that the workers' job functions, work roles and agency affiliation shape their attitudes. For example, workers who did not have contact with bioligical parents were more likely to favor termination of parental rights, to see foster care as damaging and to see children as adoptable. Similarly, those who had contact with foster/adoptive parents were more likely to favor subsidy and to favor foster parent adoptions. This is encouraging, as one would expect workers to advocate for the groups with whom they work.

Workers confirmed much of what was reported in previous chapters regarding attachment. Clearly, they saw it as an interactional process which occurred over time. Early, immediate commitments, while helpful, were seen as less important.

Workers appeared to have good support from their agencies to implement permanent plans for children. Many of the elements thought to be important in this process[6] were present in these agencies. However, major problems appear to exist in working with other agencies and systems, particularly with the courts. These data, combined with information from previous chapters regarding subsidy and termination of parental rights, lead one to conclude that there is a strong need for greater coordination between departments and agencies if adoptions by foster parents are to be completed in an efficient manner.

Workers appeared to have a good, general understanding of the factors which encourage or discourage foster parent adoptions. However, elements which emerged as important in this decision in the discriminant analysis were omitted from the workers' reports. Interestingly, the elements omitted were those over which the workers have the most control—quality of services and continuity of relationship, feelings of being "different" on the part of the family, and family contact with the biological parents.

Throughout the interview, workers seemed to inject a note of caution about foster parent adoptions. While most appeared generally to favor such adoptions, many workers felt that *some* families should not be considered for adoptive parenthood, *some* children would not profit from adoption, and that under *some* circumstances adoption should not be considered. And, it is well to point out that those workers with the most experience with these adoptions were less favorably disposed toward them than others in the sample.

Finally, workers identified many of the elements of adoption failure which were garnered in the last chapter. They also raised the issue of "forced" adoptions—adoptions which the foster parents consummate because of agency pressure and their desire to keep a child in their home. Clearly, such practices are not in anyone's best interest and should be avoided.

CHAPTER 10

Conclusions and Implications

As one considers the implications of the findings of this research, a factor of central importance to policy and practice emerges: many of the variables associated with success in developing permanent plans for children in foster care are within the control of, or may be influenced by, the sponsoring agency and its social work staff. Thoughtful, informed, and responsible social work is linked to positive outcomes. This is an enormously heartening finding. We live in a time of pervasive pessimism about the capacities of social institutions to intervene effectively in the affairs of people. The relationships between the individual, the family, and the social environment often appear to be the product of sweeping social, economic, and psychological forces only vaguely understood and seemingly not susceptible to control.

This concentration of forces confronting the social services often seems to cast doubt on the worth of available social work intervention theory. As a result, the social agency's efforts to maintain standards for the training of personnel, or to justify adherence to other principles of professional practice, are sometimes made to appear as either a futile adherence to practice myths, or as the attempts of professional groups to jealously maintain their status.

Research-based findings, such as those available from this project, strongly suggest a much more optimistic view of the contributions of skilled and dedicated social workers. Further, and also of major importance, such findings illustrate the value of systematic research-based observation and analysis of ongoing agency experience. Data so derived are rarely available. Relatively few service programs build research scrutiny designed to provide feed-back on the results of their endeavors into their programs. Funding is available for relatively few formal projects such as this. As a result, policy and practice often emerge simply out of a felt vacuum, out of competing charismas, or out of an informal, untested and often only vaguely expressed accretion of observations summed up as "practice wisdom."

Neither these research findings, nor any others, are finally definitive.

They must be tested by further systematic trial and observation. Even then, they must be applied within the context of complex professional judgments. But findings from this and similar projects do illustrate the manner in which systematic, research-based observations of our endeavors can add to the knowledge base and contribute to such judgments.

In this project, a large number of areas were probed in an effort to distinguish foster parents who chose to adopt from those who did not, and to see if there were differences in the children who were the focus of these decisions. At an exploratory level, foster parent adoptions that failed were also studied. Four domains were investigated with both the workers and the families: parent characteristics, child characteristics, parent-child interactions, and agency services. Each of these areas proved to discriminate the groups under study; the most powerful discriminator was agency services.

Some of the findings of this research confirmed impressions from practice, but to a large extent they open new areas for exploration, investigation, and perhaps action. Thus the remainder of this concluding chapter is devoted to the examination of the possible contributions of these findings to the shaping of professional practice in foster care and adoption.

The Findings

As the matrix of interacting factors associated with the formation of an adoptive family, or a foster family, began to unravel, the findings which practice wisdom had led us to anticipate did not always emerge. Who would have predicted that the actual number of previous placements the child experienced would be a less important discriminator than the reasons these previous placements terminated; that the meeting of initial parental preferences would not be an important discriminator; that early attachment to the family would be less important than the experience between the family and the child over time; or that knowing the biological family would be associated with the family's decision to adopt? Would it have been expected that those families who fostered, adopted, and then could not continue with the child would in many ways resemble those families who decided not to adopt?

Perhaps of most interest are the findings which show the importance of agency service in discriminating those who adopt from those who continue to foster. These findings were not anticipated in the literature, or by our advisory committee. Certainly the workers did not mention them. Yet discussing adoption with a worker whom the family felt knew them well, and with whom they had a continuous relationship, emerged as a major discriminator between those who adopted and those who did not. The quality of the worker's relationship with the child was also important. Families who had information about their children and their experiences prior to coming to the home were also more likely to adopt. And, there is some indication that timing of the adoption discussion may be important. All of these factors are within the control of the agency giving service.

Even more surprising was the discriminating power displayed by the variable that measured contact between the foster parents and the biological parents during the year adoption was discussed. Practice wisdom would have predicted that such contact would inhibit the adoption process, yet the opposite was found to be true. Arrangements for contact between biological and foster parents are not wholly within the control of workers, yet they have considerable power to either impede or facilitate such contacts.

Factors in the interactive process between parents and child which emerged as important in the analysis may also be, to some degree, impacted by worker activities. The establishment of a positive interactional cycle between the parent and the child and things "getting better" as the placement progressed seemed to be important. The way in which this positive cycle is initiated and maintained cannot be ascertained from these data, but there is undoubtedly a role for the social worker in helping parents to perceive the child's growth and respond to positive changes.

There were also factors unrelated to agency service which distinguish foster families who adopt. Younger foster parents with better education and higher incomes were more likely to adopt. If there were other adopted children within the home, and if the parents thought about adoption early in the placement, they were more likely to adopt. Foster parents were also likely to adopt children who were younger when placed in their homes and whose placement was planned. Children who were perceived to be of at least average intelligence, and were not perceived to have "special needs" or behavior problems at the time adoption was discussed, were more likely to be adopted. This is an identifiable constellation of factors. While they cannot be modified by the worker, they can assist a worker in discriminating, at the time of placement, those families likely to adopt and those children likely to be adopted.

Pointers Toward Adoption

Measures of initial motivation in taking children into the home were strong discriminators between the two groups. Particularly important as an indicator of intentions to adopt the study child was a previous adoption by the family. Other indicators of this motivation were reports by the families about their initial intentions; their aggressiveness in pursuing adoption with the worker; their immediate decisions about adoption; their involvement with the people and the institutions peripheral to the adoption process; and their ability to communicate their needs and wants to the worker. Thus, adopting parents appeared not only to be more motivated but also more self-confident—they knew what they wanted and pursued it. Many seemed to be using foster care an an alternate route to adoption.

Adopting parents also tended to be younger and to have better education and income, a finding supported in a recent study in England with a much larger sample.[1] Though more white families than black adopted, the important variable apparently was the higher income of the white families; this will be discussed later in the chapter, with its implications for adoption subsidies. It is possible that race had a hidden impact on the adoption decision, for the greater comfort in communicating with workers and expressing their desires, which those families who adopted exhibited, may be a measure of greater ease in negotiating with a predominantly white agency system. Nevertheless, it is apparent that young and economically secure parents, with whom young children were placed, were more likely to adopt, whatever their race.

These findings seem to indicate that agencies which differentiate short-term and long-term foster homes, and encourage long-term foster homes to think of the possibility of adoption from the start of the placement (see Chapter 2) should continue to develop these ideas, and that other agencies should begin to consider them. While there are legal and ethical considerations in the establishment of such programs,[2] it appears that many foster parents can identify themselves as either potential adopters or temporary caretakers at intake, and that agencies should capitalize on this ability. Those who wish to foster should have children placed with them who are likely to return to their biological homes. Those who are interested in adoption should have children placed in their homes for whom this might become the goal of service. And the training, services and supports provided to each type of foster parent might be different.

This idea seems to have inherent merit, for its starts conscious planning early in the placement process. For the children, the possibility that continuity of care will occur is enhanced. For the foster parents, such planning might lead to a better understanding of their role and the expectations of the agency. The agencies would be one step closer to achieving permanent plans.

In order to establish a delivery system which incorporates "three option" or "legal risk" homes, it is necessary to know which children entering foster care are in jeopardy of not returning to their biological parents. Fortunately, beginning knowledge is available in this area. Research evidence indicates that children who enter foster care at young ages are less likely to return home than other children.[3] Children who are older when they enter foster care are more likely to be visited by biological parents, and visits are associated with return home.[4] In other words, older children appear to retain their places in the biological family to a greater extent than do younger children.

There are also the more obvious cases in which the child is unlikely to return home. These include cases in which a child has been relinquished by one parent and the identity or whereabouts of the other parent is unknown; cases in which termination has been granted by the trial court but the decision is on appeal; and children from families in which others have already been freed for adoption.[5]

Other characteristics which appear to be predictive of the child's not returning home include out-of-wedlock birth, and whether the child entered care due to abandonment, neglect or abuse, or parental unwillingness to assume care.[6] These are, apparently, the parental behaviors which predict the most difficult rehabilitative task.

This is *not* to suggest that a rigid system be established. Clearly, the data from this study indicated that some foster parents eventually adopted without such initial motivation, and that some foster parents who were initially motivated decided not to adopt. More importantly, many young children, children who were abused, neglected and abandoned, and children who were born out-of-wedlock, do return to their biological parents. Therefore, any system which divides foster parents into groups *must remain fluid*. This appears to be possible, for the data showed that foster parents who were highly motivated toward adoption seemed willing to care for many children before one was freed for adoption.

Thus, what is suggested here is a method of initially screening foster parents based on their motivation to adopt and initially screening children on the likelihood of returning home, and matching them appropriately. In this way permanence is more likely to occur, although case plans will, for some, change over time.

The Partnership of Foster Parents and Social Workers

The number of service factors found to be associated with the decision to adopt, and their power to discriminate the adopting from non-adopting families, surprised even the researchers. It is anticipated that the strength and endurance of these relationships may also surprise the field, for few workers even mentioned their own potential impact on the adoption decision.

The data seemed to suggest that families and workers need time with each other. Continuity of relationship between worker and family was a strong discriminator between the adopters and the non-adopters. This suggests that agencies should strive to reduce worker turnover, a chronic problem in child welfare, and should insure, through their organizational designs, that families are not transferred from worker to worker as their status within the agency changes.

Thought must be given to ways in which fragmentation within agencies can be diminished. One possibility is for agencies to design organizational structures which do not divide responsibilities for the various members of the foster/adoptive families among different workers. The data seemed to suggest that one worker should have primary responsibility for the family and child throughout their tenure with this agency, including placement, ongoing service delivery, and, when appropriate, termination of parental rights and the transition to adoptive status. The presence of other workers, particularly workers assigned to the family at the time of adoption discussion, was associated with the decision not to adopt. This appears to be the model currently in use in the voluntary agencies that cooperated in this study, for workers in this sector reported having more varied responsibilities and less specialized tasks. Perhaps public agencies might try such a system, on a demonstration basis, to see if it is feasible within a larger, more complex organization.

Clearly, the quality of the relationship with the worker was an important discriminator between the two groups. Adopting families perceived their relationship with their workers as more open than their non-adopting counterparts. They felt free to talk with their workers and to share their concerns, hopes and fears with them. They also felt that their workers knew them well and were concerned about them. The findings confirm the need for a "partnership" relationship between worker and family. Such a partnership means mutual respect and sharing of ideas and information.

Respect is operationalized through listening to and understanding the ideas of one's partner. Little has been written about the foster parent's respect for the social worker; presumably the authority in decision making which workers possess insures that the foster parent will at least pay attention to what they say. But the data from this study showed that most foster parents were able to make their motivations, desires, preferences and needs known; that their perceptions were better predictors of adoption than worker perceptions; and that openness in communication and discussion was related to desirable outcomes. Therefore, workers must be ready to assist foster parents in meeting *their* goals. This suggests that workers must not only deliver services to foster parents but that they must also *listen* to them. Clearly they have a great deal to say, and when they are not heard the children in their care may suffer. This point was most poignantly made in the data concerning adoption failure, which intimate that these families had few of their preferences met regarding the type of child placed with them, and that some of these families were coerced into adopting.

Over and over the sharing of information emerged as a crucial variable in these data. Perhaps parents with greater knowledge of their children's experiences prior to placement in their home, and of their usual behavioral responses, are better able to care for the children, to respond to them appropriately, and to help them resolve issues from their past. They may also have fewer fantasies and fears about their biological heritage. Workers who know the children well, and with whom the foster family has shared information, appear best able to help; a lack of knowledge on the part of the worker was often present in the cases of the failed adoptions. Thus, workers should not attempt to "protect" families or insure their acceptance of a child by withholding information. Nor should they denigrate the family by assuming that the problems they face in rearing their foster children are due to their incompetence. Above all, they should view the families' requests for assistance as signs of strength and not of weakness. Without this, no true relationship can form.

Finally, if good relationships between worker and family are to develop, it appears that caseloads, particularly in the public sector, must be reduced. Within this sector many workers had caseloads of more than fifty families. Meeting the needs of that many families is a herculean task. It is to the credit of these workers that they appeared able to establish good relationships with many foster families, and to have achieved adoptions for so many children.

Preparation for Foster Care and Adoption

The data suggest a pattern which should be pursued in delivering services to families. As stated previously, there is a need for early planning on behalf of children who enter the foster care system. This idea is not new, but the data did suggest that the children for whom deliberate action was taken in a timely way (early discussion of adoption, recent termination of parental rights, etc.) were more likely to be adopted. So, also, was adoption more readily accomplished for children who were placed in their homes at young ages and who had not experienced previous traumatic separations from other foster homes. One has to wonder what would have happened had the workers of the fourteen families who initially wanted to adopt but eventually decided against it, been active and timely in their adoption planning with these families.

Good initial planning goes beyond work with a family around a particular child. It means that foster parents are well prepared for their roles and understand them. It also means that they have time to prepare for the arrival of a child who may have special needs. This did not appear to be the case for many of the families in this study. Preparation for foster parenthood seemed lacking, crisis placements were common, and home studies prior to the placement of any child seemed cursory. And the reader will recall the surprise and anger of some of the families who did not adopt when the "rules of the game" were changed and they were asked to take permanent responsibility for their children. Hopefully, these agency practices have changed in the time since the children under study were placed in these homes. Given the blurring of the distinction between foster and adoptive parenthood, it seems particularly important that these practices diminish, and more careful consideration be given to the preparation of these parents for the more complex roles which they are now being asked to undertake.

Even with better preparation and ongoing services, agencies and workers must pay special attention to the transitional period between foster and adoptive parenthood. These data confirmed that many foster parents welcomed the opportunity to adopt, and that most of these adoptions appeared successful. However, the transition was not natural or easy for some families. Poor preparation appeared to be associated with adoption failure, while intensive contact with families during this time was associated with a decision to adopt.

Full discussion of adoption issues was associated with an adoption decision. A recapitulation of the child's past history seems to be particularly important at this time; perhaps it allows parents to see their children's progress and/or to finally resolve issues about their children's past. However, in these discussions, it appears that workers should not overemphasize the difficulties the parents may face in the future. Thus, in preparing families for adoption, workers must walk the tight line of having full and realistic discussions with the foster parents without unduly raising their anxiety levels.

Such open discussions also seemed to be important to the children, and the quality of worker-child relationship was associated with the adoption decision. Children appear to need a time to recapitulate their own lives and to come to terms with the nature of their ties to their families of origin. A number of techniques have successfully been used to accomplish this. Most common is the preparation of a "life book". In such a book the child places pictures, drawings, documents and stories in time sequence. Preparation of such a book appears to help children understand what has happened to them and why, and to help clarify their relationships with the various adults in their lives.[7] Because of the intense emotional experiences a child goes through in the preparation of such a book, it has been suggested that primary work should be undertaken by the caretaker, who is available to the child twenty-four hours a day.[8] This might be a most rewarding task for the foster/adoptive parent and child to undertake together. With the help of the social worker, they could learn about the child's past and share some of the feelings associated with it.

Most importantly, foster parents must not be coerced into adoption. While foster parents must understand that a decision not to adopt might result in the child's replacement, they must be helped in *whatever* decision they make. Tendencies for workers to threaten families into an adoption for the sake of "permanency statistics" can only damage their relationship with the worker. And, according to these data, such practices may lead to adoption failure.

Finally, the data indicate that some foster parents who adopt may continue to need help from the agency. Clearly, adoption failure is most likely to occur when the child reaches adolescence, and families should be encouraged to use the services of the agencies before their family situation gets out of control and is beyond repair. Some agencies encourage this by routinely staying in contact with adoptive parents. Such contact appears to let the parents know that it is all right to need help and seems to give adoptive parents "permission" to ask for help when it is needed. Group services seem to be particularly helpful to these parents, for they allow the parents to see that the problems they face are not uniquely theirs.[9]

Clearly, more needs to be known about adoptions which fail. This study provided only a very brief "first look" at this problem, and the results are only suggestive. What they do suggest is that both parents and children may have been poorly prepared for this adoption, that family structure may be rigid, and that the child's behavior threatens the very integrity of the family. Beyond this, one can only speculate about these families, for it must be remembered that most had been successful parents to other children.

Biological Parent Involvement

The motivation and desire to adopt their foster children, which was present within the adopting group, appeared to be heightened if contacts with the biological parents took place during the year that adoption was being considered. This was an unexpected finding, differing from what practitioners expected and from the findings of a larger study of a comparable group of children, in which contact with the biological parent was associated with continued fostering.[10] Because the finding was unexpected, and because it has far-reaching policy and practice implications, this material was examined in considerable detail.

For some families in this study, contact with the biological parents was disturbing. However, even such negative contacts seemed to have positive consequences for the child; they appeared to heighten the "crisis of foster care" and enabled the parties to feel that the ongoing situation could not continue on a permanent basis. Pressure to seek more permanent solutions seemed to be exerted. For the foster families, it seemed to confirm that they were not the children's "real" parents, to bring out protective feelings toward their children, and to push them toward adoption.[11] For the biological families, it seemed to help them face the consequences of their actions.

For those adopting parents who viewed them positively, these contacts were apparently perceived as an opportunity to gather more information about their children and to resolve any remaining conflicts they might have had about their children's heritages. It seemed to help "free" them to move toward adoption, for they came to see the biological parents as real people with real problems. Some of these families have even incorporated these parents into their families. Others have gone to great effort to help their children remain in contact with their siblings. These families seem to recognize the importance of continuity of relationships for their children.

Thus, when contacts were preceived positively, there was the possibility of an "open" adoption developing. Such adoptions are likely to become more frequent as the adoption of older children by foster parents increases. The children and the foster parents are more likely to know the biological parents. Sometimes the biological parents are willing to release their children only if they can be adopted by a particular family.

Debate about the desirability of these adoptions is intense. Some believe that such a family constellation is impossible for children; that they can have ties with only one set of parents at a time.[12] Other writers view "open" adoptions as "an acceptable compromise" when biological parents cannot bring themselves to fully relinquish their responsibilities.[13] Still others believe that it is possible to consider open adoption as a plan of choice, for in such adoptions the children can be helped to understand their situations and retain a sense of continuity with their past.[14] Identification with biological parents is associated with good adjustment among foster children.[15] Is it among adopted children? Adult adopted children who have had continued contact with biological parents apparently do well.[16]

The idea of open adoptions is thought provoking. It makes one wonder if, through such arrangements, it might not be possible to help more children attain permanent security in adoptive homes. There certainly is need for further thought and investigation in this area.

Thus, no matter what the nature of the experience, it appears that contact between biological and foster parents should be encouraged by agencies. Such contact is not only associated with whether the child will be adopted within the foster home, but previous research has demonstrated that parental visiting is the best predictor of whether children will return to their biological homes from foster care.[17] Other research has demonstrated that such visiting is important to the child's developing a positive self image while in foster care.[18] Thus, no matter what the desired outcome, agencies must encourage parental visiting. The barriers which have been identified as hindrances to such visiting[19] must be removed, and agencies must encourage appropriate foster parent involvement in this process, no matter how upsetting this appears to be initially. In the long run, visiting seems critical to enhancing the possibility of good outcomes for all children in foster care, no matter what the permanency planning goal.

Attachment

The data of this study speak only indirectly to the issue of attachment, for in all of these families (except the small sample of adoption disruptions) a sufficient attachment between foster parents and their children had formed—the placements had endured for a long time, and most showed promise for the future. Nevertheless, if one can assume that stronger bonds had formed in the families that decided to adopt, one can draw some ideas about factors which facilitate attachment.

Notable in this study was the preference of a higher proportion of adopting parents for infants; the young children found in other research to be most likely to remain in a foster home.[20] Many of these infants had been abused or neglected, or were seriously ill. One can speculate that their plight called forth protectiveness and nurturing, and that the response of these infants to care cemented the attachment.

Though most children who need long term care are not needy infants, it may be possible to use these observations with a wide variety of foster home placements. Workers may need to share more information with foster parents to help them perceive the neediness of the older child, whose greatest deprivations may have been emotional. With sufficient background information about what has happened to the child prior to this placement, some knowledge about how children generally respond to such experiences, and with extensive information about this child's specific behavior patterns, the foster parents should be able to perceive and respond to the child's need in a positive way.

In addition to educating foster parents and sharing information with them, planning at the initial stages of foster care must include consideration of the "match" of child and foster family. These data show, and other research corroborates,[21] that parental perception of a likeness between themselves and the child is associated with adoption. Note that the crucial variable is parental perception, and that this includes behavioral and temperamental as well as physical traits. Physical matching may be somewhat helpful in providing a basis for initial perceptions. However, the match of emotional needs, so that each party receives something from the relationship, and the match of temperaments so that a mutual understanding can develop within the family, seems much more crucial. The consideration of what is important in a match needs much greater exploration. Unfortunately, when physical matching of infants and families fell into disrepute, the adoption field lost interest in the entire concept. Now that recent studies have highlighted the concept, one hopes it will be properly conceptualized, defined, and investigated.

In the adopting families a positive cycle of parent-child interaction appeared to have formed to a greater extent than in the non-adopting families. This positive cycle was conspicuously absent at the point of the adoption disruption in the families whose adoptions had failed. Unfortunately, all of the data were ambiguous as to who initiated the interactional cycle that was eventually established within the family, and none of the data traced the development of these cycles over time.

No matter whether one conceives this cycle as parent-initiated or child-initiated, it seems apparent that no one party is responsible for its establishment or maintenance. Parents will remain responsive to children only if they believe their efforts are justified and their children responsive. Children will respond to their parents only under similar conditions.

Seeing parent-child relationships as interactional has important implications for practice. It means that a "systems" perspective should be maintained when working with foster families. Workers must pay attention not only to the "parenting skills" of the parents and the "behaviors" of the child, but also to the interactions between them. No longer can the field automatically "blame" the foster parents if a child does not do well in their home. Nor can it assume that providing "good" foster parents will be sufficient to insure that the child will respond in a positive way.

The data also indicated that while initial positive responses on the part of the parents might auger well for the future, they did not guarantee that positive cycles would be maintained and that true attachment would occur. It will be recalled that nine of the ten failed adoptions began with the parents having uncomplicated feelings of happiness when the child was placed. Obviously, these feelings were not sustained. The workers believed that the immediate responses of the parents were less important than the ongoing interactions which occurred. It is therefore important for workers to understand that interactions develop and change over time, and that they must monitor their development and support their positive aspects.

Workers' efforts might enhance the chances that a bond between parents and child will form over time. They might help parents tailor their expectations to the capacities of the child by bringing subtle changes in the child's behavior to their attention, by helping them anticipate the child's delayed response to their caring, and by pointing out strengths within the child which the parents might not see.

Similarly, work with the child can be done in these same areas. This, hopefully, will enhance the possibility that the children in care will allow their foster parents to be incorporated into their lives.

Unfortunately, one is left wondering about the relative importance of a number of factors to the attachment process. Both this study and the study completed by Rowe and her colleagues[22] found that children with behavior problems, especially when older, tended not to be adopted. Rowe and her colleagues also found that the child's adjustment was associated with the family's expectation of a long stay in foster care.[23] Both studies indicated that children with behavior problems at the time of the adoption decision were older at placement in their foster homes and tended to exhibit behavior problems at that time. Is the nature of foster care such that children develop behavior problems? Or, is it initial behavior problems that inhibit either the parents' or the child's ability to form attachments? It is impossible to determine the causal variable.

Thus, while this research has shed some light on the attachment process between parents and children, it has left many unanswered questions. To these authors, it does not appear that retrospective studies will ever be able to truly capture this process. What appears to be called for is a better conceptualization of the elements of this process, the development of measures which are less subjective than those which have been used in adoption research, and a developmental, longitudinal study of this phenomena. Only then will initial answers be developed to questions such as "Who initiates the cycle?;" "How important is initial matching and the meeting of parental preferences?;" "How important, in the long run, are initial responses?;" and "What is the nature of the attachment process through time, and what affects its' development?"

✳Children's Special Needs

Any discussion of the implications of the findings must take note of the very real problems of some of the children in the sample. Some exhibited severe behavior problems and required special education. Others had health and physical problems. Still others were developmentally limited and may never be self-supporting.

These problems were clearly a factor in many of the parents' decisions not to adopt. It is important not to condemn parents for this decision, for the fear of raising such children without the supports available through an agency is understandable. Rather, one should look for better ways of insuring that these children receive the continuity of care that they need.

Agencies can become caught in the ideas of "permanency planning," devise monitoring and reward structures to encourage permanency, and lose sight of the fact that, for some children, continuity of care in their current foster home is a plan of choice. Restoration to the biological home is the first goal of permanency planning. However, it may be unrealistic to expect some biological parents, who have failed to cope with a young child, to take responsibility for an older child with serious problems who would have to readjust to their home. Even with massive community supports, some proportion of biological parents probably cannot provide continuity of care. If return home is not possible, termination proceedings are initiated and an adoptive home is sought. Yet there are not enough adoptive homes available for severely disturbed and impaired children. One must therefore question if adoption is the best plan for *all* children who have spent many years in foster care. Some experts in the field have raised hesitations about the assumption, prevalent in some agencies, that adoption is always preferable to long-term foster care. For example, Kudashin has stated:

> There is a further problem for the worker of violating the older child's need for stability and continuity by replacement for adoption, if the foster home in which he has lived continuously for some time is not interested in adoption. The worker faces the decision of disrupting a well-established relationship in the expectation that providing a permanent home for the child will ultimately be more beneficial. The risk for the child is a temporary discontinuity in the

hope of achieving greater permanence, with some possibility that the changeover may fail.[24]

Allen and Knitzer have raised the same issue:

> Similarly, overzealous interpretations of the law's (P.L.96–272) mandates for permanent families for children can also result in harm to children, contrary to the law's intent. For example, the law's emphasis on ensuring that children be adopted would not justify a worker's efforts to remove a fifteen-year-old adolescent from the foster home in which the youth had lived since the age of three because the foster parents wanted the youth to remain with their family but could not adopt.[25]

To these cautions, we must now add our own. While adoption would be in the child's best interest if there was a chance that the child would experience multiple placements, discontinuity of care, and traumatic separations, this was clearly not the case for most of the non-adopted children in this sample. Most of these children were deeply embedded in their foster homes, had been there for long periods, considered their foster families their "own" families, and were bonded to their foster parents. Undoubtedly, most of these children will grow up in these homes and will experience no replacements.

One must question whether agency resources should be expended on attempting to find adoptive families for children such as those in the sample who were not adopted but remained with their foster parents. Is it proper to even consider adoption in another home for older children who have been in their foster homes for a long time and are likely to remain there, but whose foster parents will not, for whatever reason, adopt them? One must also wonder if it is appropriate to ask the foster parents of children such as these to assume the sole responsibility for their care unless extensive and continuing supports can be built into the adoption situation. Perhaps these were the hesitations voiced by the workers about foster parent adoptions.

One must be very careful in identifying the children for whom long-term foster care is the plan of choice and very specific about the reasons for the appropriateness of this plan. But there are clearly some chldren who are not adoptable because they should not be moved from their foster homes. Their foster parents have become their "psychological parents,"[26] and the intent of the placement is permanence.[27]

Thus, while permanency planning and the adoption of children who cannot return to their biological homes are important and useful guiding principles, they must be applied on a *case* basis and not accepted as dogma. To these authors, while no *class* of children are unadoptable, some children who cannot be adopted by their foster parents should not be considered for adoption. Long-term foster care, in a stable environment, has not been demonstrated to be damaging to children.[28] For some children, who have spent many years in the same home, it is probably the best available option if the foster parents will not, for whatever reason, consent to an adoption. Because of this, it appears that the field must re-think the place of long-term foster care in the scheme of available options.

✳ Low Income Families

For some families in this study, low income was clearly a deterrant to adoption. The very modest income of some families (particularly those headed by women) and the expenditures which some children's conditions might necessitate appeared to dissuade some families from considering adoption, even when the child had been in the home for many years. This was especially true for the black families in the sample, whose economic means were much more modest than their white counterparts.

Adoption subsidies have been available in Illinois for some years, and a major research project documenting their usefulness in moving children into adoption (particularly in the conversion of foster homes to adoptive homes) has been completed in this state.[29] One would expect the availability of subsidies to remove many of the financial barriers to adoption.

However, it seems that there continue to be problems in the availability and use of subsidies. Although almost all of the foster parents who did not adopt (as well as some who did) stated that subsidy was important to them, a substantial minority reported that they had never discussed subsidy with their worker. And, a large minority of the workers had had trouble arranging subsidies, particularly because of the amount of paper work involved and the documentation needed to establish eligibility. Could these problems be the reason that they did not discuss subsidy with some of their families? If they were, it appears that the process of arranging subsidies must be streamlined.

There are a number of ways to accomplish such streamlining. Perhaps the most sweeping approach is to establish subsidy eligibility based on the *child's* needs rather than the parents. Currently, most states require that adoptive parents meet, and continue to meet, financial eligibility requirements in order to qualify for subsidy.[30] This involves paperwork and extensive documentation, much like an eligibility determination for other governmental programs. By attaching the subsidy to the child's need, a determination of eligibility could be made prior to or at the point that termination of parental rights is accomplished, and foster parents would not have to provide documentation as to their need nor subject themselves to an eligibility determination. Such a system would not only streamline the process, it would remove the "welfare" connotations which some parents in this and other studies[31] have attached to subsidy programs. It would also eliminate some adoptive parents' fear that subsidy would be discontinued if their income rose above the maximum level allowed under state law.[32]

Such an approach has been recommended by the federal government through its Model State Subsidized Adoption Act.[33] However, very few states have adopted this approach. In an era when available funds must be distributed to meet many needs, a reluctance to adopt such an apparently expensive and, in some respects, inequitable reform is understandable.

With the availability of federal monies for adoption subsidies, some rethinking of this issue may be appropriate. The Adoption Assistance and Child Welfare Act of 1980 (P.L. 96–272) provides federal reimbursement to states on a matching basis for adoption subsidies. It should thus lower the state costs of adopton assistance programs.

Aside from this broad-reaching solution of attaching the subsidy to the child, a number of other possibilities exist for streamlining the process of establishing subsidy eligibility and removing other objections to its use. First, states should establish clear guidelines for eligibility. This would decrease ambiguity in subsidy laws and would diminish the amount of discretion available to authorities in their application. Further, such guidelines would reduce the confusion and misinformation about subsidies expressed by some of the foster parents in this sample.

Second, it might be possible to implement a system which determines eligibility for subsidy through the filing of an affidavit. While such systems have been strongly criticized as a way of determining eligibility for public assistance, they might not meet with very much resistance as a way of establishing the need for adoption subsidy, since foster and adoptive parents are valued members of the community who provide an important service to the state. Through the use of affidavits the process of determining eligibility would be streamlined and workers would be less directly involved. This might act as an inducement for workers to discuss adoption subsidy with foster parents. It might also remove some of the objections, raised by parents in this and other studies, to the acceptance and use of subsidies.

Some parents in this study who did not adopt were worried about whether a subsidy would be sufficient to cover their children's needs, and whether it would last until they were grown. Federal funds for adoption subsidy programs should also lessen these fears by providing a broader financial base and a federal commitment to this program. However, parents must be aware of this new federal commitment, and the commitment must be sufficient to cover the children in care. Inadequate federal funds would make a charade out of this policy initiative and defeat its purpose.

Many of the children in this study who were not adopted were seriously handicapped. Securing continued medical care and special schooling for these children was a concern of their foster parents. P.L. 96–272 makes children receiving federally reimbursed subsidies automatically eligible for Medicaid, which should meet part of the problem. However, thought needs to be given to the continued responsibility of the state when it encourages the adoption of children who will be dependent throughout their lives. Subsidy payments should guarantee that the family's standard of living does not diminish because of the adoption. In order to do this, subsidies for some "children" will have to continue beyond childhood. Dependent young adults may need the care of their adoptive families, much as they did as young children.

If poverty alone should not be a reason for the removal of children from their homes, as the White House Conference on Children in 1909 stated, then surely in the 1980's economic difficulties should not be the sole reason that an adoption is not possible. In this study low income was a predictor of a decision not to adopt, and black families tended to have lower incomes than white. Resolution of some of the difficulties associated with adoption subsidies would increase the chances of children, particularly of minority backgrounds, for adoption.

Beyond the Agency

Workers in this study were almost unanimous in identifying problems in working with the courts as a major obstacle to achieving permanent adoptive homes for children. This was reported despite the fact that it had previously been observed that termination of parental rights might be accomplished more readily and comfortably when the children were already in the home in which the adoption would be finalized—the foster home.[34] The workers cited a number of reasons for the difficulties encountered in achieving termination. Many felt that the courts were biased toward the biological parents; that biological parents were afforded an undue amount of protection in termination proceedings. They cited the granting of continuances, evidential requirements, and difficulties in adhering to mandated procedures, to demonstrate this bias and to show that the courts were reluctant to move toward termination of parental rights. These problems must be addressed if foster parent adoptions are to be expedited when they are appropriate.

In the past there was great concern in the field that parental rights, particularly at the points of initial contact with the child welfare system, were being abrogated. Strong arguments were made for limiting the power of the state to intervene in family life, and for the necessity of providing services to biological families if placement in the foster care system was deemed necessary.[35] To these authors, these protections are clearly necessary. However, the question needs to be asked "when does the child's right to permanency supercede the biological parents right to their child?" This question appears to be at the heart of the issues raised by the workers.

Court decisions and their interpretations have clearly expanded the rights of parents in termination proceedings. Some feel that this has been accomplished at the expense of finding permanent homes for children.[36] Clearly, the workers in this study agreed that such delays do take place and are detrimental to children.

Problems in state statutes have also contributed to difficulties in accomplishing termination of parental rights and the achievement of permanent plans for children. As Wald states:

> Existing laws are deficient in a number of respects. First, because most statutes contain only vague definitions of the grounds for termination, *judges are prone to order termination depending on their feelings about the proper scope of deference to parental rights.* As a result, termination generally is a haphazard process.

> Second, the statutory grounds in most jurisdictions focus primarily on concepts of parental fault, rather than on whether a child can be returned. *The justifiability of termination is viewed from the parents' perspective, not the child's.*[37] (emphasis added)

Wald has suggested, and others have agreed, that current standards for termination should be replaced:

> In place of the criteria found in existing laws, I propose that termination be based on two factors: the length of time a child has been in foster care and the likelihood that termination will harm rather than help the child. *Termination would be the norm after a child has been in care a given period of time* unless there are specific reasons why terminaton would be harmful to the child.[38] (Emphasis added)

While the time frame proposed in such a standard is a matter for careful thought and debate, it seems clear that the courts should adopt the posture that, after a certain period of time during which the biological parents receive services and do not respond to them, termination of parental rights should become the norm.

The data of this study would suggest that Wald's second point may be crucial. If the concept of "fault" were dropped, and focus narrowed to the placement planning for the child, then permanent adoptive homes in which contact with the child was guaranteed to the biological parent might become a more commonly used option. Certainly, some of the difficulties with the courts reported by the workers would be mitigated if there were not a need to prove fault.

These are complex issues. While a rethinking of state statutes and the interpretation of judicial decisions is beyond the power of child welfare agencies, executives and boards of directors of these agencies can help to insure that these issues are placed on a state's policy agenda. And, with judicious experimentation and careful reporting of the outcomes of proposed solutions, the field can begin to discover which solutions seem to maximize the possibilities of permanent homes for children.

In the meantime, the data from this study suggest a number of steps which agencies can take to improve their situation *vis à vis* the courts. First, they can continue to provide legal counsel to their workers for the preparation of cases for termination proceedings. Second, workers should be trained in the legal issues involved in termination, including the laws of evidence and testimony, so that they can be more effective in their work with the court. Third, workers should be well versed in the various sub-sections of the termination statutes in their states and their applicability, for one project has demonstrated that workers have greater success in terminating parental rights when they know the provisions of the law and file petitions under its' appropriate sections.[39] Finally, workers should always attempt a voluntary agreement from the biological parents before proceeding with court action. In this study such attempts were often successful. They are beneficial to the biological parents, for they help them clarify their commitment to the child and allow them to be in better control of their own and their child's destiny. It seems that "open" adoptions are likely to occur only under these circumstances.

The Role of the Social Worker

If one of the most striking aspects of the data in this study was that the service given by the workers was a major factor in adoptive planning, another was that the workers did not recognize their own importance. Throughout this chapter, the conclusions drawn from the data have carried reflections on the role of the worker. A final examination of this crucial role is, doubtless, the appropriate ending for this study.

Child welfare workers have the responsibility and obligation to insure that a wide range of needed services are received by the children in their care. It has been suggested that in order to fulfill this function, the worker might take the role of "case manager."[40] As a case manager, the worker's responsibility is to insure that the clients' needs are assessed and met, although the worker may not directly provide all of the ongoing services to the client. Performing the functions of a case manager is by no means a simple process. It assumes that the child welfare worker has the power to monitor other service providers and to evaluate their services. This is possible only if the child welfare agency has a clear understanding or contract with provider agencies. Without this, respective responsibilities will be unclear, adherence to agreements cannot be monitored, and children will "fall between the cracks."

The data of this study suggest that, in order to be effective in making permanent plans for children, workers need to:

1. Know the children and their experiences before placement, and maintain a relationship with them during placement. Within this context the worker should help the children understand the reasons for their placement; work to resolve their feelings about their biological parents; learn their histories; develop a meaningful relationship with their foster parents; and participate appropriately in planning for their futures.

2. Know the child's biological parents; assist them in establishing a visiting pattern; help them in assessing their capacities to care for the child; and help them in making responsible plans for their future, including the possibility of continuing contact even if adoption is planned.

3. Know the foster family well; have an enduring partnership with them; include them in planning; and offer support as they care for the child.

4. Know the resources of the agency well, and know how to work effectively with other agencies, such as the court.

The data from this study suggest that it is most helpful to have a single worker perform these functions. It was important to these families to know, like, and respect their worker, and to feel that the worker knew them and their children well, was open in sharing information and ideas with them, and respected their ability to make decisions. There is no indication in these data that frequent contacts with the social worker foster dependency; rather, those families who knew their workers best were most likely to take the step into the independence of adoption.

The concept of the case manager may fit. Children, biological families, and foster/adoptive families may need a variety of specialized, intensive services. No worker can be expected to provide all of the varied and intensive therapeutic services which an emotionally troubled child may need; even fewer are trained to provide the specialized services that a physically handicapped or developmentally disabled child needs. As case manager, the social worker must see that these services are received. But in child welfare, it seems that the case manager must also work directly with the families and know them well. This case manager must actually also provide a wide variety of services.

Trained child welfare workers possess a unique body of knowledge and skills. The strongest message of these data is that this knowledge, and these particular skills, are of crucial importance in securing permanent homes for children. Social workers have a commitment to protect the powerless of our society. And, we are beginning to learn how to do it effectively.

Notes

Chapter 1

1. Alfred Kadushin, "Child Welfare Strategy in the Coming Years: An Overview," in *Child Welfare Strategy in the Coming Years* (Washington D.C.: U.S. Department of Health, Education and Welfare, DHEW Publication No. (OHDS) 78–30158, 1978), pp. 41–42.
2. Victor Pike, *Permanent Planning for Children in Foster Care: A Handbook for Social Workers* (Portland Oregon: Portland State University, Regional Institute for Human Services, 1977).
3. David Fanshel, *Computerized Information for Child Welfare Services: Foster Children and Their Foster Parents* (New York: Columbia University School of Social Work, 1979).

Chapter 2

1. An earlier and less complete version of this review has previously appeared. See William Meezan and Joan F. Shireman, "Foster Parent Adoptions: A Literature Review," *Child Welfare*, 61 (Nov. 1982), pp. 525–535. Material in this chapter is also taken from chapters by Joan F. Shireman and William Meezan which appear in *Child Welfare: Current Dilemmas, Future Directions*, edited by Brenda G. McGowan and William Meezan (Itasca, Il.: F.E. Peacock Publishers, 1983).
2. See, for example, Janet Lahti, *et. al.*, *A Follow-Up Study of the Oregon Project* (Portland, Oregon: Regional Research Institute for Human Services, Portland State University, 1978), p. 4.5.; Vivian Hargrave, Joan Shireman and Peter Connor, *Where Love and Need Are One* (Chicago: Illinois Department of Children and Family Service, 1975), p. 45; Temporary State Commission on Child Welfare, *The Children of the State: Incentives to Adoptive Placement* (Albany, N.Y.: Temporary State Commission on Child Welfare, 1977), p. 61.; *Adoption Project for Handicapped Children—Ohio District 11* (Washington, D.C.: U.S. Department of Health and Human Services, 1980).
3. David Fanshel, *Computerized Information for Child Welfare—Foster Children and Their Foster Parents* (New York: Columbia University School of Social Work, 1979), p. 38.

4. Department of Health, Education, and Welfare, "Model State Adoption Act and Model State Adoption Procedures; Request for Comment," *Federal Register*, 45 (Feb. 15, 1980), p. 10628.

5. *Ibid.*, p. 10629.

6. 42 U.S.C. Sect. 601 (C) (2) (b).

7. Trudy Festinger, "Placement Agreements with Boarding Homes: A Survey," *Child Welfare*, 53 (December 1974), pp. 646–647.

8. Elizabeth Cole, "Adoption Services Today and Tomorrow," in *Child Welfare Strategy in the Coming Years* (Washington, D.C.: U.S. Department of Health, Education and Welfare, 1978), p. 143; Lahti, *et.al.*, *Follow-Up Study of Oregon Project*, p. 2.8.; Elizabeth Herzog, *et.al.*, *Families for Black Children: The Search for Adoptive Parents—An Experience Survey* (Washington, D.C.: U.S. Government Printing Office, 1971), p. 47.

9. Cole, "Adoption Services Today and Tomorrow," p. 143.

10. Herzog, *et.al.*, *Families for Black Children*, p. 47.

11. Margaret Gill, "The Foster Care Adoptive Family: Adoption of Children Not Legally Free," *Child Welfare*, LIV (December 1975), p. 715.

12. Lahti, *et.al.*, *Follow-Up Study of the Oregon Project*, p. 2.8.

13. William Meezan, *Adoption Services in the States* (Washington, D.C.: U.S. Dept. of Health and Human Services, 1980), p. 13.

14. Lahti, *et.al.*, *Follow-Up Study of the Oregon Project*, pp. 7.2–7.9.; Kathleen Proch, "Adoption by Foster Parents," (unpublished D.S.W. Dissertation, University of Illinois at Champaign-Urbana, 1980), pp. 64 ff.

15. Elizabeth Herzog, Cecelia Sudia and Jane Harwood, "Some Opinions on Finding Families for Black Children," *Children*, 18 (July/August 1971), p. 147.

16. Gill, "The Foster Care Adoptive Family," p. 713.

17. *Ibid.*; Cornelius Hegarty, "The Family Resources Program: One Coin Two Sides of Adoption and Foster Family Care," *Child Welfare*, LII (February 1973).

18. Proch, "Adoption by Foster Parents," p. 13.

19. Kenneth Watson, "Subsidized Adoption: A Crucial Investment," *Child Welfare*, LI (April 1972), p. 224.

20. Fanshel, *Computerized Information for Child Welfare*, pp. 45–49.

21. Jane Rowe, et al., *Long Term Foster Care* (London: British Agencies for Adoption and fostering, 1984), pp. 195–205.

22. *Ibid.*, p. 205.

23. *Ibid.*, pp. 196–197.

24. Hargrave, Shireman and Connor, *Where Love and Need Are One*, pp. 65 ff.

25. Fanshel, *Computerized Information for Child Welfare*, pp. 40–43,; Hargrave, Shireman and Connor, *Where Love and Need Are One*, p. 65.; Claudia Jewitt, *Adopting the Older Child* (Harvard, Mass.: Harvard Common Press, 1978), p. 67.

26. Gill, "The Foster Care Adoptive Family," p. 713.

27. Ner Littner, "The Importance of the Natural Parents to the Child in Placement," *Child Welfare*, 54 (March 1975), pp. 175–181.

28. David Fanshel and Eugene Shinn, *Children in Foster Care: A Longitudinal Investigation* (New York: Columbia University Press, 1978).

29. Eugene Weinstein, *Self Image of the Foster Child* (New York: Russell Sage Foundation, 1960).

30. John Triseliotis, "Growing Up in Foster Care and After," in *New Developments in Foster Care and Adoption*, edited by John Triseliotis (London: Routledge & Kegan Paul, 1980), pp. 131–161.

31. Fanshel and Shinn, *Children in Foster Care*, p. 400; Triseliotis, "Growing Up in Foster Care and After," p. 157; Weinstein, *Self Image of the Foster Child*, p. 55.

32. Triseliotis, "Growing Up in Foster Care and After," p. 157.

33. Weinstein, *Self Image of the Foster Child*, p. 68.

34. Hargrave, Shireman and Connor, *Where Love and Need Are One*, p. 16.

35. Fanshel and Shinn, *Children in Foster Care*, p. 400.

36. *Ibid.*

37. Weinstein, *Self Image of the Foster Child*, pp 52–56.

38. Triseliotis, "Growing Up in Foster Care and After," p. 157.

39. Fanshel, *Computerized Information for Child Welfare*, pp. 54–65.

40. Triseliotis, "Growing Up in Foster Care and After," pp. 145–150.

41. Weinstein, *Self Image of the Foster Child*, pp. 66–70.

42. Rowe, et al., *Long Term Foster Care*, p. 88.

43. Joseph Goldstein, Anna Freud and Albert Solnit, *Beyond the Best Interests of the Child* (New York: The Free Press, 1973), p. 26.

44. Victor Pike, *Permanent Planning for Children in Foster Care: A Handbook for Social Workers* (Portland Oregon: Regional Research Institute for Human Services, Portland State University, 1977), p. i.

45. Margaret Ward, "Parental Bonding in Older Child Adoptions," *Child Welfare*, 60 (January 1981), pp. 25 ff.

46. Proch, "Adoption by Foster Parents," pp. 84–90.

47. Lois Raynor, *The Adopted Child Comes of Age*, (London: George Allen Ulwin, 1981), p. 112.

48. Hargrave, Shireman and Connor, *Where Love and Need Are One*, p. 65; Triseliotis, "Growing Up in Foster Care and After," p. 134.

49. Triseliotis, "Growing Up in Foster Care and After," pp. 144, 157.

50. Robert Holman, "Exclusive and Inclusive Concepts of Fostering," in *New Developments in Foster Care and Adoption*, edited by John Triseliotis (London: Routledge & Kegan Paul, 1980), pp. 75–80.

51. Triseliotis, "Growing Up in Foster Care and After," pp. 134–136.

52. John Triseliotis, "Growing Up Adopted or in Long Term Fostering," *Journal of Adoption and Fostering*, (in press).

53. Hargrave, Shireman and Connor, *Where Love and Need Are One*, pp. 76–78; Rita Simon and Howard Alstein, *Transracial Adoption* (New York: John Wiley and Son, 1977), p. 166.; State Commission on Child Welfare, *Incentives to Adoptive Placement*, pp. 85–104.

54. For example, in Illinois, the number of subsidized adoptions completed increased from 212 to 493 between 1979 and 1982; the amount of money available for subsidies is expected to rise from $4.84 in FY 1982 to $7.59 million in FY 1984. See, *Illinois Human Service Data Report*, Phase I, Volume I (Springfield, Il.: Department of Children and Family Service, June, 1983), pp. 93–103.

55. Alfred Kadushin and Frederick Seidl, "Adoption Failure: A Social Work Post-mortem," *Social Work*, 16 (July 1971), pp. 34–36.

56. *Ibid.*, p. 33.; *Ohio District 11*, p. 218. Christopher Unger, Gladys Dwarshuis and Elizabeth Johnson, *Chaos, Madness, and Unpredictability. . . . Placing the Child With Ears Like Uncle Harry's* (Chelsea, MI: Spaulding for Children, 1977), p. 218.

57. Kadushin and Seidl, "Adoption Failure," p. 37.; Unger, Dwarshuis and Johnson, *Chaos, Madness and Unpredictability . . .*, p. 199.; Celia Bass, "Match-maker—Matchmaker: Older Child Adoption Failures," *Child Welfare*, 54 (July1975), p. 507.

58. Sallie Churchill, "Disruption: A Risk in Adoption II," in *No Child is Unadoptable*, edited by Sallie Churchill, Bonnie Carlos, and Lynn Nybell (Beverly Hills, Cal.: Sage Publications, 1979), p. 121.; Unger, Dwarshuis and Johnson, *Chaos, Madness and Unpredictability . . .*, p. 202.

59. Hargrave, Shireman and Connor, *Where Love and Need Are One*, p. 39.; Proch, "Adoption by Foster Parents," pp. 90–92.

60. Proch, "Adoption by Foster Parents," pp. 111–112.

61. Bass, "Matchmaker — Matchmaker," pp. 508–509.; Unger, Dwarshuis and Johnson, *Chaos, Madness and Unpredictability . . .*, p. 202.

62. Churchill, "Disruption: A Risk in Adoption II," p. 122.; *Ohio District 11*, p. 26.; Unger, Dwarshuis and Johnson, *Chaos, Madness and Unpredictability . . .*, p. 196.

63. Triseliotis, "Growing Up Adopted or in Long Term Fostering."

64. Triseliotis, "Growing Up in Foster Care and After."

65. Triseliotis, "Growing Up Adopted or in Long Term Fostering."

66. Alfred Kadushin, "Children in Foster Families and Institutions," in *Social Service Research: Review of Studies*, edited by Henry Maas (Washington D.C.: National Association of Social Workers, 1978), pp. 100–101.

67. Alfred Kadushin, *Child Welfare Services* (New York: Macmillan, 1980), p. 349; Rosalie Zimmerman, *Foster Care in Retrospect* (New Orleans: Tulane Studies in Social Welfare, 1982).

68. Rowe, et al., *Long Term Foster Care*, pp. 71–92.

69. C.M. Heinicke and Ilse Westheimer, *Brief Separations* (New York: International Universities Press, 1965).

70. Weinstein, *Self Image of the Foster Child*, p. 32.

71. Carolyn B. Thomas, "The Resolution of Object Loss Following Foster Home Placement," *Smith College Studies in Social Work*, 36 (June 1967), pp. 163–234.

72. Weinstein, *Self Image of the Foster Child*, pp. 66–69.

73. Elinore Jacobson and Joanne Cockeram, "As Foster Children See It," *Children Today*, 5 (November–December 1976), pp. 32–36.
74. Fanshel and Shinn, *Children in Foster Care*, pp. 455 ff.
· 75. Ellen Rest and Kenneth Watson, "Growing Up in Foster Care," *Child Welfare*, 63 (July/August 1984), pp. 291–306.
76. Leon Eisenberg, "Deprivation and Foster Care," *Journal of the American Academy of Child Psychiatry*, 4 (1965), pp. 243–248.; Ner Littner, *Traumatic Effects of Separation and Placement* (New York: Child Welfare League of America, 1956).
77. Zimmerman, *Foster Care in Retrospect*, p. 90.
78. Fanshel and Shinn, *Children in Foster Care*, pp. 464 ff.
79. Kadushin, *Child Welfare Services*, p. 379.
80. Triseliotis, "Growing Up in Foster Care and After," p. 153.
81. Elizabeth Meier, "Current Circumstances of Former Foster Children," *Child Welfare*, 54 (April 1975), p. 206.
82. Weinstein, *The Self Image of the Foster Child*, pp. 35–36.
83. Fanshel, *Computerized Information for Child Welfare*, p. 59.
84. Martin Wolins, *Selecting Foster Parents* (New York: Columbia University Press, 1963).
85. Proch, "Adoption by Foster Parents," p. 138.
86. Kadushin, *Child Welfare Services*, pp. 524–525.
87. Raynor, *The Adopted Child Comes of Age*, pp. 69–70.
88. *Ibid.*
89. Proch, "Adoptions by Foster Parents."
90. Lahti, *et.al.*, *Follow-Up Study of the Oregon Project*, pp. 7.11–7.12.

Chapter 3

1. The major modification of this design was that, because of anticipated high refusal rate among families whose adoptions had failed, these families were interviewed before their workers, reversing the usual pattern.
2. We are grateful to Dr. Ner Littner, whose consultation on developing this schedule and others was most helpful.
3. See William Meezan, "Program Orientation as a Factor in Workers' Attitudes and Perceptions of the Need for Placement in Child Welfare" (unpublished DSW Dissertation, Columbia University, 1978); and Deborah Shapiro, *Agencies and Foster Children* (New York: Columbia University Press, 1976).
4. David Fanshel, *Computerized Information for Child Welfare—Foster Children and Their Foster Parents*, (New York: Columbia University School of Social Work, 1979), Instruments used for data collection, pp. 10ff.
5. Fanshel, *Computerized Information*, Instrument used for data collection, pp. 10ff.
6. *SAS Users Guide* (Cary, N.C.: SAS Institute Inc., 1979).

7. Norman H. Nie, *et.al.*, *Statistical Package for the Social Sciences* (New York: McGraw-Hill, Inc., 1975 and Updates).

Chapter 6

1. See, for example, Mary Ann Jones, Stephen Magura, and Ann W. Shyne, "Effective Practice with Families in Protective and Preventive Service: What Works?" *Child Welfare*, 60 (Feb. 1981), pp. 67–80.

Chapter 7

1. Stepwise discriminant analysis using Wilks' Lambda as the criteria for entrance into the equation was utilized in all analyses.
2. For a full discussion of this technique see William R. Klecka, *Discriminant Analysis* (Beverly Hills: Sage Publications, 1980).
3. Fred Kerlinger. *Foundations of Behavioral Research* (New York: Holt, Rinehart and Winston, 1973).
4. This technical note is based on comments made by Professor John Schuerman, School of Social Service Administration, University of Chicago. The authors are most grateful to him for calling these limitations of the analysis to our attention and for his other helpful comments on this chapter.
5. Trudy Festinger. "Placement Agreement With Boarding Home: A Survey," *Child Welfare*, 52 (December 1974), pp. 646–647.
6. An additional discriminant analysis was run with both of the estimates of intelligence included. Both appeared as important discriminators, but did not alter either the other discriminators present in the analysis or their relative importance to any degree. In this analysis the intelligence estimate of the family was the stronger discriminator. Thus the worker's estimate was removed from the analysis presented in the text. The analysis containing both measures of intelligence correctly classified 85 percent of the cases.
7. Because of the questionable reliability of the interviewers judgment (See Chapter 5) a second discriminant analysis was performed using only information provided directly by the parents. All four of these variables appeared as discriminators and their relative importance remained the same. The one family-reported variable not included in the analysis presented in Table 7.3, whether the child was perceived as different from other children, was the least important discriminator in this second analysis. This second analysis correctly classified 66 percent of the cases, a decrease of 15 percent from the analysis presented. Thus, the presence of the judgment data added to the ability of the parent-child interaction variables to correctly discriminate between the two groups.

8. For a complete review of the literature on this topic, see Alfred Kadushin and Judith Martin, *Child Abuse: An Interactional Event* (New York: Columbia University Press, 1983), pp. 47–90.

9. The reader will note that in both this analysis and Figure 1 the interviewer judgments of quality of help received by the family were not included. This was done to allow the analysis to be based solely on reports of the family and worker since, unlike family-child interactions, agency service variables were probed extensively in the interview.

10. See, for example, Mary Ann Jones, Stephen Magura and Ann Shyne, "Effective Practice With Families in Protective and Preventive Services: What Works?" *Child Welfare*, 60 (February 1981), pp. 67–80.

Chapter 8

1. See, for instance, Christopher Unger, Gladys Dwarshuis and Elizabeth Johnson, *Chaos, Madness and Unpredictability. . . . Placing the Child With Ears Like Uncle Harry's* (Chelsea, MI: Spaulding for Children, 1977), pp. 196–229.

Chapter 9

1. David Fanshel, *Computerized Information for Child Welfare—Foster Children and Their Foster Parents* (New York: Columbia University School of Social Work, 1979), p. 38.

2. See William Meezan "Program Orientation as a Factor in Workers' Attitudes and Perceptions of the Need for Placement in Child Welfare," (unpublished D.S.W. Dissertation, Columbia University, 1978), pp. 38–64; and Deborah Shapiro, *Agencies and Foster Children* (New York: Columbia University Press, 1976), pp. 142–150.

3. This was done through the program provided in the SPSS data analysis package (Norman H. Nie, *et al.*, *Statistical Package for the Social Sciences* [New York: McGraw Hill, 1975 and Updates]) which provides item-criteria correlations, the Chronbach Alpha for the index, and the Chronbach Alpha for the index if an item was deleted. Items were deleted from an index if they had both a low item-criteria correlation and their elimination would raise the Alpha. By repeating this procedure a number of times, those items which were most internally consistent for measuring a specific area were eventually chosen.

4. Shapiro, *Agencies and Foster Children*, pp. 187–188.

5. Vivian Hargrave, Joan Shireman and Peter Connor, *Where Love and Need Are One* (Chicago: Illinois Department of Children and Family Services, 1975), p. 39; Kathleen Proch "Adoption by Foster Parents" (unpublished D.S.W. Dissertation, University of Illinois-Urbana, 1980), pp. 90–92.

6. Joan Shireman "Achieving Permanence After Placement" in *Child Welfare: Current Dilemmas—Future Directions* edited by Brenda G. McGowan and William Meezan (Itasca, Il.: F.E. Peacock, 1983), pp. 412–415.

Chapter 10

1. Jane Rowe, et al., *Long Term Foster Care*, (London: British Agencies for Adoption and Fostering, 1984), p. 195.
2. Robert E. Lee and Ruth K. Hall, "Legal, Casework and Ethical Issues in 'Risk Adoption'," *Child Welfare*, 62 (Sept/Oct 1983), pp. 450–454.
3. David Fanshel, "Preschoolers Entering Foster Care in New York City: The Need to Stress Plans for Permanency," *Child Welfare*, 58 (Feb. 1979), p. 68.
4. David Fanshel and Eugene Shinn, *Children in Foster Care: A Longitudinal Investigation* (New York: Columbia University Press, 1978), pp. 98–106. This has also been the finding of other investigations of foster care in the United States. These are summarized in Alfred Kadusin, *Child Welfare Services* (New York: MacMillan Publishing Co., 1980), p. 363.
5. Margaret M. Gill and Carol Amadio, "Social Work and Law in Foster Care/Adoption Programs," *Child Welfare* 62 (Sept/Oct 1983), pp. 455–467.
6. David Fanshel, "Status Changes of Children in Foster Care: Final Results of the Columbia Unversity Longitudinal Study," *Child Welfare*, 55 (March 1976), pp. 146–150; and Fanshel and Shinn, *Children in Foster Care*, pp. 116–130.
7. Claudia Jewitt, *Adopting the Older Child* (Cambridge, Mass.: Harvard Common Press, 1978), pp. 70ff; Martha Jones, "Preparing School Aged Children for Adoption," *Child Welfare*, 58 (January 1979), p. 29.
8. *Cambridge Cottage Pre-Fostering and Adoption Unit*, Barnardo's Social Work Papers No. 16 (London: Barnardo's, 1982).
9. Christopher Unger, Gladys Dwarshuis, and Elizabeth Johnson, *Chaos, Madness and Unpredictability. . . . Placing the Child With Ears Like Uncle Harry's* (Chelsea, Mich.: Spaulding for Children, 1977), pp. 162–163.
10. Rowe, et al., *Long Term Foster Care*, p. 203.
11. Kenneth Watson, "A Bold New Model for Foster Family Care," *Public Welfare*, 40 (Spring 1982), p. 19.
12. For example, Joseph Goldstein, Anna Freud and Albert J. Solnit, *Beyond the Best Interests of the Child* (New York: Free Press, 1973), pp. 48–49.
13. Kadushin, *Child Welfare Service*, p. 501.
14. Robert Borgman, "The Consequences of Open and Closed Adoption for Older Children," *Child Welfare*, 61 (April 1982), pp. 217–225.
15. Eugene Weinstein, *The Self Image of the Foster Child* (New York: Russell Sage Foundation, 1960), pp. 67–70.
16. Lois Raynor, *The Adopted Child Comes of Age* (London: George, Allen & Ulwin, 1980), p. 89.
17. Fanshel and Shinn, *Children in Foster Care*, pp. 92–108.

18. Weinstein, *Self Image of the Foster Child*, pp. 48–69.
19. See, for example, Joan Shireman, "Achieving Permanence After Placement," in *Child Welfare: Current Dilemmas—Future Directions*, edited by Brenda G. McGowan and William Meezan (Itasca, Il.: F.E. Peacock, 1983), pp. 387–388.
20. For example, Fanshel, "Preschoolers Entering Foster Care," p. 68.
21. Raynor, *The Adopted Child Comes of Age*, pp. 47–48; also pp. 75–76 discusses the adult adopted children's perception of likeness.
22. Rowe, et al., *Long Term Foster Care*, p. 203–204.
23. *Ibid.*, p. 88.
24. Kadushin, *Child Welfare Services*, p. 559.
25. MaryLee Allen and Jane Knitzer. "Child Welfare: Examining the Policy Framework," in *Child Welfare: Current Dilemmas—Future Directions*, edited by Brenda G. McGowan and William Meezan (Itasca, Il.: F.E. Peacock, 1983), p. 128.
26. A term developed in Goldstein, Freud, and Solnit, *Beyond the Best Interests of the Child*.
27. A definition of permanence developed by Victor Pike, et al., *Permanent Planning for Children in Foster Care: A Handbook for Social Workers* (Portland, Oregon: Portland State University, Regional Institute for Human Services, 1977) p. i.
28. Fanshel and Shinn, *Children in Foster Care*, p. 491. In addition, studies of former foster children as adults show generally satisfactory adult adjustment. These are reviewed by Kadushin, *Child Welfare Services*, p. 379.
29. Vivian Hargrave, Joan Shireman and Peter Connor, *Where Love and Need Are One* (Chicago: Illinois Department of Children and Family Services, 1975).
30. William Meezan, "Toward an Expanded Role for Adoption Services," in *Child Welfare: Current Dilemmas—Future Directions*, edited by Brenda G. McGowan and William Meezan (Itasca, Il.: F.E. Peacock, 1983), p. 437.
31. Hargrave, Shireman and Connor, *Where Love and Need Are One*.
32. Kadushin, *Child Welfare Services*, p. 558.
33. Sanford Katz and Ursula Gallagher. "Subsidized Adoption in America," *Family Law Quarterly*, 10 (Spring 1976), pp. 3–54.
34. Margaret Gill, "The Foster Care/Adoptive Family: Adoption of Children Not Legally Free," *Child Welfare*, 59 (December 1975), pp. 712 ff.
35. See, for example, Goldstein, Freud and Solnit, *Beyond the Best Interest of the Child*; Michael Wald, "State Intervention on Behalf of 'Neglected Children'," *Stanford Law Review*, 28 (April 1976), pp. 625–706.
36. Allen and Knitzer, "Child Welfare: Examining the Policy Framework," pp. 109–110.
37. Wald, "State Intervention on Behalf of Neglected Children," pp. 688–690.
38. *Ibid.*, pp. 690–691.
39. Theodore Stein, Eileen Gambrill and Kermit Wiltse, *Children in Foster Homes: Achieving Continuity in Care* (New York: Praeger Publishers, 1978), pp. 60–62.
40. James Intagliata, "Operationalizing a Case Management System: A Multi-Level Approach," in *Case Management: State of the Art* (Columbus, Ohio: National Conference on Social Welfare, 1981), pp. 103–104.

Index